Golf Course Guide

Published by AA Publishing (a trading name of AA Media Limited, whose registered office is Fanum House, Basingstoke, Hampshire RG21 4EA. Registered number 06112600).

Editorial: lifestyleguides@theAA.com

Cover and introduction pictures: sourced from Corbis UK

Photographs in the gazetteer are provided by the establishments.

Printed and bound by Luk Ka, China

ISBN: 978-0-7495-5833-8

A04513

Contents

How to Use the Guide

❶ Town name

❷ Club name and contact details
Where the club name appears in italic we have been unable to verify current course details with the club. You should check any details with the club before your visit.

❸ Description The description highlights the significant features of the course or courses.

❹ Course statistics The number of holes, distance, par, Standard Scratch Score, Course Record, and the number of club members.

❺ Visitor information Playing days, booking requirements or restrictions are noted. A small number of courses in the guide are not open to visitors and we have included their details for information only.

❻ Society information Booking requirements or restrictions for societies.

❼ Green fees The most up-to-date green fees are given, including any variations or restrictions. Where green fees are not confirmed you should contact the club for current rates. An asterisk * denotes 2007 fees.

❽ Professional The name of the club professional(s).

❾ Facilities See the key to symbols on page 4.

❿ Conference facilities The available conference facilities are noted, and corporate hospitality days.

⓫ Location The location of the club is given in relation to the nearest town or motorway junction. Many golf courses are in rural locations and we do not provide detailed directions in the guide.
You should contact the club for further details, or use the AA Route Planner at www.theAA.com.

⓬ Accommodation An AA recognised hotel is provided for most entries. This does not imply that the hotel offers special terms for the golf club, though in some cases the golf course is in the grounds of the hotel. The Star rating, Quality Assessment (%) score and AA Rosette restaurant award appear as applicable. Contact details and the number of rooms are given. Where there is no nearby AA recognised hotel, an AA guest accommodation is recommended. Where golf courses offer club accommodation the bed symbol appears under Facilities. Unless the club accommodation has an AA Star classification, the only AA recognised accommodation is the hotel or guest house that follows the entry.

Golf courses and hotels in the guide can illustrate their entry with a photograph or an advertisement.

Championship courses
Major championship courses have a full-page entry in the guide with an extensive description. .

---

❶ HARTLEY WINTNEY

❷ Hartley Wintney London Rd RG27 8PT
☎ 01252 844211 (Sec/Gen Mgr) 🖹 01252 844211
e-mail: office@hartleywintneygolfclub.com
web: www.hartleywintneygolfclub.com
❸ Easy walking parkland and partly wooded course in pleasant countryside. Provides a challenging test for golfers of all abilities with many mature trees and water hazards.

❹ *18 holes, 6240yds, Par 71, SSS 71, Course record 63. Club membership 750.*
❺ Visitors Mon-Sun & BHs Booking required Sat, Sun & BHs. Handicap certificate. Dress code. **❻ Societies** Booking required **❼ Green Fees** £45 per day, £30 per 18 holes (£50/£35 weekends and Bank holidays). **❽ Prof** Martin Smith **❾ Facilities** ⑪ 🍴 ⚲ ☕ 🍸 👜 🏌 🚗 **Leisure** indoor teaching studio. **❿ Conf** facs Corporate Hospitality Days **⓫ Location** NE of village on A30
Hotel ★★★ 78% HL The Elvetham, HARTLEY WINTNEY - 01252 844871 41 en suite 29 annexe en suite

---

Key to symbols

☎	Phone number
🖹	Fax number
€	Euro (Republic of Ireland)
⊘	No credit card
⑪	Lunch
🍴	Dinner
⚲	Bar snacks
☕	Tea/coffee
🍸	Bar open midday and evenings
◇	Accommodation at club
⚲	Changing rooms
👜	Well stocked shop
🏌	Clubs for hire
🏌	Motorized cart/trolley for hire
🚗	Buggies for hire
🏌	Trolley for hire
🏌	Driving range
★	AA Star Hotel
Ⓤ	Hotel not yet rated by the AA
◎	AA Rosettes indicate an award for food

BEDFORDSHIRE

ASPLEY GUISE

Aspley Guise & Woburn Sands
West Hill MK17 8DX
☎ 01908 583596
🖥 01908 583596 (Secretary)

A fine undulating course in expansive heathland interspersed with many attractive clumps of gorse, broom and bracken. Some well-established silver birch is a feature. The really tough 7th, 8th and 9th holes complete the first half.

18 holes, 6079yds, Par 71, SSS 70, Course record 65. Club membership 590.

Visitors may play Mon-Sun except BHs. Advance booking required Sat & Sun). Handicap certificate required. Dress code. **Societies** advance booking required. **Green Fees** not confirmed. **Prof** Colin Clingan **Course Designer** Sandy Herd **Facilities** ⓦ ⓘⓞⓛ 🝙 ♥ 🏌 ⚐ ☂ 🛥 ⚌ **Conf** Corporate Hospitality Days **Location** M1 junct 13, 2m W

Hotel ★★★ 70% HL Best Western Moore Place Hotel, The Square, ASPLEY GUISE ☎ 01908 282000 35 en suite 27 annexe en suite

DUNSTABLE

Dunstable Downs
Whipsnade Rd LU6 2NB
☎ 01582 604472
🖥 01582 478700
e-mail: dunstabledownsgc@btconnect.com
web: www.dunstable-golf.co.uk

A fine downland course set on two levels with far-reaching views and frequent sightings of graceful gliders. The 9th hole is one of the best short holes in the country.

18 holes, 6320yds, Par 70, SSS 70, Course record 64. Club membership 600.

Visitors Mon-Fri & BHs. Dress code. **Societies** Welcome. **Green Fees** £30 per round. ⊕ **Prof** Darren Charlton **Course Designer** James Braid **Facilities** ⓦ ⓘⓞⓛ 🝙 ♥ 🏌 ⚐ 🛥 ⚌ **Conf** Corporate Hospitality Days **Location** 2m S off B4541

Hotel ★★★ 72% HL Old Palace Lodge, Church St, DUNSTABLE ☎ 01582 662201 68 en suite

BERKSHIRE

ASCOT

Berkshire
Swinley Rd SL5 8AY
☎ 01344 621495
🖥 01344 623328

Two classic heathland courses, with splendid tree-lined fairways, that have remained the same since they were constructed in 1928. The Red Course, on slightly higher ground, is a little longer than the Blue. It has an unusual assortment of holes, six Par 3s, six Par 4s and six Par 5s,

the short holes, particularly the 10th and 16th, being the most intimidating. The Blue Course starts with a Par 3 and shares with the 16th the reputation of being the finest holes of the 18.

Red Course: 18 holes, 6379yds, Par 72, SSS 71.
Blue Course: 18 holes, 6260yds, Par 71, SSS 71.

Visitors Mon-Fri except BHs. Booking required. Dress code. **Societies** Booking required. **Green Fees** £115 per day, £85 per round. **Prof** P Anderson **Course Designer** H Fowler **Facilities** ⓦ ⓛ 🝙 ♥ 🏌 🛥 ⚐ ☂ ⚌ 🏌 **Conf** Corporate Hospitality Days **Location** M3 junct 3, 2.5m NW on A332

Hotel ★★★★ 78% HL Macdonald Berystede Hotel & Spa, Bagshot Rd, Sunninghill, ASCOT ☎ 0870 400 8111 126 en suite

Swinley Forest
Coronation Rd SL5 9LE
☎ 01344 874979 (Secretary)
🖥 01344 874733
e-mail: swinleyfgc@tiscali.co.uk

An attractive and immaculate course of heather and pine situated in the heart of Swinley Forest. The 17th is as good a short hole as can be found, with a bunkered plateau green, and the 12th is one of the most challenging Par 4s.

18 holes, 6100yds, Par 69, SSS 70, Course record 62. Club membership 350.

Visitors may play Mon-Fri except BHs. Booking required. Handicap certificate. Dress code. **Societies** Welcome. **Green Fees** £135 per day. **Prof** Stuart Hill **Course Designer** Harry Colt **Facilities** ⓦ 🝙 🏌 🛥 ♥ ⚐ ⚌ **Leisure** Video studio. **Conf** Corporate Hospitality Days **Location** 2m S of Ascot, off A30

Hotel ★★★★ 78% HL Macdonald Berystede Hotel & Spa, Bagshot Rd, Sunninghill, ASCOT ☎ 0870 400 8111 126 en suite

CROWTHORNE

East Berkshire
Ravenswood Ave RG45 6BD
☎ 01344 772041
🖥 01344 777378
e-mail: thesecretary@eastberksgc.fsnet.co.uk
web: www.eastberkshiregolfclub.co.uk

An attractive heathland course with an abundance of heather and pine trees. Walking is easy and the greens are exceptionally good. Some fairways become tight where the heather encroaches on the line of play. The course is testing and demands great accuracy.

18 holes, 6236yds, Par 69, SSS 70, Course record 65. Club membership 766.

Visitors may play Mon-Fri. Handicap certificate required. Dress code
Societies Booking required. **Green Fees** £60 per day, £40 per round. ⊕ **Prof** Jason Brant **Course Designer** P Paxton **Facilities** ⓦ ⓘⓞⓛ 🝙 ♥ 🏌 🛥 ⚌ **Conf** Corporate Hospitality Days **Location** W side of town centre off B3348

Hotel ★★★★★ HL Pennyhill Park Hotel & The Spa, London Rd, BAGSHOT ☎ 01276 471774 26 en suite 97 annexe en suite

MAIDENHEAD

Maidenhead
Shoppenhangers Rd SL6 2PZ
☎ 01628 624693
🖷 01628 780758
e-mail: manager@maidenheadgolf.co.uk
web: www.maidenheadgolf.co.uk
Pleasant parkland with excellent greens and some challenging holes. The long Par 4 4th and short Par 3 13th are only two of the many outstanding aspects of this course. Fairway irrigation installed 2006.
18 holes, 6364yds, Par 70, SSS 70.
Club membership 750.
Visitors Mon-Sun & BHs. Booking required Sat, Sun & BHs. Handicap certificate required. Dress code. **Societies** Booking required.
Green Fees £46 per day, £36 per round (£46 per round weekends).
Prof Steve Geary **Course Designer** Alex Simpson **Facilities** ⊕ ⭗ ⓡ ⓓ ☝ ⚒ ⛨ ✐ ✐ **Conf** facs Corporate Hospitality Days
Location S side of town centre off A308
Hotel ★★★★ HL Fredrick's Hotel, Restaurant & Spa, Shoppenhangers Rd, MAIDENHEAD ☎ 01628 581000   34 en suite

Temple
Henley Rd, Hurley SL6 5LH
☎ 01628 824795
🖷 01628 828119
e-mail: templegolfclub@btconnect.com
web: www.templegolfclub.co.uk
Open parkland with extensive views over the Thames Valley. Firm, relatively fast greens, natural slopes and subtle contours provide a challenging test to golfers of all abilities. Excellent drainage assures play during inclement weather.
18 holes, 6266yds, Par 70, SSS 70.
Club membership 480.
Visitors Mon-Sun & BHs. Booking required. Handicap certificate required. Dress code. **Societies** Booking required. **Green Fees** £56 per day; £44 per round (£60/ £50 weekends). **Prof** James Whiteley
Course Designer Willie Park (Jnr) **Facilities** ⊕ ⭗ by prior arrangement ☝ ⓓ ⓡ ⚒ ⛨ ✐ ✐ **Conf** Corporate Hospitality Days **Location** M4 junct 8/9, A404M then A4130, signed Henley **Hotel** ★★★★ 80% HL Macdonald Compleat Angler, Marlow Bridge, MARLOW ☎ 0870 400 8100   64 en suite

MORTIMER

Wokefield Park
Wokefield Park RG7 3AE
☎ 0118 933 4072
🖷 0118 933 4031
e-mail: wokgolfteam@deverevenues.co.uk
web: www.deverevenues.co.uk
Set in a prime location amid the peaceful and picturesque Berkshire countryside. The course architect has retained the numerous mature trees, and these, together with the winding streams, nine lakes and large bunkers, contribute to the beauty and challenge of this championship course.
18 holes, 6579yds, Par 72, SSS 72, Course record 65.
Club membership 350.
Visitors Mon-Fri & BHs. After noon Sat & Sun. Dress code.
Societies Booking required. **Green Fees** £25 (£35 Sat & Sun).
Course Designer Jonathan Gaunt **Facilities** ⊕ ⭗ ☝ ⓓ ⓡ ⚒ ☝ ⛨ ⚒ ✐ ⛨ **Leisure** heated indoor swimming pool, fishing, sauna, gymnasium, jacuzzi. **Conf** facs Corporate Hospitality Days **Location** M4 junct 11, A33 towards Basingstoke. 1st rdbt, 3rd exit towards Grazeley. After 2.5m right bend, club on right **Hotel** ★★★ 70% HL Romans Hotel, Little London Rd, SILCHESTER ☎ 0118 970 0421   11 en suite   14 annexe en suite

READING

Calcot Park
Bath Rd, Calcot RG31 7RN
☎ 0118 942 7124
🖷 0118 945 3373
e-mail: info@calcotpark.com
web: www.calcotpark.com
A delightfully picturesque, slightly undulating parkland course just outside the town, which celebrated its 75th anniversary in 2005. The subtle borrows on the greens challenge all categories of golfer. Hazards include streams, a lake and many trees. The 6th is a 503yd Par 5, with the tee shot hit downhill over cross-bunkers to a well-guarded green; the 7th (156yds) is played over the lake to an elevated green and the 13th (also 156yds) requires a carry across a valley to a plateau green.
18 holes, 6216yds, Par 70, SSS 70, Course record 63.
Club membership 730.
Visitors may play Mon-Fri. Booking required. Handicap certificate required. Dress code. **Societies** Booking required.
Green Fees £50 per day/round. Enquire for off peak rates. ⭗
Prof Mark Grieve
Course Designer H S Colt **Facilities** ⊕ ⭗ ☝ ⓓ ⓡ ⚒ ☝ **Leisure** fishing. **Conf** facs Corporate Hospitality Days
Location 1.5m from M4 junct 12 on A4 towards Reading
Hotel ★★★ 70% HL Best Western Calcot Hotel, 98 Bath Rd, Calcot, READING ☎ 0118 941 6423   78 en suite

SONNING

Sonning
Duffield Rd RG4 6GJ
☎ 0118 969 3332
🖷 0118 944 8409
e-mail: secretary@sonning-golf-club.co.uk
web: www.sonning-golf-club.co.uk
A quality parkland course and the scene of many county championships. Wide fairways, not over-bunkered, and very good greens. holes of changing character through wooded belts. Four challenging Par 4s over 450yds.
continued

SUNNINGDALE

Ridgemount Rd SL5 9RR
☎ **01344 621681** 📄 **01344 624154**
web: **www.sunningdalegolfclub.co.uk**
Old Course: 18 holes, 6308yds, Par 70,
SSS 70. **New Course:** 18 holes, 6443yds,
Par 71, SSS 72. **Club membership 1000.**
Visitors may play Mon-Thu. Advance
booking required. Handicap certificate
required. Dress code. **Societies** advance
booking required. **Green Fees** Old Course:
£165 per round; New Course £125 per
round. 36 holes £225. **Prof** Keith Maxwell
Course Designer W Park **Facilities** 🍴 ⛳ ☕
🍷 🏌 🏪 🛒 🛈 ⛳
Conf Corporate Hospitality Days
Location 1m S off A30

Sunningdale Golf Club has two championship
courses, laid out on the most glorious piece of
heathland and both have their own individual
characteristics. The Old Course, founded
in 1900, was designed by Willie Park. It is a
classic course at just 6308yds long, with gorse
and pines, silver birch, heather and
immaculate turf. The New Course was
created by H S Colt in 1922. At 6443yds, it is
a mixture of wood and open heath with long
carries and tight fairways.

18 holes, 6366yds, Par 70, SSS 70, Course record 65. Club membership 750.
Visitors may play Mon-Fri. Handicap certificate required. Dress code. **Societies** Booking required. **Green Fees** £40.50 before 10.30am or £30.50 after 10.30am. ☺ **Prof** R McDougall **Course Designer** J H Taylor **Facilities** ⓘ 🍴 🍺 ⌨ ☎ 🏌 🚗 ♂ **Conf** facs Corporate Hospitality Days **Location** 1m S off A4 **Hotel** ★★★ 78% HL The French Horn, SONNING ON THAMES ☎ 0118 969 2204 13 en suite 8 annexe en suite

STREATLEY

Goring & Streatley
RG8 9QA
☎ 01491 873229
🖨 01491 875224
e-mail: secretary@goringgc.org
web: www.goringgc.org
A parkland and moorland course that requires negotiating. Four well-known holes lead up to the heights of the 5th tee, to which there is a 300ft climb. Wide fairways, not over-bunkered, with nice rewards on the way home down the last few holes. A delightful course that commands magnificent views of the Ridgeway & the River Thames.
18 holes, 6355yds, Par 71, SSS 70, Course record 65. Club membership 740.
Visitors Mon-Fri. Handicap certificate. **Societies** Booking required. **Green Fees** Phone. **Prof** Jason Hadland **Course Designer** Tom Morris **Facilities** ⓘ 🍴 🍺 ⌨ ☎ 🏌 🚗 ♂ **Location** N of village off A417
Hotel ★★★★ 73% HL The Swan at Streatley, High St, STREATLEY ☎ 01491 878800 45 en suite

BRISTOL

BRISTOL

Bristol and Clifton
Beggar Bush Ln, Failand BS8 3TH
☎ 01275 393474
🖨 01275 394611
e-mail: mansec@bristolgolf.co.uk
web: www.bristolgolf.co.uk
Utilising the aesthetics and hazards of a former quarry, a valley, stone walls and spinneys of trees, the course is a stern challenge but one always in tip top condition, due in summer to the irrigation and in winter to the natural draining land upon which it is situated. Par 3s from 120 to 220yds, dog-legs which range from the gentle to the brutal and a collection of natural obstacles and hazards add to the charm of the layout.
18 holes, 6387yds, Par 70, SSS 71, Course record 63. Club membership 850.
Visitors may play Mon-Sun & BHs. Booking required. Handicap certificate. Dress code. **Societies** Booking required. **Green Fees** £40 per day (£45 weekends). **Prof** Paul Mitchell **Facilities** ⓘ 🍴 🍺 ⌨ 🏌 🚗 ☎ 🐴 ♂ ♂ ♣ **Leisure** chipping green, practice

bunkers. **Conf** facs Corporate Hospitality Days **Location** M5 junct 19, A369 for 4m, onto B3129, club 1m on right
Hotel ★★★ 70% HL Redwood Hotel & Country Club, Beggar Bush Ln, Failand, BRISTOL ☎ 0870 609 6144 112 en suite

Henbury
Henbury Hill, Westbury-on-Trym BS10 7QB
☎ 0117 950 0044 & 950 2121 (Prof)
🖨 0117 959 1928
e-mail: thesecretary@henburygolfclub.co.uk
web: www.henburygolfclub.co.uk
A parkland course tree-lined and on two levels. The River Trym comes into play on the 7th drop-hole with its green set just over the stream. The last nine holes have the beautiful Blaise Castle woods for company.
18 holes, 6007yds, Par 69, SSS 70, Course record 65. Club membership 825.
Visitors Mon-Fri except BHs. Booking required. Handicap certificate. Dress code. **Societies** Booking required. **Green Fees** £30 per day.
Prof Nick Riley **Facilities** ⓘ 🍴 by prior arrangement 🍺 ⌨ 🏌 🚗 ☎ 🐴 ♂ **Conf** facs Corporate Hospitality Days **Location** 3m NW of city centre on B4055 off A4018
Hotel ★★★ 66% HL Henbury Lodge Hotel, Station Rd, Henbury, BRISTOL ☎ 0117 950 2615 12 en suite 9 annexe en suite

Knowle
West Town Ln, Brislington BS4 5DF
☎ 0117 977 0660
🖨 0117 972 0615
e-mail: mike@knowlegolfclub.co.uk
web: www.knowlegolfclub.co.uk
Parkland with nice turf. The first five holes climb up and down hill but the remainder are on a more even plane.

18 holes, 6006yds, Par 69, SSS 69, Course record 61. Club membership 700.
Visitors may play Mon-Sun & BHs. Advance booking required. Handicap certificate required. Dress code. **Societies** advance booking required. **Green Fees** not confirmed. ☺ **Prof** Robert Hayward
Course Designer Hawtree/J H Taylor **Facilities** ⓘ 🍴 🍺 ⌨ 🏌 🚗 🐴 🚗 ♂ **Location** 3m SE of city centre off A37
Hotel ★★★ 82% CHH Hunstrete House Hotel, HUNSTRETE ☎ 01761 490490 25 en suite

BUCKINGHAMSHIRE

AYLESBURY

Ellesborough
Wendover Rd, Butlers Cross HP17 0TZ
☎ 01296 622114
🖺 01296 622114
e-mail: admin@ellesboroughgolf.co.uk
web: www.ellesboroughgolf.co.uk
Once part of the property of Chequers, and under the shadow of the famous Coombe monument at the Wendover end of the Chilterns. A downland course, it is rather hilly with most holes enhanced by far-ranging views over the Aylesbury countryside.
18 holes, 6360yds, Par 71, SSS 71, Course record 64. Club membership 700.
Visitors Mon-Fri except BHs. Booking required. Handicap certificate. Dress code. **Societies** Booking required. **Green Fees** £50 per day; £30 per round. ☺ **Prof** Mark Squire **Course Designer** James Braid **Facilities** ⑪ ⓑ ♥ ✎ ⚐ ☖ ⚘ ✓ **Conf** Corporate Hospitality Days **Location** 1m W of Wendover on B4010 towards Princes Risborough
Hotel BUD Innkeeper's Lodge Aylesbury South, 40 Main St, Weston Turville, AYLESBURY ☎ 0845 112 6095 16 en suite

BEACONSFIELD

Beaconsfield
Seer Green HP9 2UR
☎ 01494 676545
🖺 01494 681148
e-mail: secretary@beaconsfieldgolfclub.co.uk
web: www.beaconsfieldgolfclub.co.uk
An interesting and, at times, testing tree-lined and parkland course which frequently plays longer than appears on the card. Each hole differs to a considerable degree and here lies the charm. Walking is easy, except perhaps to the 6th and 8th. Well bunkered.
18 holes, 6506yds, Par 72, SSS 71, Course record 63. Club membership 900.
Visitors Mon-Fri except BHs. Handicap certificate. Dress code. **Societies** Booking required. **Green Fees** £60 per day; £50 per round. ☺ **Prof** Michael Brothers **Course Designer** H S Colt **Facilities** ⑪ ⓑ ♥ ✎ ⚐ ☖ ⚘ ✓ ✂ **Conf** Corporate Hospitality Days **Location** M40 junct 2, next to Seer Green railway station
Hotel BUD Innkeeper's Lodge Beaconsfield, Aylesbury End, BEACONSFIELD ☎ 0845 112 6096 32 en suite

BURNHAM

Burnham Beeches
Green Ln SL1 8EG
☎ 01628 661448
🖺 01628 668968
e-mail: enquiries@bbgc.co.uk
web: www.bbgc.co.uk
Wooded parkland on the edge of the historic Burnham Beeches Forest with a good variety of holes.
18 holes, 6449yds, Par 70, SSS 71, Course record 66. Club membership 670.
Visitors Mon-Fri excepr BHs. Handicap certificate. Dress code. **Societies** Booking required. **Green Fees** not confirmed. ☺ **Prof** Ronnie Bolton **Course Designer** J H Taylor **Facilities** ⑪ 🍽 ⓑ ♥ ✎ ⚐ ☖ ⚘ ✓ ✂ **Conf** Corporate Hospitality Days **Location** 0.5m NE of Burnham
Hotel ★★★ 72% HL Burnham Beeches Hotel, Grove Rd, BURNHAM ☎ 0870 609 6124 82 en suite

DENHAM

Denham
Tilehouse Ln UB9 5DE
☎ 01895 832022
🖺 01895 835340
e-mail: club.secretary@denhamgolfclub.co.uk
web: www.denhamgolfclub.co.uk
18 holes, 6462yds, Par 70, SSS 71, Course record 66.
Course Designer H S Colt **Location** 0.5m N of North Orbital Road, 2m from Uxbridge
Telephone for further details
Hotel ★★★ 77% HL Barn Hotel, West End Rd, RUISLIP ☎ 01895 636057 59 en suite

GERRARDS CROSS

Gerrards Cross
Chalfont Park SL9 0QA
☎ 01753 883263 (Sec) & 885300 (Pro)
🖺 01753 883593
e-mail: secretary@gxgolf.co.uk
web: www.gxgolf.co.uk
A wooded parkland course that has been modernised in recent years and is now a very pleasant circuit with infinite variety and fine views.

continued

CHAMPIONSHIP COURSE

WOBURN

MK17 9LJ
☎ 01908 370756 ▤ 01908 378436
e-mail: enquiries@woburngolf.com
web: www.discoverwoburn.co.uk
Duke's Course: 18 holes, 6973yds, Par 72, SSS 74, Course record 62.
Duchess Course: 18 holes, 6651yds, Par 72, SSS 72. **Marquess Course:** 18 holes, 7214yards, Par 72, SSS 74.
Visitors Mon-Fri except BHs. Booking required. Handicap certificate required. Dress code. **Societies** Booking required.
Green Fees May-Oct £140-£155 per day including lunch. Nov-Feb £75/ Mar £95/ Apr £115. Aug & Oct £105-£120 per round including lunch. **Prof** Luther Blacklock **Course Designer** Charles Lawrie/Peter Alliss & others
Facilities ⑪ ▯ ▯ ⚐ ☂ 🖥 ⛳ ◆ 🛺 ◆ ⛳ **Conf** Corporate Hospitality Days **Location** M1 junct 13, 4m W off A5130

Easily accessible from the M1, Woburn is famed not only for its golf courses but also for the magnificent stately home and wildlife park, which are both well worth a visit. Charles Lawrie of Cotton Pennink designed two great courses here among trees and beautiful countryside. From the back tees they are rather long for the weekend amateur golfer. The Duke's Course is a tough challenge for golfers at all levels. The Duchess Course, although relatively easier, still demands a high level of skills to negotiate the fairways guarded by towering pines. A third course, the Marquess, opened in June 2000 and has already staged the British Masters twice. The town of Woburn and the abbey are in Bedfordshire, while the golf club is over the border in Buckinghamshire.

18 holes, 6212yds, Par 69, SSS 70, Course record 64. Club membership 700.
Visitors Mon-Fri. Handicap certificate. Dress code. **Societies** Booking required. **Green Fees** £55 per day, £45 per round. **Prof** Matthew Barr **Course Designer** Bill Pedlar **Facilities** ⊕ ⓛ ⊡ ⊡ ⅄ ☎ 🕈 **Location** NE side of town centre off A413 **Hotel** ★★ 71% HL The Ethorpe Hotel, Packhorse Rd, GERRARDS CROSS ☎ 01753 882039 32 en suite

STOKE POGES

Stoke Poges
Stoke Park, Park Rd SL2 4PG
☎ 01753 717171
📄 01753 717181
e-mail: info@stokeparkclub.com
web: www.stokeparkclub.com
Course 1: 18 holes, 6721yds, Par 71, SSS 72, Course record 65.
Course 2: 18 holes, 6551yds, Par 72, SSS 73.
Course 3: 18 holes, 6318yds, Par 71, SSS 70.
Course Designer Harry Shapland Colt **Location** Off A4 at Slough onto B416 Stoke Poges Ln, club 1.5m on left
Telephone for further details
Hotel ★★★★ 75% HL Slough/Windsor Marriott Hotel, Ditton Rd, Langley, SLOUGH ☎ 0870 400 7244 382 en suite

STOWE

Silverstone Silverstone Rd MK18 5LH
☎ 01280 850005
📄 01280 850156
e-mail: proshop@silverstonegolfclub.co.uk
18 holes, 6472yards, Par 72, SSS 71, Course record 65.
Course Designer David Snell **Location** From Silverstone signs to Grand Prix track. Club 1m past entrance on right
Telephone for further details
Hotel ★★★★ 74% HL Villiers Hotel, 3 Castle St, BUCKINGHAM ☎ 01280 822444 46 en suite

CAMBRIDGESHIRE

BAR HILL

Menzies Cambridgeshire
Bar Hill CB3 8EU
☎ 01954 780098 & 249971
📄 01954 780010
e-mail: cambridge@menzies-hotels.co.uk
web: www.bookmenzies.com
Mature undulating parkland course with tree-lined fairways, easy walking. Challenging opening and closing holes with water on the right and out of bounds on the left of both.
18 holes, 6575yds, Par 71, SSS 72, Course record 68. Club membership 600.
Visitors Mon-Sun & BHs. Booking required Sat, Sun & BHs. Dress code. **Societies** Booking required. **Green Fees** £30 per

round (£40 weekends & bank holidays). Winter £25/£30. **Prof** Mike Clemons **Facilities** ⊕ ⓛ ⓛ ⊡ ⊡ ⅄ ☎ 🕈 ◇ ☎ **Leisure** hard tennis courts, heated indoor swimming pool, sauna, solarium, gymnasium. **Conf** facs Corporate Hospitality Days **Location** M11/A14, then B1050 (Bar Hill)
Hotel ★★★★ 80% HL Hotel Felix, Whitehouse Ln, CAMBRIDGE ☎ 01223 277977 52 en suite

CAMBRIDGE

Gog Magog
Shelford Bottom CB2 4AB
☎ 01223 247626
📄 01223 414990
e-mail: secretary@gogmagog.co.uk
web: www.gogmagog.co.uk
Situated just outside the centre of the university town, Gog Magog, established in 1901, is known as the nursery of Cambridge undergraduate golf. The chalk downland courses are on high ground, and it is said that if you stand on the highest point and could see far enough to the east the next highest ground would be the Ural Mountains. The courses are open but there are enough trees and other hazards to provide plenty of problems. Views from the high parts are superb. The nature of the ground ensures good winter golf. The area has been designated a Site of Special Scientific Interest.
Old Course: 18 holes, 6398yds, Par 70, SSS 70, Course record 62.
Wandlebury: 18 holes, 6735yds, Par 72, SSS 72, Course record 67. Club membership 1400.
Visitors Mon-Fri except BHs. Advance booking required. Handicap certificate required. Dress code. **Societies** Booking required.
Green Fees £60 per day, £45 per round (£65 per round weekends and bank holidays). ☺ **Prof** Ian Bamborough **Course Designer** Hawtree Ltd **Facilities** ⊕ ⓛ ⓛ ⊡ ⊡ ⅄ ☎ 🕈 ✔ ☎ ✔ **Conf** Corporate Hospitality Days **Location** 3m SE on A1307
Hotel ★★★ 78% HL Best Western The Gonville Hotel, Gonville Place, CAMBRIDGE ☎ 01223 366611 & 221111 📄 01223 315470 73 en suite

GIRTON

Girton
Dodford Ln CB3 0QE
☎ 01223 276169
📄 01223 277150
e-mail: secretary@girtongolfclub.sagehost.co.uk
web: www.club-noticeboard.co.uk
Flat, open, easy walking parkland with many trees and ditches.
18 holes, 6012yds, Par 69, SSS 69, Course record 66. Club membership 800.
Visitors Mon-Fri except BHs. Booking required. Dress code. **Societies** Booking required. **Green Fees** £25 weekdays. ☺ **Prof** Scott Thomson **Course Designer** Allan Gow

continued

Facilities ⓣ ⓘ ⓘ ⓘ ⓘ ⓘ ⓘ ⓘ ⓘ ⓘ ⓘ **Location** 3m from Cambridge. Just off A14 junct 31

Hotel ★★★★ 80% HL Hotel Felix, Whitehouse Ln, CAMBRIDGE ☎ 01223 277977 52 en suite

CHESHIRE

DELAMERE

Delamere Forest
Station Rd CW8 2JE
☎ 01606 883264 & 883800
🖹 01606 889444
e-mail: info@delameregolf.co.uk
web: www.delameregolf.co.uk
Played mostly on undulating open heath there is great charm in the way this course drops down into the occasional pine sheltered valley. Six of the first testing nine holes are from 420 to 455yds in length.

18 holes, 6348yds, Par 72, SSS 71, Course record 65. Club membership 500.
Visitors may play Tue-Fri. Dress code. **Societies** Booking required. **Green Fees** not confirmed. ⊛ **Prof** Ellis B Jones **Course Designer** H Fowler **Facilities** ⓣ ⓘ by prior arrangement ⓘ ⓘ ⓘ ⓘ ⓘ ⓘ ⓘ ⓘ **Conf** Corporate Hospitality Days **Location** 1.5m NE, off B5152
Hotel ★★★ 78% CHH Willington Hall, Willington, TARPORLEY ☎ 01829 752321 10 en suite

KNUTSFORD

Mere Golf & Country Club
Chester Rd, Mere WA16 6LJ
☎ 01565 830155
🖹 01565 830713
e-mail: enquiries@meregolf.co.uk
web: www.meregolf.co.uk
A gracious parkland championship course designed by James Braid in the Cheshire sand belt, with several holes close to a lake. The round has a tight finish with four testing holes.

18 holes, 6817yds, Par 71, SSS 73, Course record 64. Club membership 550.
Visitors Mon, Tue & Thu except BHs. Booking required. Handicap certificate. Dress code. **Societies** Booking required **Green Fees** £70 per day (£50 Oct-Mar). **Prof** Peter Eyre **Course Designer** James Braid/George Duncan **Facilities** ⓣ ⓘ ⓘ ⓘ ⓘ ⓘ ⓘ ⓘ ⓘ ⓘ ⓘ **Leisure** hard tennis courts, heated indoor swimming pool, squash, sauna, solarium, gymnasium. **Conf** facs Corporate Hospitality Days
Location M6 junct 19, 1m E. M56 junct 7, 1m W
Hotel ★★★★ 78% HL Cottons Hotel & Spa, Manchester Rd, KNUTSFORD ☎ 01565 650333 109 en suite

MACCLESFIELD

Tytherington
Dorchester Way, Tytherington SK10 2JP
☎ 01625 506000
🖹 01625 506040
e-mail: tytherington.events@clubhaus.com
web: www.clubhaus.com
18 holes, 6765yds, Par 72, SSS 74.
Course Designer Dave Thomas/Patrick Dawson **Location** 1m N of Macclesfield off A523
Telephone for further details
Hotel ★★★★ 74% HL Shrigley Hall Hotel Golf & Country Club, Shrigley Park, Pott Shrigley, MACCLESFIELD ☎ 01625 575757 150 en suite

ENGLAND

PRESTBURY

Prestbury
Macclesfield Rd SK10 4BJ
☎ 01625 828241
🖷 01625 828241
e-mail: office@prestburygolfclub.com
web: www.prestburygolfclub.com
Undulating parkland with many plateau greens. The 9th
hole has a challenging uphill three-tier green and
the 17th is over a valley. Host to county and inter-county
championships, including hosting an Open qualifying
event annually until 2008.

*18 holes, 6371yds, Par 71, SSS 71, Course record 64.
Club membership 730.*
Visitors Mon-Fri except BHs. Booking required Tue & Thu.
Dress code. **Societies** Booking required. **Green Fees** £50 per
day. **Prof** Nick Summerfield **Course Designer** Harry S Colt
Facilities ⊕ ⏍ 🛢 ☞ ⋒ ⚐ 🛆 🖻 ✐ ⋔ **Conf** Corporate Hospitality
Days **Location** S side of village off A538
Hotel ★★★★ 80% HL De Vere Mottram Hall, Wilmslow Rd,
Mottram St Andrew, Prestbury, WILMSLOW ☎ 01625 828135
131 en suite

SANDIWAY

Sandiway
Chester Rd CW8 2DJ
☎ 01606 883247 (Secretary)
🖷 01606 888548
e-mail: info@sandiwaygolf.fsnet.co.uk
web: www.sandiwaygolf.co.uk
Delightful undulating wood and heathland course with
long hills up to the 8th, 16th and 17th holes. Many
dog-leg and tree-lined holes give opportunities for the
deliberate fade or draw. True championship test and one
of the finest inland courses in north-west England.
*18 holes, 6404yds, Par 70, SSS 71, Course record 65.
Club membership 750.*
Visitors Mon-Sun & BHs. Handicap certificate. Dress code.
Societies Booking required. **Green Fees** £55 per day, £45
per round (£60 per round weekends). ⊛ **Prof** William Laird
Course Designer Ted Ray **Facilities** ⊕ ⏍ 🛢 ☞ ⋒ 🛆 🖻 ⋔ ✐
Conf Corporate Hospitality Days **Location** 2m W of Northwich
on A556

Hotel ★★★★ HL Nunsmere Hall Country House Hotel,
Tarporley Rd, SANDIWAY ☎ 01606 889100 36 en suite

WARRINGTON

Leigh
Kenyon Hall, Broseley Ln, Culcheth WA3 4BG
☎ 01925 762943 (Secretary)
🖷 01925 765097
e-mail: golf@leighgolf.fsnet.co.uk
web: www.leighgolf.co.uk
This compact parkland course has benefited in recent
years from intensive tree planting and extra drainage. An
interesting course to play with narrow fairways making
accuracy from the tees essential.
*18 holes, 5853yds, Par 69, SSS 69, Course record 64.
Club membership 850.*
Visitors Mon-Sun & BHs. Booking required. Dress code
Societies Booking required. **Green Fees** Summer: £30 per
day, £28 per 18 holes. Winter £15 per 18 holes. ⊛ **Prof** Andrew
Baguley **Course Designer** Harold Hilton **Facilities** ⊕ ⏍ 🛢 ⚐
⋔ 🛆 🖻 ✐ **Conf** Corporate Hospitality Days **Location** 5m NE
off A579
Hotel ★★★ 77% HL Best Western Fir Grove Hotel, Knutsford
Old Rd, WARRINGTON ☎ 01925 267471 52 en suite

WILMSLOW

Wilmslow
Great Warford, Mobberley WA16 7AY
☎ 01565 872148
🖷 01565 872172
e-mail: info@wilmslowgolfclub.co.uk
web: www.wilmslowgolfclub.co.uk
Peaceful parkland in the heart of the Cheshire
countryside offering golf for all levels.
*18 holes, 6607yds, Par 72, SSS 72, Course record 62.
Club membership 800.*
Visitors contact club for details. Handicap certificate required.
Dress code. **Societies** advance booking required. **Green Fees**
not confirmed. **Prof** John Nowicki **Facilities** ⊕ ⏍ 🛢 ⚐ ⋔ 🛆
🖻 ⋒ 🖻 ✐ **Conf** Corporate Hospitality Days **Location** 2m SW
off B5058
Hotel ★★★ 83% HL Alderley Edge Hotel, Macclesfield Rd,
ALDERLEY EDGE ☎ 01625 583033 50 en suite

ST MELLION

PL12 6SD
☎ **01579 351351** 📄 **01579 350537**
e-mail: **stmellion@crown-golf.co.uk**
web: **www.st-mellion.co.uk**
Nicklaus Course: 18 holes, 6592yds, Par 72, SSS 74, Course record 63.
The Old Course: 18 holes, 5782yds, Par 68, SSS 68, Course record 60.
Club membership 1000.
Visitors Mon-Sun & BHs. Advance booking required. Dress code. **Societies** Booking required. **Green Fees** Nicklaus Course: £85 per day, £59 per round: Old Course:£70 per day, £40 per round. **Prof** David Moon **Course Designer** Old Course H J Stutt/Jack Nicklaus **Facilities** ⑪ 🍴 🛒 🖥️ 🏌️ ⚖ 🏠 🎯 ♦ 🏌 🚌
♦ 🏌 **Leisure** hard tennis courts, heated indoor pool, squash, sauna, solarium, gym.
Conf facs Corporate Hospitality Days **Location** A38 to Saltash, onto A388 to Callington

Set among 450 acres of glorious Cornish countryside, St Mellion with its two outstanding courses is heralded as the premier golf and country club in the south-west. The Old Course is perfect for golfers of all abilities. Complete with well-sited bunkers, strategically tiered greens and difficult water features, this is definitely not a course to be overlooked. But if you really want to test your game, then head to the renowned Nicklaus Course, designed by the great man himself. On its opening in 1998 Jack declared, 'St Mellion is potentially the finest golf course in Europe'. The spectacularly sculptured fairways and carpet greens of the Nicklaus Course are a challenge and an inspiration to all golfers.

CORNWALL & ISLES OF SCILLY

BUDE

Bude & North Cornwall Burn View EX23 8DA
☎ 01288 352006 📠 01288 356855
e-mail: secretary@budegolf.co.uk
web: www.budegolf.co.uk
A traditional links course established in 1891. Situated in the centre of Bude with magnificent views to the sea. A challenging course with super greens and excellent drainage enables course to be playable throughout the year off regular tees and greens.
18 holes, 6057yds, Par 71, SSS 70.
Club membership 800.
Visitors Mon-Sun & BHs. Dress code. **Societies** Booking required.
Green Fees £27 per day (£27 per round weekends & bank holidays). **Prof** John Yeo **Course Designer** Tom Dunn **Facilities** ⑪ ⑩ 🍴 ⎓ 🏌 △ 🛄 🎯 ⛳ **Leisure** snooker room. **Conf** facs Corporate Hospitality Days **Location** N side of town

CAMELFORD

Bowood Park Hotel
Lanteglos PL32 9RF
☎ 01840 213017
📠 01840 212622
e-mail: info@bowoodpark.org
web: www.bowoodpark.org
A rolling parkland course set in 230 acres of ancient deer park once owned by the Black Prince; 27 lakes and ponds test the golfer and serve as a haven for wildlife.
18 holes, 6736yds, Par 72, SSS 72, Course record 68.
Club membership 350.
Visitors Mon-Sun & BHs. Booking required. Handicap certificate. Dress code. **Societies** Booking required. **Green Fees** £40 per day, £30 Apr & Oct. **Prof** Tony Nash **Course Designer** Sandow **Facilities** ⑪ ⑩ 🍴 ⎓ 🏌 △ 🛄 🎯 ◇ ⛳ 🎯 **Leisure** fishing.
Conf facs Corporate Hospitality Days **Location** Through Camelford, 0.5m turn right Tintagel/Boscastle B3266, 1st left at garage
Hotel ★★★ 73% HL Bowood Park Hotel & Golf Course, Lanteglos, CAMELFORD ☎ 01840 213017 31 en suite

CARLYON BAY

Carlyon Bay Hotel
Beach Rd PL25 3RD
☎ 01726 814250
📠 01726 814250
e-mail: golf@carlyonbay.com
web: www.carlyonbay.com
A championship-length, clifftop parkland course, running east to west and back again - and also uphill and down a fair bit. The fairways stay in excellent condition all year as they have since the course was laid down in 1925. Magnificent views from the course across St Austell Bay;

particularly from the 9th green, where an approach shot remotely to the right will plummet over the cliff edge.

18 holes, 6597yds, Par 72, SSS 71, Course record 63.
Club membership 500.
Visitors may play Mon-Sun & BHs. Booking required. Handicap certificate. Dress code. **Societies** Booking required. **Green Fees** from £25-£42 per round depending on season. £10 for extra round. **Prof** Mark Rowe **Course Designer** Hamilton Stutt **Facilities** ⑪ ⑩ 🍴 ⎓ 🏌 △ 🛄 🎯 ◇ ⛳ 🎯 ⛳ **Leisure** hard tennis courts, outdoor and indoor heated swimming pools, sauna, solarium, 9 hole Par 3 course. **Conf** Corporate Hospitality Days **Location** 3m SE of St Austell off A390, signposted
Hotel ★★★★ 80% HL Carlyon Bay Hotel, Sea Rd, Carlyon Bay, ST AUSTELL ☎ 01726 812304 87 en suite

CONSTANTINE BAY

Trevose
PL28 8JB
☎ 01841 520208
📠 01841 521057
e-mail: info@trevose-gc.co.uk
web: www.trevose-gc.co.uk
Well-known links course with early holes close to the sea on excellent springy turf. A championship course affording varying degrees of difficulty appealing to both the professional and higher handicap player. It is a good test with well-positioned bunkers, and a meandering stream, and the wind playing a decisive role in preventing low scoring. Hosts for the English Amateur Stroke Play championship 2007.

continued

Championship Course: 18 holes, 6863yds, Par 72, SSS 73, Course record 66. New Course: 9 holes, 3031yds, Par 35. Short Course: 9 holes, 1360yds, Par 29. Club membership 1650.
Visitors may play Mon-Sun & BHs. Advance booking required. Handicap certificate required. Dress code. **Societies** advance booking required. **Green Fees** not confirmed. **Prof** Gary Lenaghan **Course Designer** H S Colt **Facilities** ⊕ ℩◎℩ ♨ ⚑ ▱ ⛳ 🏌
🏖🍴🏐✎⛵🏨✎🏌 **Leisure**
hard tennis courts, heated outdoor swimming pool, self catering accommodation & a la carte restaurant, snooker room. **Conf** facs Corporate Hospitality Days **Location** 4m W of Padstow on B3276, to St Merryn, 500yds past x-rds turn, signed
Hotel ★★★★ 74% HL Treglos Hotel, CONSTANTINE BAY
☎ 01841 520727 42 en suite

HOLYWELL BAY

Holywell Bay TR8 5PW
☎ 01637 830095 🖹 01637 831000
e-mail: golf@trevornick.co.uk
web: www.holywellbay.co.uk/golf
Situated beside a family fun park with many amenities. The course is an 18-hole Par 3 with excellent sea views. Fresh Atlantic winds make the course hard to play and there are several tricky holes, particularly the 18th over the trout pond. The site also has an excellent 18-hole Pitch and Putt course for the whole family.
18 holes, 2784yds, Par 61, Course record 58. Club membership 100.
Visitors may play Mon-Sun & BHs. **Societies** welcome. **Green Fees** not confirmed. **Course Designer** Hartley **Facilities** ⊕ ℩◎℩
♨ ▱ 🏌🏖🏐✎ **Leisure** heated outdoor swimming pool, fishing, touring & camping facilities. **Location** Off A3075 Newquay-Perranporth road
Hotel ★★★ 72% HL Barrowfield Hotel, Hilgrove Rd, NEWQUAY
☎ 01637 878878 81 en suite

LELANT

West Cornwall
TR26 3DZ
☎ 01736 753401
🖹 01736 758468
e-mail: secretary@westcornwallgolfclub.co.uk
web: www.westcornwallgolfclub.co.uk
A seaside links with sandhills and lovely turf adjacent to the Hayle estuary and St Ives Bay. A real test of the player's skill, especially Calamity Corner starting at the 5th on the lower land by the River Hayle.
18 holes, 5884yds, Par 69, SSS 69, Course record 63. Club membership 813.
Visitors Mon-Sun & BHs. Handicap certificate required. Dress code **Societies** advance booking required. **Green Fees** £28 per day (£33 weekends & BHs). **Prof** Jason Broadway **Course Designer** Reverend Tyack **Facilities** ⊕ ℩◎℩ ♨ ▱ 🏌🏖🏐✎
Location N side of village off A3074

Hotel ★★ 79% HL Pedn-Olva Hotel, West Porthminster Beach, ST IVES ☎ 01736 796222 31 en suite

MULLION

Mullion
Cury TR12 7BP
☎ 01326 240685 (sec) & 241176 (pro)
🖹 01326 241527
e-mail: secretary@mulliongolfclub.plus.com
Founded in 1895, a clifftop and links course with panoramic views over Mounts Bay. A steep downhill slope on 6th and the 10th descends to the beach with a deep ravine alongside the green. Second most southerly course in the British Isles.
18 holes, 6083yds, Par 70, SSS 70. Club membership 800.
Visitors Mon-Sun & BHs. Handicap certificate required. Dress code. **Societies** Booking required. **Green Fees** £30 per day, £25 per
round (£35/£30 weekends & bank holidays). **Prof** Ian Harris **Course Designer** W Sich **Facilities** ⊕ ℩◎℩ ♨ ▱ 🏖🏐
🏌✎🏖✎ **Leisure** indoor computerised teaching academy.
Location 1.5m NW of Mullion, off A3083
Hotel ★★★ 77% HL Polurrian Hotel, MULLION ☎ 01326 240421 39 en suite

PORTWRINKLE

Whitsand Bay Hotel Golf & Country Club PL11 3BU
☎ 01503 230276 🖹 01503 230329
e-mail: whitsandbayhotel@btconnect.com
web: www.whitsandbayhotel.co.uk
Testing seaside course laid out on cliffs overlooking Whitsand Bay. Easy walking after first hole. The Par 3 3rd hole is acknowledged as one of the most attractive holes in Cornwall.
18 holes, 6030yds, Par 69, SSS 68, Course record 62. Club membership 400.
Visitors may play Mon-Sun & BHs. Dress code. **Societies** Booking required. **Green Fees** £22 per round (£28 weekends). **Prof** Steve Dougan **Course Designer** Fernie **Facilities** ⊕ ℩◎℩ ♨ ▱ 🏖
🏖🏐◇✎🏖✎ **Leisure** heated indoor swimming pool, sauna, solarium, gymnasium, spa centre. **Conf** Corporate Hospitality Days **Location** from Tamar Bridge, turn left at Treulefoot roundabout for Polbathic. After 2m turn right to Crafthole then Portwrinkle. Golf course on right.
Hotel ★★★ 74% HL Whitsand Bay Hotel & Golf Club, PORTWRINKLE
☎ 01503 230276 32 en suite

ROCK

St Enodoc
PL27 6LD
☎ 01208 863216
🖹 01208 862976
e-mail: enquiries@st-enodoc.co.uk
web: www.st-enodoc.co.uk

Classic links course with huge sand hills and rolling fairways. James Braid laid out the original 18 holes in 1907 and changes were made in 1922 and 1935. On the Church, the 10th is the toughest Par 4 on the course and on the 6th is a truly enormous sand hill known as the Himalayas. The Holywell is not as exacting as the Church; it is less demanding on stamina but still a real test of skill for golfers of any handicap.

Church Course: 18 holes, 6406yds, Par 69, SSS 70, Course record 64.
Holywell Course: 18 holes, 4142yds, Par 63, SSS 61.
Club membership 1300.

Visitors may play Mon-Fri, Sun & BHS. Handicap certificate required. **Societies** advance booking required. **Green Fees** Church Course:£65 per day, £50 per round (£60 per round Sun). Holywell Course: £25 per day, £16 per round. **Prof** Nick Williams **Course Designer** James Braid **Facilities** ⓣ 🕽 ⮣ ♥ 🕽 ♨ 🖰 ⮟ ✑ ✑ ✑ **Location** W side of village

Hotel ★★★ 70% HL Old Custom House Inn, South Quay, PADSTOW ☎ 01841 532359 24 en suite

CUMBRIA

APPLEBY-IN-WESTMORLAND

Appleby
Brackenber Moor CA16 6LP
☎ 017683 51432
🖹 017683 52773
e-mail: enquiries@applebygolfclub.co.uk
web: www.applebygolfclub.co.uk

This remotely situated heather and moorland course offers interesting golf with the rewarding bonus of several long Par 4 holes that will be remembered and challenging Par 3s. There are superb views of the Pennines and the Lakeland hills. Renowned for the excellent greens and very good drainage.

18 holes, 5901yds, Par 68, SSS 68, Course record 61.
Club membership 800.

Visitors Mon-Sun & BHs. **Societies** Booking required. **Green Fees** £28 per day, £22 per round (£34/£27 Sat, Sun & BHs). 🈂 **Prof** James Taylor **Course Designer** Willie Fernie **Facilities** ⓣ 🕽 ⮣ ♥ 🕽 ♨ 🖰 ⮟ ✑ **Leisure** buggy for disabled use. **Conf** Corporate Hospitality Days **Location** 2m E of Appleby 0.5m off A66

Hotel ★★★ 85% HL Best Western Appleby Manor Country House Hotel, Roman Rd, APPLEBY-IN-WESTMORLAND ☎ 017683 51571 23 en suite 7 annexe en suite

BOWNESS-ON-WINDERMERE

Windermere
Cleabarrow LA23 3NB
☎ 015394 43123
🖹 015394 43123
e-mail: windermeregc@btconnect.com
web: www.windermeregolfclub.net

Located in the heart of the Lake District, just 2m from Windermere. The course offers some of the finest views in the country. Not a long course but makes up for its lack of distance with heather and tight undulating fairways. The 6th hole has nerve-racking but exhilarating blind shots - 160yds over a rocky face to a humpy fairway with a lake to avoid on the second shot.

18 holes, 5122yds, Par 67, SSS 65, Course record 58.
Club membership 890.

Visitors may play Mon-Sun & BHs. Advance booking required. Handicap certificate required. Dress code. **Societies** welcome. **Green Fees** not confirmed. **Prof** W S M Rooke **Course Designer** G Lowe **Facilities** ⓣ 🕽 ⮣ ♥ 🕽 ♨ 🖰 ⮟ ✑ ✑ **Leisure** snooker. **Conf** Corporate Hospitality Days **Location** B5284 1.5m from Bowness

Hotel ★★★ 78% HL Best Western Famous Wild Boar Hotel, Crook, WINDERMERE ☎ 015394 45225 36 en suite

BRAMPTON

Brampton
Tarn Rd CA8 1HN
☎ 016977 2255
🖹 01900 822917
e-mail: secretary@bramptongolfclub.com
web: www.bramptongolfclub.com

Undulating heathland course set in rolling fell country. A number of particularly fine holes, the pick of which may arguably be the lengthy 3rd and 11th. The challenging nature of the course is complemented by unspoilt panoramic views of the Lake District, Pennines and southern Scotland.

18 holes, 6407yds, Par 72, SSS 71, Course record 64.
Club membership 800.

Visitors Mon-Sun & BHs. Advance booking required Fri-Sun & BHs. Handicap certificate. Dress code. **Societies** Booking required. **Green Fees** £35 per day £28 round (£42/£35 Sat, Sun & BHs). **Prof** Stewart Wilkinson **Course Designer** James Braid

continued

Facilities ⊕ ⏀ ⊫ ⊡ ⊷ ⚐ ☎ ☞ ✔ ⊭ **Leisure** games room. **Conf** Corporate Hospitality Days **Location** 1.5m SE of Brampton on B6413

Hotel ★★★ HL Farlam Hall Hotel, BRAMPTON ☎ 016977 46234 11 en suite 1 annexe en suite

CARLISLE

Carlisle
Aglionby CA4 8AG
☎ 01228 513029 (secretary)
📄 01228 513303
e-mail: secretary@carlislegolfclub.org
web: www.carlislegolfclub.org
Majestic, long-established parkland course with great appeal providing a secure habitat for red squirrels and deer. A complete but not too severe test of golf, with fine turf, natural hazards, a stream and many beautiful trees; no two holes are similar.
18 holes, 6263yds, Par 71, SSS 70, Course record 63. Club membership 700.
Visitors may play Mon, Wed-Sun & BHs. Booking required. Handicap certificate. Dress code. **Societies** Booking required. **Green Fees** £50 per day; £35 per round. **Prof** Graeme Lisle **Course Designer** Mackenzie Ross **Facilities** ⊕ ⏀ ⊫ ⊡ ⊷ ⚐ ☎ ☞ ✔ **Conf** facs Corporate Hospitality Days **Location** M6 junct 43, 0.5m E on A69
Hotel ★★★ 77% HL Crown Hotel, Wetheral, CARLISLE ☎ 01228 561888 49 en suite 2 annexe en suite

GRANGE-OVER-SANDS

Grange Fell
Fell Rd LA11 6HB
☎ 015395 32536
e-mail: grangefellgc@aol.com
A fell course with no excessive climbing and dependant on how straight you hit the ball. Fine views in all directions.
9 holes, 5292yds, Par 70, SSS 66, Course record 65. Club membership 300.
Visitors may play Mon & Wed-Sat except BHs. Dress code. **Green Fees** £15 per day (£20 weekends & bank holidays). ⊛ **Course Designer** A B Davy **Facilities** ⊡ ⚐ **Location** 1m W on Grange-Over-Sands/Cartmel
Hotel ★★★ 80% HL Netherwood Hotel, Lindale Rd, GRANGE-OVER-SANDS ☎ 015395 32552 32 en suite

PENRITH

Penrith
Salkeld Rd CA11 8SG
☎ 01768 891919
📄 01768 891919
e-mail: golf@penrithgolfclub.co.uk
A beautiful and well-balanced course, always changing direction, and demanding good length from the tee. It is

set on rolling moorland with occasional pine trees and some fine views.
18 holes, 6047yds, Par 69, SSS 69, Course record 63. Club membership 850.
Visitors may play Mon-Sun & BHs. Handicap certificate required. Dress code. **Societies** telephone in advance. **Green Fees** not confirmed. ⊛ **Prof** Garry Key **Facilities** ⚐ ☎ ☞ ✔ **Conf** facs **Location** M6 junct 41, A6 to Penrith, left after 30mph sign

SEASCALE

Seascale
The Banks CA20 1QL
☎ 019467 28202
📄 019467 28042
e-mail: seascalegolfclub@aol.com
web: www.seascalegolfclub.co.uk
A tough links requiring length and control. The natural terrain is used to give a variety of holes and considerable character. Undulating greens add to the challenge. Fine views of the western fells, the Irish Sea and the Isle of Man.
18 holes, 6416yds, Par 71, SSS 71, Course record 64. Club membership 700.
Visitors may play Mon, Tue, Thu-Sun & BHs. Booking required. Handicap certificate. Dress code. **Societies** Booking required. **Green Fees** £33 per day; £28 per round (£38/£33 Sat, Sun & BHs). **Course Designer** Willie Campbell **Facilities** ⊕ ⏀ ⊫ ⊡ ⊷ ⚐ ☎ ☞ ✔ ⊭ **Conf** facs **Location** NW side of village off B5344
Hotel ★★ 74% HL Low Wood Hall Hotel & Restaurant, NETHER WASDALE ☎ 019467 26100 7 en suite 6 annexe en suite

SILLOTH

Silloth on Solway
The Clubhouse CA7 4BL
☎ 016973 31304
📄 016973 31782
e-mail: office@sillothgolfclub.co.uk
web: www.sillothgolfclub.co.uk
Billowing dunes, narrow fairways, heather and gorse and the constant subtle problems of tactics and judgement make these superb links on the Solway an exhilarating and searching test. The 13th is a good long hole. Superb views.
18 holes, 6041yds, Par 72, SSS 69, Course record 59. Club membership 700.
Visitors Mon-Sun & BHs. Booking required. Handicap certificate. Dress code. **Societies** Booking required. **Green Fees** £37 per day (£50 per round weekends). **Prof** J Graham **Course Designer** David Grant/Willie Park Jnr **Facilities** ⊕ ⏀ ⊫ ⊡ ⊷ ⚐ ☎ ✔ **Conf** facs **Location** S side of village off B5300
Hotel Golf Hotel, Criffel St, SILLOTH ☎ 016973 31438 22 en suite

ULVERSTON

Ulverston

Bardsea Park LA12 9QJ

☎ 01229 582824

🖷 01229 588910

e-mail: enquiries@ulverstongolf.co.uk

web: www.ulverstongolf.co.uk

Undulating parkland course overlooking Morecambe Bay with extensive views to the Lakeland Fells.

18 holes, 6201yds, Par 71, SSS 70, Course record 64. Club membership 808.

Visitors may play Mon-Fri. Advance booking required. Handicap certificate required. Dress code. **Societies** advance booking required. **Green Fees** not confirmed. **Prof** P A Stoller **Course Designer** A Herd/H S Colt **Facilities** ⑪ ⑩ ⅬⅬ ⌸ ⅋⅃ ⅄ 🖿 ⅌ ⅋ **Leisure** practice ball dispensing machine. **Conf** Corporate Hospitality Days **Location** 2m S off A5087

Hotel ★★★ 73% HL Whitewater Hotel, The Lakeland Village, NEWBY BRIDGE ☎ 015395 31133 35 en suite

18 holes, 5721yds, Par 68, SSS 68, Course record 61. Club membership 650.

Visitors Mon-Sun & BHs. Booking required Sat & Sun. Handicap certificate required. Dress code. **Societies** Booking required. **Green Fees** Phone. **Prof** Simon Townend **Course Designer** Dr Mackenzie **Facilities** ⑪ by prior arrangement ⑩ by prior arrangement ⅬⅬ ⌸ ⅋⅃ ⅄ 🖿 ⅌ ⅋ ⅋ ⅌ **Conf** Corporate Hospitality Days **Location** 0.75m W of town centre off A53

Hotel ★★★ 78% HL Best Western Lee Wood Hotel, The Park, BUXTON ☎ 01298 23002 35 en suite 5 annexe en suite

DERBYSHIRE

ASHBOURNE

Ashbourne Wyaston Rd DE6 1NB

☎ 01335 347960 (pro shop) 🖷 01335 347937

e-mail: sec@ashbournegc.fsnet.co.uk

web: www.ashbournegolfclub.co.uk

With fine views over surrounding countryside, the course uses natural contours and water features.

18 holes, 6308yds, Par 71, SSS 71. Club membership 650.

Visitors may play Mon-Sun except BHs. Booking required. Dress code. **Societies** Booking required. **Green Fees** £40 per 36 holes, £28 per 18 holes (£35 per 18 holes Sat & Sun). ⊛ **Prof** Andrew Smith **Course Designer** D Hemstock **Facilities** ⑪ ⑩ ⅬⅬ ⌸ ⅋⅃ ⅄ 🖿 ⅌ **Leisure** snooker table. **Location** Off Wyaston Rd, club signed

Hotel ★★★ 80% CHH Callow Hall, Mappleton Rd, ASHBOURNE ☎ 01335 300900 16 en suite

BUXTON

Cavendish

Gadley Ln SK17 6XD

☎ 01298 79708

🖷 01298 79708

e-mail: admin@cavendishgolfcourse.com

web: www.@cavendishgolfcourse.com

This parkland and moorland course with its comfortable clubhouse nestles below the rising hills. Generally open to the prevailing west wind, it is noted for its excellent surfaced greens which contain many deceptive subtleties. Designed by Dr Alastair McKenzie, good holes include the 8th, 9th and 18th.

KEDLESTON

Kedleston Park

DE22 5JD

☎ 01332 840035

🖷 01332 840035

e-mail: secretary@kedleston-park-golf-club.co.uk

web: www.kedlestonparkgolf.co.uk

The course is laid out in flat mature parkland with fine trees and background views of historic Kedleston Hall (National Trust). Many testing holes are included in each nine and there is an excellent modern clubhouse.

18 holes, 6430yds, Par 72, SSS 71. Club membership 697.

Visitors Mon, Tue, Thu-Sun & BHs. Booking required Sat, Sun & BHs. Handicap certificate. Dress code. **Societies** Booking required. **Green Fees** £55 per day; £45 per round. **Prof** Paul Wesselingh **Course Designer** James Braid **Facilities** ⑪ ⑩ ⅬⅬ ⌸ ⅋⅃ ⅄ 🖿 ⅌ ⅋ 🖿 ⅋ **Leisure** sauna. **Conf** Corporate Hospitality Days **Location** Signposted Kedleston Hall from A38

Hotel ★★★ 67% HL International Hotel, 288 Burton Rd, DERBY ☎ 01332 369321 41 en suite 21 annexe en suite

DEVON

BUDLEIGH SALTERTON

East Devon
Links Rd EX9 6DG
☎ 01395 443370
🖷 01395 445547
e-mail: secretary@edgc.co.uk
web: www.edgc.co.uk
An interesting course with downland turf, much heather and gorse, and superb views over the bay. Laid out on cliffs 250 to 400 feet above sea level, the early holes climb to the cliff edge. The downhill 17th has a heather section in the fairway, leaving a good second to the green. In addition to rare orchids, the course enjoys an abundance of wildlife including deer and peregrine falcons.
18 holes, 6231yds, Par 70, SSS 70, Course record 61. Club membership 850.
Visitors may play Mon-Sun & BHs. Advance booking required. Handicap certificate required. Dress code. **Societies** Booking required. **Green Fees** £48 per 27/36 holes; £36 per 18 holes. **Prof** Trevor Underwood **Facilities** ⑪ ⦿ 🝩 ⬜ 🍴 ⚘ 🖳🏌 ✧ **Conf** Corporate Hospitality Days **Location** W side of town centre
Hotel ★★★ 75% HL Royal Beacon Hotel, The Beacon, EXMOUTH ☎ 01395 264886   60 en suite

CHURSTON FERRERS

Churston
Dartmouth Rd TQ5 0LA
☎ 01803 842751 & 842218
🖷 01803 845738
e-mail: manager@churstongc.freeserve.co.uk
web: www.churstongolfclublimited.co.uk
18 holes, 6219yds, Par 70, SSS 70, Course record 64.
Location NW side of village on A379
Telephone for further details
Hotel ★★★ 70% HL Berry Head Hotel, Berry Head Rd, BRIXHAM ☎ 01803 853225   32 en suite

MORETONHAMPSTEAD

Bovey Castle
TQ13 8RE
☎ 01647 445009
🖷 01647 440961
e-mail: richard.lewis@boveycastle.com
web: www.boveycastle.com
This enjoyable parkland course has enough hazards to make any golfer think. Most hazards are natural such as the Rivers Bowden and Bovey which meander through the first eight holes.
18 holes, 6303yds, Par 70, SSS 70, Course record 63. Club membership 320.

Visitors may play Mon-Sun & BHs. Advance booking required. Dress code. **Societies** Booking required **Green Fees** £100 per round. **Prof** Richard Lewis **Course Designer** J Abercrombie **Facilities** ⑪ ⦿ 🝩 ⬜ 🍴 ⚘ 🖳🏌 ✧ ✿ 🖳 ✧ 🝩 **Leisure** hard and grass tennis courts, outdoor and indoor heated swimming pools, fishing, sauna, solarium, gymnasium. **Conf** facs Corporate Hospitality Days **Location** 2m W of Moretonhampstead, off B3212
Hotel ★★★★★ 84% HL Bovey Castle, Dartmoor National Park, North Bovey, MORETONHAMPSTEAD ☎ 01647 445000   58 en suite   7 annexe en suite

SAUNTON

Saunton
EX33 1LG
☎ 01271 812436
🖷 01271 814241
e-mail: info@sauntongolf.co.uk
web: www.sauntongolf.co.uk
Two traditional championship links courses. The opening 4 holes of the East course total over one mile in length. The Par 3 5th and 13th holes are short but testing with undulating features and the 16th is notable. On the West course club selection is paramount as positioning the ball is the key to success. The loop on the back nine, comprising the 12th, 13th and 14th is as testing as it is pleasing to the eye.

East Course: 18 holes, 6427yds, Par 71, SSS 71, Course record 64.
West Course: 18 holes, 6138yds, Par 71, SSS 70, Course record 63. Club membership 1450.
Visitors Mon-Sun & BHs. Booking required. Handicap certificate. Dress code. **Societies** Booking required. **Green Fees** £85 per day; £60 per round. **Prof** A T MacKenzie **Course Designer** F Pennick/W H Fowler **Facilities** ⑪ ⦿ by prior arrangement 🝩 ⬜ 🍴 ⚘ 🖳🏌 ✿ ✧ ✿ **Conf** Corporate Hospitality Days **Location** S side of village off B3231
Hotel ★★★★ 79% HL Saunton Sands Hotel, SAUNTON ☎ 01271 890212   92 en suite

TAVISTOCK

Tavistock
Down Rd PL19 9AQ
☎ 01822 612344
🗎 01822 612344
e-mail: tavygolf@hotmail.org
web: www.tavistockgolfclub.org.uk
Set on Whitchurch Down in south-west Dartmoor with easy walking and magnificent views over rolling countryside into Cornwall. Downland turf with some heather, and interesting holes on undulating ground.
18 holes, 6495yds, Par 71, SSS 71, Course record 60. Club membership 700.
Visitors may play Mon-Fri. Handicap certificate. Dress code **Societies** Booking required. **Green Fees** £28 per day/round (£36 weekends and bank holidays). ☻ **Prof** D Rehaag **Course Designer** H Fowler
Facilities ⊕ ⍟ ⅃ ☐ ⅌ ⏃ 🏠 ✐ **Conf** Corporate Hospitality Days **Location** 1m SE of town centre, on Whitchurch Down
Hotel ★★★ 70% HL Bedford Hotel, 1 Plymouth Rd, TAVISTOCK ☎ 01822 613221 29 en suite

TEIGNMOUTH

Teignmouth
Haldon Moor TQ14 9NY
☎ 01626 777070
🗎 01626 777304
e-mail: tgc@btconnect.com
web: www.teignmouthgolfclub.co.uk
This fairly flat heathland course is high up with fine panoramic views of sea, moors and river valley. Good springy turf with some heather and an interesting layout makes for very enjoyable holiday golf. Designed by Dr A MacKenzie, the world famous architect who also designed Augusta GC USA.
18 holes, 6200yds, Par 69, SSS 69, Course record 63. Club membership 900.
Visitors Mon-Sun & BHs. Handicap certificate required. Dress code. **Societies** Booking required. **Green Fees** £40 per day. **Prof** Rob Selley **Course Designer** Dr Alister Mackenzie
Facilities ⊕ ⍟ ⅃ ☐ ⅌ ⏃ 🏠 ✐ **Conf** facs Corporate Hospitality Days **Location** 2m NW off B3192
Hotel ★★ 68% HL Cockhaven Manor Hotel, Cockhaven Rd, BISHOPSTEIGNTON ☎ 01626 775252 12 en suite

THURLESTONE

Thurlestone
TQ7 3NZ
☎ 01548 560405
🗎 01548 562149
e-mail: secretary@thurlestonegc.co.uk
web: www.thurlestonegc.co.uk
Situated on the edge of the cliffs with downland turf and good greens. The course, after an interesting opening

hole, rises to higher land with fine sea views, and finishes with an excellent 502yd downhill hole to the clubhouse.
18 holes, 6340yds, Par 71, SSS 70, Course record 65. Club membership 770.
Visitors Mon-Sun & BHs. Booking required. Handicap certificate. Dress code. **Green Fees** £36 per day/round. **Prof** Peter Laugher **Course Designer** Harry S Colt **Facilities** ⊕ ⍟ by prior arrangement ⅃ ☐ ⅌ ⏃ 🏠 ✐ **Leisure** hard and grass tennis courts. **Location** S side of village
Hotel ★★★★ 79% HL Thurlestone Hotel, THURLESTONE ☎ 01548 560382 64 en suite

TIVERTON

Tiverton
Post Hill EX16 4NE
☎ 01884 252187
🗎 01884 251607
e-mail: tivertongolfclub@lineone.net
web: www.tivertongolfclub.co.uk
Parkland with many different species of tree, and lush pastures that ensure some of the finest fairways in the south-west. The undulating ground provides plenty of variety and there are a number of interesting holes which visitors will find a real challenge.
18 holes, 6236yds, Par 71, SSS 71, Course record 65. Club membership 750.
Visitors Mon-Fri & Sun. Booking required. Handicap certificate. Dress code. **Societies** Booking required. **Green Fees** £32 per 18 holes. ☻ **Prof** Michael Hawton **Course Designer** Braid **Facilities** ⊕ ⍟ ⅃ ☐ ⅌ ⏃ 🏠 ✐ **Conf** Corporate Hospitality Days **Location** 3m E of Tiverton. M5 junct 27, through Sampford Peverell & Halberton
Hotel ★★★ 72% HL Best Western The Tiverton Hotel, Blundells Rd, TIVERTON ☎ 01884 256120 69 en suite

WESTWARD HO!

Royal North Devon
Golf Links Rd EX39 1HD
☎ 01237 473817
🗎 01237 423456
e-mail: info@royalnorthdevongolfclub.co.uk
web: www.royalnorthdevongolfclub.co.uk
Oldest links course in England with traditional links features and a museum in the clubhouse.
18 holes, 6665yds, Par 72, SSS 72, Course record 65. Club membership 1150.
Visitors Mon-Sun & BHs. Booking required. Handicap certificate. Dress code. **Societies** Booking required. **Green Fees** £44 per day; £38 per round (£50/£44 weekends & bank holidays). **Prof** Iain Parker **Course Designer** Old Tom Morris **Facilities** ⊕ ⍟ ⅃ ☐ ⅌ ⏃ 🏠 ✐ **Leisure** Museum of Golf Memorabilia, snooker. **Conf** facs Corporate Hospitality Days **Location** N side of village off B3236
Guesthouse ★★★ GH Culloden House, Fosketh Hill, WESTWARD HO! ☎ 01237 479421 5 en suite

YELVERTON

Yelverton
Golf Links Rd PL20 6BN
☎ 01822 852824
📠 01822 854869
e-mail: secretary@yelvertongc.co.uk
web: www.yelvertongc.co.uk
An excellent course on Dartmoor with plenty of gorse and heather. Tight lies in the fairways, fast greens and challenging hazards. Three of the best holes in Devon (12th, 13th and 16th) and outstanding views.
18 holes, 6353yds, Par 71, SSS 71, Course record 64. Club membership 650.
Visitors Mon-Fri, Sun & BHs. Handicap certificate. Dress code. **Societies** Booking required. **Green Fees** £34 per day. **Prof** Tim McSherry **Course Designer** Herbert Fowler **Facilities** ⊕ ⋮◎⋮ ⬚ ⊡ ⋔⬚ ⚒ ⬚ ⋔ ✔ **Leisure** indoor golf academy. **Conf** facs Corporate Hospitality Days **Location** 1m S of Yelverton, off A386
Hotel ★★★ 74% HL Moorland Links Hotel, YELVERTON
☎ 01822 852245   44 en suite

DORSET

BRIDPORT

Bridport & West Dorset The Clubhouse, Burton Rd DT6 4PS
☎ 01308 421491 & 421095 📠 01308 421095
e-mail: secretary@bridportgolfclub.org.uk
web: www.bridportgolfclub.org.uk
Seaside links course on the top of the east cliff, with fine views over Lyme Bay and surrounding countryside. The signature 6th hole, known as Port Coombe, is only 133yds but dropping from the top of the cliff to a green almost at sea level far below. Fine sea views along the Chesil Bank to Portland Bill and across Lyme Bay.
18 holes, 5875yds, Par 70, SSS 68. Club membership 600.
Visitors Mon-Sun & BHs. Dress code. **Societies** Booking required. **Green Fees** £28 per day; £22 after 2pm, £14 after 5pm. **Prof** David Parsons **Course Designer** Hawtree **Facilities** ⊕ ⬚ ⊡ ⋔⬚ ⚒ ⬚⋔ ✔ ✔ **Leisure** pitch & putt (holiday season). **Conf** Corporate Hospitality Days **Location** 1m E of Bridport on B3157
Hotel ★★★ 68% HL Haddon House Hotel, West Bay, BRIDPORT
☎ 01308 423626 & 425323 📠 01308 427348   12 en suite

BERE REGIS

Dorset Golf & Country Club
BH20 7NT
☎ 01929 472244
📠 01929 471294
e-mail: admin@dorsetgolfresort.com
web: www.dorsetgolfresort.com
Lakeland/Parkland is the longest course in Dorset. Designed by Martin Hawtree with numerous interconnected water features, carefully planned bunkers and sculptured greens. A player who completes a round within handicap has every reason to celebrate. The Woodland course, although shorter, is equally outstanding with rhododendron and tree-lined fairways.
Lakeland/Parkland Course: 18 holes, 6580yds, Par 72, SSS 73, Course record 69.
Woodland Course: 9 holes, 5032yards, Par 66, SSS 64. Club membership 600.
Visitors may play Mon-Sun & BHs. Advance booking required. Dress code. **Societies** advance booking required. **Green Fees** not confirmed. **Prof** Scott Porter **Course Designer** Martin Hawtree **Facilities** ⊕ ◎ ⬚ ⊡ ⋔⬚ ⚒ ⬚⋔ ✔ ✔ ✔ **Leisure** fishing. **Conf** facs Corporate Hospitality Days **Location** 5m from Bere Regis on Wool Road
Hotel ★★ 72% CHH Kemps Hotel, East Stoke, WAREHAM
☎ 01929 462563   4 en suite   10 annexe en suite

BROADSTONE

Broadstone (Dorset) Wentworth Dr BH18 8DQ
☎ 01202 692595
📠 01202 642520
e-mail: admin@broadstonegolfclub.com
web: www.broadstonegolfclub.com
Undulating and demanding heathland course with the 2nd, 7th, 13th and 16th being particularly challenging holes.

18 holes, 6349yds, Par 70, SSS 70, Course record 63. Club membership 620.
Visitors Mon-Sun except BHs. Booking required. Handicap certificate. Dress code. **Societies** Booking required. **Green Fees** £72 per 27/36 holes, £48 per round (£62 per round weekends). **Prof** Matthew Wilson **Course Designer** Colt/Dunn **Facilities** ⊕ ◎ ⬚ ⊡ ⋔⬚ ⚒ ⬚⋔ ✔ ✔ **Conf** Corporate Hospitality Days **Location** N side of village off B3074
Guesthouse ★★★★ GA Ashton Lodge, 10 Oakley Hill, WIMBORNE ☎ 01202 883423 5 rms (2 en suite)

DORCHESTER

Came Down
Higher Came DT2 8NR
☎ 01305 813494 (manager)
🖹 01305 815122
e-mail: manager@camedowngolfclub.co.uk
web: www.camedowngolfclub.co.uk
Scene of the West of England championships on
several occasions, this fine course lies on a high plateau
commanding glorious views over Portland. Three
Par 5 holes add interest to a round. The turf is of the
springy, downland type.
18 holes, 6255yds, Par 70, SSS 70.
Club membership 750.
Visitors Mon-Sun & BHs. Handicap certificate required. Dress
code. **Societies** Booking required. **Green Fees** £32 per
day weekdays (£38 Sat & Sun). **Prof** Nick Rodgers **Course
Designer** J H Taylor/H S Colt **Facilities** ⑪ ⫯ ⬛ ⌷ ⬗ 쓰 ⛟ ⛳
⛳ **Location** 2m S off A354
Guesthouse ★★★★★ GH Yalbury Cottage Hotel & Restaurant,
Lower Bockhampton, DORCHESTER ☎ 01305 262382 8 en suite

FERNDOWN

Ferndown
119 Golf Links Rd BH22 8BU
☎ 01202 874602
🖹 01202 873926
e-mail: ferndowngc@lineone.net
web: www.ferndown-golf-club.co.uk
Fairways are gently undulating among heather, gorse
and pine trees, giving the course a most attractive
appearance. There are a number of dog-leg holes.
Championship Course: 18 holes, 6505yds, Par 71,
SSS 71, Course record 63.
Presidents Course: 9 holes, 5604yds, Par 70, SSS 68.
Club membership 600.
Visitors Booking required. Handicap certificate. Dress code.
Societies Booking required. **Green Fees** Championship: £80
per day, £60 per round. **Prof** Neil Pike **Course Designer**
Harold Hilton **Facilities** ⑪ ⫯ ⬛ ⌷ ⬗ 쓰 ⛟ ⛳ **Conf**
Corporate Hospitality Days **Location** S side of town centre off
A347
Hotel BUD Premier Travel Inn Bournemouth/ Ferndown,
Ringwood Rd, Tricketts Cross, FERNDOWN ☎ 08701 977102
32 en suite

POOLE

Parkstone
Links Rd, Parkstone BH14 9QS
☎ 01202 707138
🖹 01202 706027
e-mail: admin@parkstonegolfclub.co.uk
web: www.parkstonegolfclub.co.uk
Very scenic heathland course with views of Poole Bay.
Designed in 1909 by Willie Park Jnr and enlarged in 1932

by James Braid. The result of this highly imaginative
reconstruction was an intriguing and varied test of golf
set among pines and heather fringed fairways where
every hole presents a different challenge.
18 holes, 6241yds, Par 72, SSS 70. Course record 63.
Club membership 700.
Visitors Mon-Sun & BHs. Booking required. Handicap certificate.
Dress code. **Societies** Booking required. **Green Fees** £80 per
day; £55 per round (£90/£65 Sat, Sun & BHs). **Prof** Martyn
Thompson **Course Designer** Willie Park Jnr **Facilities** ⑪ ⬛ ⌷
⬗ 쓰 ⛟ ⛳ ⛳ **Conf** Corporate Hospitality Days **Location** E
side of town centre off A35
Hotel ★★★ 68% HL Arndale Court Hotel, 62/66 Wimborne Rd,
POOLE ☎ 01202 683746 39 en suite

SHERBORNE

Sherborne
Higher Clatcombe DT9 4RN
☎ 01935 814431
🖹 01935 814218
web: www.sherbornegolfclub.co.uk
Beautiful mature parkland to the north of Sherborne
on the Dorset-Somerset border, with extensive views.
Recently extended to 6414yds.
18 holes, 6414yds, Par 72, SSS 71, Course record 62.
Club membership 600.
Visitors Booking required. **Societies** Wwelcome. **Green
Fees** £30 per day, £25 per round (£36 per round weekends).
Prof Alistair Tresidder **Course Designer** James Braid (part)
Facilities ⑪ ⫯ ⬛ ⌷ ⬗ 쓰 ⛟ ⛳ **Location** 2m N off B3145
Hotel ★★★ 73% HL Eastbury Hotel, Long St, SHERBORNE
☎ 01935 813131 21 en suite

SWANAGE

Isle of Purbeck
BH19 3AB
☎ 01929 450361 & 450354
🖹 01929 450501
e-mail: iop@purbeckgolf.co.uk
web: www.purbeckgolf.co.uk
A heathland course sited on the Purbeck Hills with grand
views across Swanage and Poole Harbour. holes of note
include the 5th, 8th, 14th, 15th, and 16th where trees,
gorse and heather assert themselves. The very attractive
clubhouse is built of local stone.

Purbeck Course: 18 holes, 6295yds, Par 70, SSS 70, Course record 66.
Dene Course: 9 holes, 4014yds, Par 60.
Club membership 500.
Visitors Booking required. **Societies** Booking required.
Green Fees Phone. **Prof** Ian Brake **Course Designer** H Colt
Facilities ⊕ ⚲ by prior arrangement ⚑ ⚐ ⚒ ⚞ ⚟ ⚐ ♨ ✆
Location 2.5m N on B3351
Hotel ★★★ 71% HL The Pines Hotel, Burlington Rd, SWANAGE
☎ 01929 425211   49 en suite

CO DURHAM

BARNARD CASTLE

Barnard Castle
Harmire Rd DL12 8QN
☎ 01833 638355
🖹 01833 695551
e-mail: sec@barnardcastlegolfclub.org.uk
web: www.barnardcastlegolfclub.org.uk
Flat parkland in open countryside. Plantations and
natural water add colour and interest to this classic
course.

18 holes, 6406yds, Par 73, SSS 71, Course record 63.
Club membership 650.
Visitors Mon-Sun & BHs. Booking required Sat, Sun & BHs.
Dress code. **Societies** Welcome. **Green Fees** £22 per round
(£35 Sat, Sun & BHs). ⚅ **Prof** Darren Pearce **Course Designer**
A Watson **Facilities** ⊕ ⚲ ⚑ ⚐ ⚒ ⚞ ♨ ✆ **Conf**
Corporate Hospitality Days **Location** 1m N of town centre on
B6278
Hotel ★★ HL Rose & Crown Hotel, ROMALDKIRK
☎ 01833 650213 7 en suite 5 annexe en suite

BISHOP AUCKLAND

Bishop Auckland
High Plains, Durham Rd DL14 8DL
☎ 01388 661618
🖹 01388 607005
e-mail: enquiries@bagc.co.uk
web: www.bagc.co.uk
A parkland course with many well-established trees
offering a challenging round. A small ravine adds
interest to several holes including the short 7th, from

a raised tee to a green surrounded by a stream, gorse
and bushes. Pleasant views over the Wear Valley and
over the residence of the Bishop of Durham. Has the
distinction of having five Par 5 holes and five Par 3s.
18 holes, 6379yds, Par 72, SSS 70, Course record 63.
Club membership 950.
Visitors Mon-Sun except BHs. Booking required Tue, Sat & Sun.
Handicap certificate. Dress code. **Societies** Booking required.
Green Fees £30 per day, £25 per round. **Prof** David Skiffington
Course Designer James Kay **Facilities** ⊕ ⚲ ⚑ ⚐ ⚒ ⚞ ⚟
♨ ✆ **Leisure** snooker. **Conf** facs Corporate Hospitality Days
Location 1m NE on A689
Hotel ★★★ 77% CHH BW Whitworth Hall Hotel, Whitworth Hall
Country Park, SPENNYMOOR ☎ 01388 811772 29 en suite

EAGLESCLIFFE

Eaglescliffe and District
Yarm Rd TS16 0DQ
☎ 01642 780238 (office)
🖹 01642 780238
e-mail: eaglescliffegcsec@tiscali.co.uk
web: www.eaglescliffegolfclub.co.uk
Undulating wooded parkland with views over the River
Tees to the Cleveland Hills. A tee on the riverbank makes
for a daunting tee shot at the 14th signature hole.
18 holes, 6275yds, Par 72, SSS 70, Course record 64.
Club membership 970.
Visitors Mon-Sun & BHs. Booking required Tue, Sat, Sun & BHs.
Handicap certificate. Dress code. **Societies** Welcome. **Green
Fees** £40 per day; £32 per round (£55/£40 Sun). ⚅ **Prof**
Graeme Bell **Course Designer** J Braid/H Cotton **Facilities** ⊕
⚲ ⚑ ⚐ ⚒ ⚞ ♨ ✆ ⚐ ✆ **Conf** Corporate Hospitality Days
Location On E side of A135 between Yarm -on-Tees
Hotel ★★★★ 79% HL Best Western Parkmore Hotel & Leisure
Park, 636 Yarm Rd, Eaglescliffe, STOCKTON-ON-TEES
☎ 01642 786815 55 en suite

HARTLEPOOL

Hartlepool
Hart Warren TS24 9QF
☎ 01429 274398
🖹 01429 274129
e-mail: hartlepoolgolf@btconnect.com
web: www.hartlepoolgolfclub.co.uk
A seaside course, half links, overlooking the North Sea. A
good test and equally enjoyable to all handicap players.
The 10th, Par 4, demands a precise second shot over a
ridge and between sand dunes to a green down near
the edge of the beach, alongside which several holes
are played.
18 holes, 6200yds, Par 70, SSS 70, Course record 62.
Club membership 700.
Visitors Mon-Sat except BHs. Booking required. Dress code.
Societies Booking required. **Green Fees** £34 per day (£44
weekends). **Prof** Graham Laidlaw **Course Designer** Partly

Braid **Facilities** ⊕ ⊖ ⊾ ⊏ ⊡ ⊿ ⊜ ✓ **Location** N of
Hartlepool, off A1086
Hotel BUD Premier Travel Inn Hartlepool, Maritme Av,
Hartlepool Marina, HARTLEPOOL ☎ 08701 977127 40 en suite

MIDDLETON ST GEORGE

Dinsdale Spa
Neasham Rd DL2 1DW
☎ 01325 332297
🖹 01325 332297
Mainly flat parkland on high land above the River Tees
with views of the Cleveland Hills. Water hazards in front
of the 15th tee and green; the prevailing west wind
affects the later holes. There is a practice area by the
clubhouse.
18 holes, 6107yds, Par 71, SSS 69, Course record 65.
Club membership 870.
Visitors Mon & Wed-Fri except BHs. Booking required. Handicap
certificate. Dress code. **Societies** Booking required. **Green Fees**
£25 per day. ⊛ **Prof** Martyn Stubbings **Facilities** ⊕ ⊖ ⊾ ⊏ ⊡
⊿ ⊜ ✓ **Conf** Corporate Hospitality Days **Location** 1.5m SW
Hotel ★★★ 74% HL Best Western Croft, Croft-on-Tees,
DARLINGTON ☎ 01325 720319 20 en suite

SEATON CAREW

Seaton Carew
Tees Rd TS25 1DE
☎ 01429 266249
🖹 01429 267952
e-mail: seatoncarewgolf@btconnect.com
web: www.seatoncarewgolfclub.co.uk
A championship links course taking full advantage of
its dunes, bents, whins and gorse. Renowned for its
Par 4 17th; just enough fairway for an accurate drive
followed by another precise shot to a pear-shape sloping
green that is severely trapped.
The Old Course: 18 holes, 6622yds, Par 72, SSS 72.
Brabazon Course: 18 holes, 6857yds, Par 73, SSS 73.
Club membership 700.
Visitors Mon-Fri. Limited play Sat, Sun & BHs. Booking required.
Handicap certificate. Dress code. **Societies** Booking required.
Green Fees Phone. ⊛ **Prof** Mark Rogers **Course Designer**
McKenzie **Facilities** ⊕ ⊖ ⊾ ⊏ ⊡ ⊿ ⊜ ✓ ⊜ ✓ **Conf**
Corporate Hospitality Days **Location** SE side of village off A178
Hotel BUD Premier Travel Inn Hartlepool, Maritme Av,
Hartlepool Marina, HARTLEPOOL ☎ 08701 977127 40 en suite

ESSEX

ABRIDGE

Abridge Golf and Country Club
Epping Ln, Stapleford Tawney RM4 1ST
☎ 01708 688396
🖹 01708 688550
e-mail: info@abridgegolf.com
web: www.abridgegolf.com
Easy walking parkland. The quick drying course is a
challenge for all levels. This has been the venue of
several professional tournaments. Abridge is a golf and
country club and has all the attendant facilities.
18 holes, 6704yds, Par 72, SSS 72. Course record 67.
Club membership 600.
Visitors may play Mon & Wed-Fri except BHs, Tue, Sat & Sun pm
only. Advance booking required. Handicap certificate required.
Dress code. **Societies** advance booking required. **Green Fees**
not confirmed. **Prof** Stuart Layton **Course Designer** Henry
Cotton **Facilities** ⊕ ⊾ ⊏ ⊡ ⊿ ⊜ ✓ ⊜ ✓ ⊱ **Leisure** swimming
pool, 3 snooker tables.
Conf facs Corporate Hospitality Days **Location** 1.75m NE
Hotel BUD Premier Travel Inn Romford West, Whalebone Ln
North, Chadwell Heath, ROMFORD ☎ 0870 9906450 40 en suite

CHELMSFORD

Chelmsford
Widford Rd CM2 9AP
☎ 01245 256483
🖹 01245 256483
e-mail: office@chelmsfordgc.co.uk
web: www.chelmsfordgc.co.uk
An undulating parkland course, hilly in parts, with
three holes in woods and four difficult Par 4s. From the
reconstructed clubhouse there are fine views over the
course and the wooded hills beyond.
18 holes, 5981yds, Par 68, SSS 69, Course record 61.
Club membership 650.
Visitors Mon-Fri except BHs. Handicap certificate required.
Dress code. **Societies** Booking required. **Green Fees** £40
per round. ⊛ **Prof** Mark Welch **Course Designer** Tom Dunn
Facilities ⊕ ⊾ ⊏ ⊡ ⊿ ⊜ ✓ ⊜ ✓ **Location** 1.5m S of town
centre off A12
Hotel ★★★ 75% HL Pontlands Park Country Hotel, West
Hanningfield Rd, Great Baddow, CHELMSFORD ☎ 01245 476444
36 en suite

CHIGWELL

Chigwell
High Rd IG7 5BH
☎ 020 8500 2059
020 8501 3410
e-mail: info@chigwellgolfclub.co.uk
web: www.chigwellgolfclub.co.uk
A course of high quality, mixing meadowland with parkland. For those who believe 'all Essex is flat' the undulating nature of Chigwell will be a refreshing surprise. The greens are excellent and the fairways tight with mature trees.
18 holes, 6296yds, Par 71, SSS 70, Course record 66. Club membership 800.
Visitors may play Mon, Wed, Thu & Tue pm only. Advance booking required. Handicap certificate required. Dress code. **Societies** advance booking required. **Green Fees** not confirmed. **Prof** James Fuller **Course Designer** Hawtree/Taylor **Facilities** **Conf** facs Corporate Hospitality Days **Location** 0.5m S on A113
Hotel BUD Premier Travel Inn Romford Central, Mercury Gardens, ROMFORD ☎ 08701 977220 64 en suite

INGRAVE

Thorndon Park
CM13 3RH
☎ 01277 810345
01277 810645
e-mail: office@thorndonpark.com
web: www.thorndonparkgolfclub.com
Course is playable even at the wettest time of the year. holes stand on their own surrounded by mature oaks, some of which are more than 700 years old. The lake in the centre of the course provides both a challenge and a sense of peace and tranquillity. The Palladian Thorndon Hall, site of the old clubhouse, is the magnificent backdrop to the closing hole.
18 holes, 6512yds, Par 71, SSS 71, Course record 68. Club membership 600.
Visitors Mon-Fri except BHs. Booking required. Handicap certificate. Dress code. **Societies** Booking required. **Green Fees** Phone. **Prof** Brian White **Course Designer** Colt/Alison **Facilities** **Conf** Corporate Hospitality Days **Location** W side of village off A128
Hotel ★★★ 77% HL BW Weald Park Hotel, Golf & Country Club, Coxtie Green Rd, South Weald, BRENTWOOD ☎ 01277 375101 32 annexe en suite

ORSETT

Orsett
Brentwood Rd RM16 3DS
☎ 01375 891352
01375 892471
e-mail: enquiries@orsettgolfclub.co.uk
web: www.club-noticeboard.co.uk/orsett
18 holes, 6614yds, Par 72, SSS 72, Course record 65.
Course Designer James Braid **Location** Junct A13 , S towards Chadwell St Mary
Telephone for further details

STOCK

Crondon Park Stock Rd CM4 9DP
☎ 01277 843027 01277 841356
e-mail: paul@crondon.com
web: www.crondon.com
Undulating parkland with many water hazards, set in the Crondon valley.
18 holes, 6627yards, Par 72, SSS 72, Course record 67. Club membership 700.
Visitors Mon-Fri. Booking required. Dress code. **Societies** Welcome. **Green Fees** Phone. **Prof** Chris Wood/Freddie Sunderland **Course Designer** Mr M Gillet **Facilities** **Conf** facs Corporate Hospitality Days **Location** On B1007, between Stock and Ingatestone
Hotel ★★★★ 71% CHH Greenwoods Hotel Spa & Retreat, Stock Rd, STOCK ☎ 01277 829990 39 en suite

THEYDON BOIS

Theydon Bois
Theydon Rd CM16 4EH
☎ 01992 812460 (pro) & 813054 (office)
01992 815602
e-mail: theydonboisgolf@btconnect.com
web: www.theydongolf.co.uk
The course was originally nine holes built into Epping Forest. It was later extended to 18 holes which were well-planned and well-bunkered but in keeping with the Forest tradition. The old nine in the Forest are short and have two bunkers between them, but even so a wayward shot can be among the trees. The autumn colours here are truly magnificent.

18 holes, 5490yds, Par 68, SSS 67, Course record 64. Club membership 600.
Visitors Mon, Tue & Fri except BHs. Dress code. **Societies** Booking required. **Green Fees** £30 per round. **Prof** R Hall **Course Designer** James Braid **Facilities** **Location** M25 junct 26, 2m
Hotel BUD Travelodge Harlow North Weald, A414 Eastbound, Tylers Green, North Weald, HARLOW ☎ 08700 850 950 60 en suite

GLOUCESTERSHIRE

CHIPPING SODBURY

Chipping Sodbury

Trinity Ln BS37 6PU
☎ 01454 319042
🖹 01454 320052
e-mail: info@chippingsodburygolfclub.co.uk
web: www.chippingsodburygolfclub.co.uk
Founded in 1905, a parkland course of championship
proportions on the edge of the Cotswolds. The easy
walking terrain, delicately interrupted by a medley
of waterways and lakes, is complimented by a stylish
clubhouse.
Beaufort Course: 18 holes, 6912yds, Par 73, SSS 73,
Course record 65. Club membership 800.
Visitors may play Mon-Fri except BHs. Dress code. **Societies**
Welcome. **Green Fees** £32 per round. **Prof** Mike Watts
Course Designer Hawtree **Facilities** ⊕ ⍩ ⌾ 🏌 ⌷ 🖦 ☶ ☂ ⛳
✐ 🦽 ✐ **Leisure** 6 hole academy course. **Conf** facs Corporate
Hospitality Days **Location** 0.5m N
Hotel ★★ 78% HL Best Western Compass Inn, TORMARTON
☎ 01454 218242 & 218577 🖹 01454 218741 26 en suite

COALPIT HEATH

The Kendleshire

Henfield Rd BS36 2TG
☎ 0117 956 7007
🖹 0117 957 3433
e-mail: info@kendleshire.com
web: www.kendleshire.com
Opened in 1997, the course has 27 holes with water
coming into play on 18 holes. Notable holes are the 11th,
the 16th and the 27th. The 11th is a short hole with
an island green set in a 3-acre lake and the 16th has
a second shot played over water. The course is never
short of interest and the greens have been built to USGA
specification.
18 holes, 6567, Par 71, SSS 72, Course record 63.
18 holes, 6249, Par 71, SSS 70, Course record 68.
18 holes, 6353, Par 70, SSS 70, Course record 68.
Club membership 900.
Visitors Mon-Sun & BHs. Booking required. Dress code.
Societies Booking required. **Green Fees** £35 per round (£40
weekends). **Prof** Tony Mealing **Course Designer** A Stiff/P
McEvoy **Facilities** ⊕ ⍩ ⌾ 🏌 ⌷ 🖦 ☶ ☂ ⛳ ✐ 🦽 ✐ ⛳ **Conf** facs
Corporate Hospitality Days **Location** M32 junct 1, on Avon Ring
Road
Hotel ★★★★ 72% HL Jurys Bristol Hotel, Prince St, BRISTOL
☎ 0117 923 0333 192 en suite

DURSLEY

Stinchcombe Hill

Stinchcombe Hill GL11 6AQ
☎ 01453 542015
🖹 01453 549545
e-mail: secretary@stinchcombehill.plus.com
web: www.stinchcombehillgolfclub.com
High on the hill with splendid views of the Cotswolds,
the River Severn and the Welsh hills. A downland course
with good turf, some trees and an interesting variety of
greens. Protected greens make this a challenging course
in windy conditions.
18 holes, 5734yds, Par 68, SSS 68, Course record 63.
Club membership 550.
Visitors Mon-Sun & BHs. Booking required. Handicap certificate
required. Dress code. **Societies** Booking required. **Green Fees**
£34 per day, £28 per 18 holes (£42/£36 weekends and bank
holidays). ⊛
Prof Paul Bushell **Course Designer** Arthur Hoare **Facilities**
⊕ ⍩ ⌾ by prior arrangement 🖦 ⌷ 🏌 ☶ ☂ ⛳ **Conf** Corporate
Hospitality Days **Location** 1m W off A4135
Hotel ★★★ 68% HL Prince of Wales Hotel, BERKELEY ROAD
☎ 01453 810474 43 en suite

GLOUCESTER

Ramada Gloucester

Matson Ln, Robinswood Hill GL4 6EA
☎ 01452 525653
🖹 01452 307212
web: www.gloucestergolf.com
Undulating, wooded course, built around a hill with
superb views over Gloucester and the Cotswolds.
The 12th is a drive straight up a hill, nicknamed
'Coronary Hill'.
18 holes, 6170yds, Par 70, SSS 69, Course record 65.
Club membership 600.
Visitors Mon-Sun & BHs. Dress code. **Societies** Welcome.
Green Fees Phone. **Prof** Keith Wood **Facilities** ⊕ ⍩ ⌾ 🖦 ⌷ 🏌
☶ ☂ ⛳ ◇ ✐ 🦽 ✐ ⛳ **Leisure** hard tennis courts, heated indoor
swimming pool, squash, sauna, solarium, gymnasium, 9 hole
Par 3 course. **Location** 2.5m SE of Gloucester, off B4073
Hotel ★★★ 68% HL Ramada Hotel & Resort Gloucester, Matson
Ln, Robinswood Hill, GLOUCESTER ☎ 01452 525653 97 en suite

Rodway Hill

Newent Rd, Highnam GL2 8DN
☎ 01452 384222
🖹 01452 313814
e-mail: info@rodway-hill-golf-course.co.uk
web: www.rodway-hill-golf-course.co.uk
A challenging 18-hole course with superb panoramic views.
Testing front five holes and the Par 3 13th and Par 5 16th
affected by strong crosswinds off the River Severn.

continued

18 holes, 6040yds, Par 70, SSS 69, Course record 66. Club membership 400.
Visitors Mon-Sun & BHs. Boking required. Dress code. **Societies** Booking required. **Green Fees** £15 per 18 holes, £9 per 9 holes (£17-£18/£9-£10 Sat & Sun). **Prof** Chris Murphy **Course Designer** John Gabb **Facilities** ⑪ ⑩ ⑩ ▙ ◻ ⑩ ⏚ 🛒 ⚑ ◈ 🛒 ⚑ **Conf** Corporate Hospitality Days **Location** 2m outside Gloucester on B4215
Hotel ★★★ 70% HL Macdonald Hatherley Manor, Down Hatherley Ln, GLOUCESTER ☎ 0870 1942126 52 en suite

TEWKESBURY

Tewkesbury Park Hotel Golf & Country Club
Lincoln Green Ln GL20 7DN
☎ 01684 295405
🖨 01684 292386
e-mail: tewkesburypark@foliohotels.com
web: www.foliohotels.com/tewkesburypark

The course offers many interesting and testing holes, with wooded areas and water hazards early in the round, opening up onto spacious fairways on the back nine of the undulating course.
18 holes, 6533yds, Par 73, SSS 72, Course record 66. Club membership 550.
Visitors Mon-Sun & BHs. Booking required. Dress code. **Societies** Booking required. **Green Fees** Phone. **Prof** Marc Cottrell **Course Designer** Frank Pennick **Facilities** ⑪ ⑩ ⑩ ▙ ◻ ⑩ ⏚ 🛒 ⚑ ◈ 🛒 ⚑ **Leisure** hard tennis courts, heated indoor swimming pool, squash, sauna, solarium, gymnasium. **Conf** facs Corporate Hospitality Days **Location** 1m SW off A38 **Hotel** ★★★ 72% HL Tewkesbury Park Hotel Golf & Country Club, Lincoln Green Ln, TEWKESBURY ☎ 0870 609 6101 80 en suite

WICK

Park Resort
Tracy Park Estate, Bath Rd BS30 5RN
☎ 0117 937 1800
🖨 0117 937 1813
e-mail: info@tpresort.com
web: www.theparkresort.com
Two 18-hole championship courses on the south-western escarpment of the Cotswolds, affording fine views. Both courses present a challenge to all levels of player, with water playing a part on a number of occasions. The elegant clubhouse dates from 1600, set in the 240-acre estate of this golf and country club.
Crown Course: 18 holes, 6201yds, Par 69, SSS 70.
Cromwell Course: 18 holes, 6157yds, Par 71, SSS 70.
Club membership 1000.
Visitors Mon-Sun & BHs. Booking required. Dress code. **Societies** Booking required. **Green Fees** £18-£38 per 18 holes. **Prof** Richard Berry **Facilities** ⑩ ⑩ ▙ ◻ ⑩ ⏚ 🛒 ◈ 🛒 ⚑ **Conf** facs Corporate Hospitality Days **Location** M4 junct 18, then follow A46 towards Bath followed by A420. Course off A420 E of village of Wick
Hotel ★★★ HL The Queensberry Hotel, Russel St, BATH ☎ 01225 447928 820830 🖨 01225 446065 29 en suite

GREATER LONDON

ADDINGTON

The Addington
205 Shirley Church Rd CR0 5AB
☎ 020 8777 1055
🖨 020 8777 6661
e-mail: info@addingtongolf.com
web: www.addingtongolf.com
This heather and woodland course is considered to be one of the best laid out courses in Southern England with the world famous 13th, Par 3 at 230yds. A good test of golfing ability with no two holes the same.

The Addington

18 holes, 6338yds, Par 69, SSS 71, Course record 66.
Visitors Mon-Fri. Restricted play Sat, Sun & BHs. Booking required. required. Dress code **Societies** Booking required. **Green Fees** Phone. **Prof** M Churchill **Course Designer** J F Abercromby **Facilities** ⑪ ⑩ ⑩ ▙ ◻ ⑩ ⏚ 🛒 ⚑ ◈ 🛒 **Conf**

Corporate Hospitality Days **Location** M25 junct 7, 3m from Croydon

Hotel ★★★★ 73% HL Selsdon Park Hotel & Golf Club, Addington Rd, Sanderstead, CROYDON ☎ 020 8657 8811 204 en suite

BECKENHAM

Langley Park
Barnfield Wood Rd BR3 6SZ
☎ 020 8658 6849
📄 020 8658 6310
e-mail: manager@langleyparkgolf.co.uk
web: www.langleyparkgolf.co.uk

A pleasant but difficult, well-wooded parkland course. Natural hazards include a lake at the Par 3 18th hole. Although most fairways are bordered by woodland, they are wide with forgiving rough and friendly bunkers.
18 holes, 6453yds, Par 69, SSS 71, Course record 65. Club membership 700.
Visitors Mon-Fri except BHs. Handicap certificate. Dress code. **Societies** Booking required. **Green Fees** £60 per day, £40 per round. **Prof** Colin Staff **Course Designer** J H Taylor **Facilities** ⑪ ⑩ 🍴 ⬜ ➰ 🏌 🏠 ⛳ 🛒 **Conf** Corporate Hospitality Days **Location** 0.5 N of Beckenham on B2015
Hotel ★★★ 77% HL Best Western Bromley Court Hotel, Bromley Hill, BROMLEY ☎ 020 8461 8600 114 en suite

BROMLEY

Sundridge Park
Garden Rd BR1 3NE
☎ 020 8460 0278
📄 020 8289 3050
e-mail: gm@spgc.co.uk
web: www.spgc.co.uk

The East Course is longer than the West but many think the shorter of the two courses is the more difficult. The East is surrounded by trees while the West is more hilly, with good views. Both are certainly a good test of golf. An Open qualifying course with year round irrigation of fairways.
East Course: 18 holes, 6516yds, Par 71, SSS 71, Course record 63.
West Course: 18 holes, 6019yds, Par 69, SSS 69, Course record 65. Club membership 1200.
Visitors Mon-Fri. Handicap certificate. Dress code. **Societies** Booking required. **Green Fees** £85 per day, £65 per round **Prof** Stuart Dowsett **Course Designer** Willie Park **Facilities** ⑪ ⑩ 🍴 ⬜ ➰ 🏌 🏠 🛒 **Conf** facs Corporate Hospitality Days **Location** N side of town centre off A2212
Hotel ★★★ 77% HL Best Western Bromley Court Hotel, Bromley Hill, BROMLEY ☎ 020 8461 8600 114 en suite

CROYDON

Shirley Park
194 Addiscombe Rd CR0 7LB
☎ 020 8654 1143
📄 020 8654 6733
e-mail: secretary@shirleyparkgolfclub.co.uk
web: www.shirleyparkgolfclub.co.uk

The parkland course lies amid fine woodland with good views of Shirley Hills. The more testing holes come in the middle section of the course. The remarkable 7th hole calls for a 187yd iron or wood shot diagonally across a narrow valley to a shelved green set right-handed into a ridge. The 13th hole, 160yds, is considered to be one of the finest short holes in the county.
18 holes, 6210yds, Par 71, SSS 69, Course record 64. Club membership 600.
Visitors may play Mon-Fri except BHs & Sun. Dress code. **Societies** Booking required. **Green Fees** £40 weekday (£48 Sun). **Prof** Michael Taylor **Course Designer** Tom Simpson/Herbert Fowler **Facilities** ⑪ ⑩ 🍴 ⬜ ➰ 🏌 🏠 ⛳ 🛒 **Leisure** snooker. **Conf** Corporate Hospitality Days **Location** E of town centre on A232
Hotel ★★★★ 73% HL Selsdon Park Hotel & Golf Club, Addington Rd, Sanderstead, CROYDON ☎ 020 8657 8811 204 en suite

HADLEY WOOD

Hadley Wood
Beech Hill EN4 0JJ
☎ 020 8449 4328 & 4486
📄 020 8364 8633
e-mail: gm@hadleywoodgc.com
web: www.hadleywoodgc.com

Parkland on the north-west edge of London. The gently undulating fairways have a friendly width inviting the player to open his shoulders, though the thick rough can be very punishing to the unwary. The course is pleasantly wooded and there are some admirable views.

Club membership 650.

continued

Visitors may play Mon-Fri & Sun except BHs. Advance booking required. Handicap certificate required. Dress code. **Societies** advance booking required. **Green Fees** not confirmed. **Prof** Peter Jones **Course Designer** Alister Mackenzie **Facilities** ⑪ ⑩ ⓛ ☐ ⑪ 丿 ⑥ ⑥ ⑥ **Conf** facs Corporate Hospitality Days **Location** M25 junct 24, take A111 to Cockforsters, 2m to 3rd turning right

Hotel ★★★★ 77% HL West Lodge Park Hotel, Cockfosters Rd, HADLEY WOOD ☎ 020 8216 3900 46 en suite 13 annexe en suite

KINGSTON UPON THAMES

Coombe Hill
Golf Club Dr, Coombe Ln West KT2 7DF
☎ 020 8336 7600
▤ 020 8336 7601
e-mail: thesecretary@chgc.net
web: www.coombehillgolfclub.com
Charming heathland course featuring a fine display of rhododendrons during May and June. The course presents a challenge to golfers of all standards offering superb greens, quality short holes and a number of testing long holes requiring approach shots to elevated greens.
18 holes, 6293yds, Par 71, SSS 71, Course record 67. Club membership 550.
Visitors may play Mon, Tue, Thu-Sun & BHs. Wed pm only. Booking required. Handicap certificate. Dress code. **Societies** Welcome. **Green Fees** £100 per 36 holes, £80 per 18 holes. **Prof** Andy Dunn **Course Designer** J F Abercromby **Facilities** ⑪ ⓛ ☐ ⑪ ⓛ ☐ ⑪ ⑥ **Leisure** sauna. **Conf** Corporate Hospitality Days **Location** 1.75m E on A238
Hotel BUD Travelodge London Kingston Upon Thames, 21-23 London Rd, KINGSTON-UPON-THAMES ☎ 08700 850 950 72 en suite

NORTHWOOD

Northwood
Rickmansworth Rd HA6 2QW
☎ 01923 821384
▤ 01923 840150
e-mail: secretary@northwoodgolf.co.uk
web: www.northwoodgolf.co.uk
A high quality parkland course. The course provides a good test of golf to the experienced golfer and can hold many surprises for the unsuspecting. The Par 4 10th hole, Death or Glory, has wrecked many good cards in the past, while the long Par 4 5th hole requires two very good shots to make par.
18 holes, 6535yds, Par 71, SSS 71, Course record 67. Club membership 650.
Visitors may play Mon, Thu, Fri. Advance booking required. Dress code. **Societies** advance booking required. **Green Fees** not confirmed. **Prof** C J Holdsworth **Course Designer** James Braid **Facilities** ⑪ ⑩ ⓛ ☐ ⑪ ⓛ ☐ ⑥ **Conf** Corporate Hospitality Days **Location** On A404

Hotel ★★★ 74% HL Quality Harrow Hotel, 12-22 Pinner Rd, HARROW ☎ 020 8427 3435 79 en suite

Sandy Lodge
Sandy Lodge Ln HA6 2JD
☎ 01923 825429
▤ 01923 824319
e-mail: info@sandylodge.co.uk
web: www.sandylodge.co.uk
A links-type, very sandy, heathland course.
18 holes, 6347yds, Par 71, SSS 71, Course record 64. Club membership 780.
Visitors Mon-Fri. Handicap certificate required. Dress code. **Societies** Booking required. **Green Fees** £45 per round. **Prof** Jeff Pinsent **Course Designer** H Vardon **Facilities** ⑪ ⑩ ⓛ ☐ ⑪ ⓛ ☐ ⑥ ⑥ ⑥ **Conf** Corporate Hospitality Days **Location** N of town centre off A4125
Hotel ★★★ 71% HL Best Western The White House, Upton Rd, WATFORD ☎ 01923 237316 57 en suite

RICHMOND (UPON THAMES)

Richmond
Sudbrook Park, Petersham TW10 7AS
☎ 020 8940 4351 (office) & 8940 7792 (shop)
▤ 8940 8332/7914
e-mail: admin@richmondgolfclub.com
web: www.the richmondgolfclub.com
Beautiful and historic parkland on the edge of Richmond Park dating from 1891 and extensively modernised in recent years. The clubhouse is one of the most-distinguished small Georgian mansions in England.
18 holes, 6100yds, Par 70, SSS 70, Course record 65. Club membership 650.
Visitors may play Mon-Fri except BHs. Advance booking required Wed. Handicap certificate required. Dress code. **Societies** advance booking required. **Green Fees** not confirmed. **Prof** Steve Burridge **Course Designer** Tom Dunn **Facilities** ⑪ ⑩ by prior arrangement ⓛ ☐ ⑪ ⓛ ☐ ⑥ ⑥ ⑥ **Conf** facs Corporate Hospitality Days **Location** 1.5m S off A307 between KIngston & Richmond
Hotel ★★★★ 71% HL Richmond Hill Hotel, Richmond Hill, RICHMOND UPON THAMES ☎ 020 8940 2247 138 en suite

Royal Mid-Surrey
Old Deer Park, Twickenham Rd TW9 2SB
☎ 020 8940 1894
▤ 020 8939 0150
e-mail: secretary@rmsgc.co.uk
web: www.rmsgc.co.uk
A long playing historic parkland course. The flat fairways are cleverly bunkered. The 1st hole at 245yds from the medal tees is a tough Par 3 opening hole. The 18th provides an exceptionally good Par 4 finish with a huge bunker before the green to catch the not quite perfect long second. The Inner Course, while shorter than the Outer, offers a fair challenge to all golfers. Again the 18th offers a strong Par 4 finish with bunkers threatening

from the tee. A long second to a sloping, well-bunkered green will reward the accurate player.

Outer Course: 18 holes, 6343yds, Par 69, SSS 71, Course record 62.
Inner Course: 18 holes, 5544yds, Par 68, SSS 67.
Club membership 1400.

Visitors Mon-Fri except BHs. Booking required. Handicap certificate. Dress code. **Societies** Booking required. **Green Fees** Phone. **Prof** Matthew Paget **Course Designer** J H Taylor **Facilities** ⑪ 🍴 🍺 🏌 🛒 ♂ ♂ **Leisure** snooker. **Conf** facs Corporate Hospitality Days **Location** 0.5m N of Richmond off A316

Hotel ★★★★ 71% HL Richmond Hill Hotel, Richmond Hill, RICHMOND UPON THAMES ☎ 020 8940 2247 138 en suite

ROMFORD

Romford
Heath Dr, Gidea Park RM2 5QB
☎ 01708 740986 📄 01708 752157
18 holes, 6410yds, Par 72, SSS 70, Course record 64.
Course Designer H Colt **Location** 1m NE on A118
Telephone for further details
Hotel BUD Premier Travel Inn Romford Central, Mercury Gardens, ROMFORD ☎ 08701 977220 64 en suite

GREATER MANCHESTER

BOLTON

Bolton
Lostock Park, Chorley New Rd BL6 4AJ
☎ 01204 843067 & 843278
📄 01204 843067
e-mail: secretary@boltongolfclub.co.uk
This well-maintained heathland course is always a pleasure to visit. The 12th hole should be treated with respect and so too should the final four holes which have ruined many a card.
18 holes, 6237yds, Par 70, SSS 70, Course record 64.
Club membership 612.
Visitors may play Mon, Wed-Fri except BHs. Booking required. Dress code. **Societies** Booking required. **Green Fees** £35 per day, £30 per round. ☜ **Prof** R Longworth **Facilities** ⑪ 🍴 🍺 🏌 🍴 🛒 ♂

Conf Corporate Hospitality Days **Location** 3m W of Bolton on A673
Hotel BUD Premier Travel Inn Bolton, 991 Chorley New Rd, Horwich, BOLTON ☎ 08701 977282 40 en suite

MIDDLETON

Manchester
Hopwood Cottage, Rochdale Rd M24 6QP
☎ 0161 643 3202
📄 0161 643 9174
e-mail: secretary@mangc.co.uk
web: www.mangc.co.uk
Moorland golf of unique character over a spaciously laid out course with generous fairways sweeping along to large greens. A wide variety of holes will challenge the golfer's technique, particularly the testing last four holes.
18 holes, 6491yds, Par 72, SSS 72, Course record 63.
Club membership 650.
Visitors Mon-Fri, Sun & BHs. Advance booking required. Handicap certificate. Dress code. **Societies** Booking required. **Green Fees** £45 per day, £35 per round (£50 per round Sun & BHs). **Prof** Brian Connor **Course Designer** Shapland Colt **Facilities** ⑪ 🍴 🍺 🏌 🍴 🛒 ♂ ♂ **Leisure** snooker. **Conf** facs Corporate Hospitality Days **Location** 1m S of M62 junct 20 on A664
Hotel ★★★★ 77% HL Mercure Norton Grange Hotel & Spa, Manchester Rd, Castleton, ROCHDALE ☎ 0870 1942119 81 en suite

SWINTON

Swinton Park
East Lancashire Rd M27 5LX
☎ 0161 794 0861
📄 0161 281 0698
e-mail: info@spgolf.co.uk
web: www.spgolf.co.uk
One of Lancashire's longest inland courses. Designed and laid out in 1926 by James Braid.

18 holes, 6472yds, Par 73, SSS 71.
Club membership 600.
Visitors Mon-Wed & Fri except BHs. Booking required. Handicap certificate. Dress code. **Societies** Booking required. **Green Fees** £30 per day/round. **Prof** James Wilson **Course Designer** James Braid
Facilities ⑪ 🍴 🍺 🏌 🍴 🛒 ♂ **Conf** facs Corporate Hospitality Days **Location** Entrance off A580
Hotel ★★★ 68% HL Novotel Manchester West, Worsley Brow, WORSLEY119 en suite

HAMPSHIRE

BARTON-ON-SEA

Barton-on-Sea
Milford Rd BH25 5PP
☎ 01425 615308
🖹 01425 621457
e-mail: admin@barton-on-sea-golf.co.uk
web: www.barton-on-sea-golf.co.uk
A cliff top course with 3 loops of nine giving a great
variety and challenge to golfers of all handicaps. Fine
views over the Solent and Isle of Wight.
9 holes, 3182yds, Par 36.
Needles: 9 holes, 3339yds, Par 36.
Stroller: 9 holes, 3114yds, Par 36.
Club membership 750.
Visitors Mon-Sun & BHs. Booking required. Handicap certificate.
Dress code. Must contact in advance. **Societies** Booking
required.
Green Fees £44 per day (£55 Sat, Sun & BHs). **Prof** Peter
Rodgers **Course Designer** Vardon/Colt/Stutt **Facilities** ⊕ ⊺⊙⊺
by prior arrangement ⅃⊾ ⊑ ⊺⅃ ⊿ ⊜ ⊷ ⚡ **Leisure** snooker
tables.
Conf Corporate Hospitality Days **Location** B3058 SE of town
Hotel ★★★★★ HL Chewton Glen Hotel, Christchurch Rd, NEW
MILTON ☎ 01425 275341 58 en suite

BASINGSTOKE

Basingstoke
Kempshott Park RG23 7LL
☎ 01256 465990
🖹 01256 331793
e-mail: enquiries@basingstokegolfclub.co.uk
web: www.basingstokegolfclub.co.uk
A well-maintained parkland course. Excellent bunkering
requires good course management from the tee and all
clubs will be required with many long testing Par 4's.
A true test of golf, yet fair and playable for the less
experienced golfer.
18 holes, 6350yds, Par 70, SSS 70, Course record 63.
Club membership 700.
Visitors Mon-Fri except BHs. Handicap certificate. Dress code.
Societies Booking required. **Green Fees** £50 per day, £40
per round. Reduced winter fees. **Prof** Richard Woolley **Course
Designer** James Braid **Facilities** ⊕ ⊺⊙⊺ ⅃⊾ ⊑ ⊺⅃ ⊿ ⊜ ⊷ ⚡ ⊜
⚡ **Conf** facs Corporate Hospitality Days **Location** M3 junct 7,
1m SW on A30
Hotel ★★★★ 76% HL Apollo Hotel, Aldermaston Roundabout,
BASINGSTOKE ☎ 01256 796700 125 en suite

BORDON

Blackmoor
Firgrove Rd, Whitehill GU35 9EH
☎ 01420 472775
🖹 01420 487666
e-mail: admin@blackmoorgolf.co.uk
web: www.blackmoorgolf.co.uk
A first-class moorland course with a great variety
of holes. Fine greens and wide pine tree-lined fairways
are a distinguishing feature. The ground is mainly flat
and walking easy.
18 holes, 6164yds, Par 69, SSS 70, Course record 63.
Club membership 750.
Visitors Mon-Fri except BHs. Booking required. Handicap
certificate. Dress code. **Societies** Booking required. **Green
Fees** £49 per 36 holes; £39 per 18 holes. ⊕ **Prof** Stephen
Clay **Course Designer** H S Colt **Facilities** ⊕ ⊺⊙⊺ by prior
arrangement ⅃⊾ ⊑ ⊺⅃ ⊿ ⊜ ⚡
Conf Corporate Hospitality Days **Location** 6m S from Farnham
on A325, through Whitehill, right at rdbt
Hotel ★★★ 72% HL Alton House Hotel, Normandy St, ALTON
☎ 01420 80033 43 en suite

BROCKENHURST

Brokenhurst Manor
Sway Rd SO42 7SG
☎ 01590 623332 (Secretary)
🖹 01590 624691
e-mail: secretary@brokenhurst-manor.org.uk
web: www.brokenhurst-manor.org.uk
An attractive forest course set in the New Forest, with
the unusual feature of three loops of six holes each
to complete the round. Fascinating holes include the
short 5th and 12th, and the 4th and 17th, both dog-legs.
A stream also features on seven of the holes.
18 holes, 6222yds, Par 70, SSS 70, Course record 63.
Club membership 700.
Visitors Mon-Sun & BHs. Booking required Thu. Handicap
certificate.
Dress code. **Societies** Booking required. **Green Fees** £67 per
day; £49 per round (£78/£60 Sat, Sun & BHs). **Prof** Bruce Parker
Course Designer H S Colt **Facilities** ⊕ ⊺⊙⊺ ⅃⊾ ⊑ ⊺⅃ ⊿ ⊜ ⚡
Conf Corporate Hospitality Days **Location** 1m S on B3055

Hotel ★★ 65% SHL Watersplash Hotel, The Rise, BROCKENHURST ☎ 01590 622344 23 en suite

Brokenhurst Manor

FLEET

North Hants
Minley Rd GU51 1RF
☎ 01252 616443
🖹 01252 811627
e-mail: secretary@north-hants-fleetgc.co.uk
web: www.northhantsgolf.co.uk
Picturesque tree-lined course with much heather and gorse close to the fairways. The club is currently completing a woodland management scheme which will give new views and incorporate a review of fairway and greenside bunkering. A testing first hole to the course is a 214 yd followed by many other testing holes around the course. The ground is rather undulating and, though not tiring, does offer some excellent blind shots, and more than a few surprises in judging distance.

18 holes, 6472yds, Par 70, SSS 72, Course record 65. Club membership 600.
Visitors Mon-Sun & BHs. Booking required. Handicap certificate. Dress code. **Societies** Booking required. **Green Fees** Phone. **Prof** Steve Porter **Course Designer** James Braid **Facilities** ⊕ ⊚ ⌷ ⌑ ⌑ ⌑ ♨ ♨ ✠ **Conf** Corporate Hospitality Days **Location** 0.25m N of Fleet station on B3013
Hotel ★★★ 67% HL Falcon Hotel, 68 Farnborough Rd, FARNBOROUGH ☎ 01252 545378 30 en suite

HAYLING ISLAND

Hayling
Links Ln PO11 0BX
☎ 023 9246 4446
🖹 023 9246 1119
e-mail: generaloffice@haylinggolf.co.uk
web: www.haylinggolf.co.uk
A delightful links course among the dunes offering fine seascapes and views of the Isle of Wight. Varying sea breezes and sometimes strong winds ensure that the course seldom plays the same two days running. Testing holes at the 12th and 13th, both Par 4. Club selection is important.
18 holes, 6531yds, Par 71, SSS 71, Course record 65. Club membership 1000.
Visitors Mon-Fri except BHs. Handicap certificate. Dress code. **Societies** Welcome. **Green Fees** £62 per day; £49 per round. **Prof** Raymond Gadd **Course Designer** Taylor 1905, Simpson 1933 **Facilities** ⊕ ⌑ ⌷ ⌑ ⌑ ⌑ ♨ ✠ **Conf** facs Corporate Hospitality Days **Location** SW side of island at West Town
Hotel ★★★ 75% HL Brookfield Hotel, Havant Rd, EMSWORTH ☎ 01243 373363 40 en suite

KINGSCLERE

Sandford Springs
RG26 5RT
☎ 01635 296800 & 296808 (Pro Shop)
🖹 01635 296801
e-mail: alicew@sandfordspringsgolf.co.uk
web: www.sandfordsprings.co.uk
The course has unique variety in beautiful surroundings and offers three distinctive loops of nine holes. There are water hazards, woodlands and gradients to negotiate, providing a challenge for all playing categories.

The Park: 9 holes, 2963yds, Par 34.
The Lakes: 9 holes, 3042yds, Par 35.
The Wood: 9 holes, 3180yds, Par 36.
Club membership 700.

continued

Visitors Mon-Fri except BHs. Booking required. Dress code. **Societies** Booking required. **Green Fees** not confirmed. **Prof** Neal Granville **Course Designer** Hawtree & Son **Facilities** ⑨ ⑩ ⓛ ⏍ ⓣ⏌ ⏃ ⏢ ⑨⏂ ⑩ ⏢ ⑨ ⓯ **Conf** facs Corporate Hospitality Days **Location** On A339 between Basingstoke & Newbury **Hotel** ★★★★ 76% HL Apollo Hotel, Aldermaston Roundabout, BASINGSTOKE ☎ 01256 796700 125 en suite

LIPHOOK

Liphook
Wheatsheaf Enclosure GU30 7EH
☎ 01428 723271 & 723785
📄 01428 724853
e-mail: secretary@liphookgolfclub.com
web: www.liphookgolfclub.com
Heathland course with easy walking and fine views.
18 holes, 6167yds, Par 70, SSS 69, Course record 67.
Club membership 800.
Visitors Booking required. Handicap certificate. Dress code.
Societies Booking required. **Green Fees** £63 per day, £50 per round (£70/£60 Sat, £70 Sun & bank holidays pm only). **Prof** Ian Mowbray **Course Designer** A C Croome **Facilities** ⓛ ⏍ ⓣ⏌ ⏃ ⏢ ⑨⏂ ⑨ ⑩ ⑨ ⓯ **Conf** Corporate Hospitality Days **Location** 1m S on B2070
Hotel ★★★★ 77% HL Lythe Hill Hotel & Spa, Petworth Rd, HASLEMERE ☎ 01428 651251 41 en suite

Old Thorns Golf & Country Estate
Griggs Green GU30 7PE
☎ 01428 724555
📄 01428 725036
e-mail: sales@oldthorns.com
web: www.oldthorns.com
A challenging 18-hole championship course with rolling hills, undulating greens, demanding water features and magnificent views. A challenge to any level of golfer.
18 holes, 6461yds, Par 72, SSS 72.
Club membership 200.
Visitors may play Mon-Sun & BHs. Advance booking required.
Societies advance booking required. **Green Fees** not confirmed.
Prof Steven Hall **Course Designer** Peter Alliss **Facilities** ⑨ ⑩ ⓛ ⏍ ⓣ⏌ ⏃ ⏢ ⑨⏂ ⑨ ⑩ ⑨ ⓯ **Leisure** hard tennis courts, heated indoor swimming pool, fishing, sauna, solarium, gymnasium. **Conf** Corporate Hospitality Days **Location** Off A3 at Griggs Green, S of Liphook, signed Old Thorns
Hotel ★★★ 79% Old Thorns Hotel Golf & Country Estate, Griggs Green, LIPHOOK ☎ 01428 724555 29 en suite 4 annexe rms (3 en suite)

LYNDHURST

Bramshaw
Brook SO43 7HE
☎ 023 8081 3433
📄 023 8081 3460
e-mail: golf@bramshaw.co.uk
web: www.bramshaw.co.uk
Manor Course: 18 holes, 6527yds, Par 71, SSS 71, Course record 65.
Forest Course: 18 holes, 5774yds, Par 69, SSS 68, Course record 65.
Location M27 junct 1, 1m W on B3079
Telephone for further details
Hotel ★★★ 70% HL Bell Inn, BROOK ☎ 023 8081 2214 25 en suite

New Forest
Southampton Rd SO43 7BU
☎ 023 8028 2752
📄 023 8028 4030
e-mail: tonyatnfgc@aol.com
web: www.newforestgolfclub.co.uk
This picturesque heathland course is laid out in a typical stretch of the New Forest on high ground a little above the village of Lyndhurst. The first two holes are somewhat teasing, as is the 485yd (Par 5) 9th. Walking is easy.
18 holes, 5526yds, Par 69, SSS 67.
Club membership 500.
Visitors may play Mon, Wed & Fri. Limited play Tue, Thu, Sat, Sun & BHs. Booking required. Dress code. **Societies** Welcome.
Green Fees £17 per 18 holes (£23 weekends and bank holidays.
Prof Colin Murray **Facilities** ⑨ ⓛ ⏍ ⓣ⏌ ⏃ ⏢ ⑨⏂ ⑨ **Conf** Corporate Hospitality Days **Location** 0.5m NE off A35)
Hotel ★★★ 75% HL Best Western Crown Hotel, High St, LYNDHURST ☎ 023 8028 2922 39 en suite

ROWLAND'S CASTLE

Rowland's Castle

31 Links Ln PO9 6AE

☎ 023 9241 2784

🖹 023 9241 3649

e-mail: manager@rowlandscastlegolfclub.co.uk

web: www.rowlandscastlegolfclub.co.uk

Reasonably dry in winter, the flat parkland course is a testing one with a number of tricky dog-legs and bunkers much in evidence. The Par 4 13th is a signature hole necessitating a drive to a narrow fairway and a second shot to a two-tiered green. The 7th, at 522yds, is the longest hole on the course and leads to a well-guarded armchair green.

18 holes, 6630yds, Par 72, SSS 72, Course record 68. Club membership 800.

Visitors may play Sun-Fri & BHs. Advance booking required. Handicap certificate required. Dress code. **Societies** advance booking required. **Green Fees** not confirmed. **Prof** Peter Klepacz **Course Designer** Colt **Facilities** ⊕ ⌾ ⅃ ⅂ ⮌ ⊣ ⚲ ⬛ ⚋ ⬛ **Conf** Corporate Hospitality Days **Location** W of village off B2149

Hotel ★★★ 75% HL Brookfield Hotel, Havant Rd, EMSWORTH ☎ 01243 373363 40 en suite

SHEDFIELD

Marriott Meon Valley Hotel & Country Club

Sandy Ln SO32 2HQ

☎ 01329 833455

🖹 01329 834411

It has been said that a golf-course architect is as good as the ground on which he has to work. Here Hamilton Stutt had magnificent terrain at his disposal and a very good and lovely parkland course is the result. There are three holes over water. The hotel provides many sports facilities.

Meon Course: 18 holes, 6520yds, Par 71, SSS 71, Course record 66.

Valley Course: 9 holes, 2721yds, Par 35, SSS 33. Club membership 700.

Visitors Mon-Sun & BHs. Booking required. Dress code. **Societies** Welcome. **Green Fees** £44 per 18 holes (£54 Sat, Sun & BHs). **Prof** Neal Grist **Course Designer** Hamilton Stutt **Facilities** ⊕ ⌾ ⅃ ⅂ ⮌ ⊣ ⚲ ⬛ ⮌ ◇ ⚋ ⬛ ⚋ **Leisure** hard tennis courts, heated indoor swimming pool, sauna, solarium, gymnasium. **Conf** facs Corporate Hospitality Days **Location** M27 junct 7, off A334 between Botley & Wickham

Hotel ★★★★ 74% HL Marriott Meon Valley Hotel & Country Club, Sandy Ln, SHEDFIELD ☎ 01329 833455 113 en suite

SOUTHAMPTON

Stoneham

Monks Wood Close, Bassett SO16 3TT

☎ 023 8076 9272

🖹 023 8076 6320

e-mail: richard.penley-martin@stonehamgolfclub.org.uk

web: www.stonehamgolfclub.org.uk

Undulating through an attractive parkland and heathland setting with views over the Itchen valley towards Winchester, this course rewards brains over brawn. It is unusual in having 5 Par 5's and 5 Par 3's and no two holes alike. The quality of the course means that temporary greens are never used and the course is rarely closed.

18 holes, 6392yds, Par 72, SSS 70, Course record 63. Club membership 800.

Visitors Mon-Sun & BHs. Booking required. Handicap certificate. Dress code. **Societies** Booking required. **Green Fees** £50 per day, £45 per round (£60/£50 Sat, Sun & BHs). **Prof** Ian Young **Course Designer** Willie Park Jnr **Facilities** ⊕ ⌾ ⅃ ⅂ ⮌ ⊣ ⚲ ⬛ ⮌ ⚋ **Conf** facs Corporate Hospitality Days **Location** 4m N of city centre off A27

Hotel ★★★ 75% HL Chilworth Manor, CHILWORTH ☎ 023 8076 7333 95 en suite

WINCHESTER

Royal Winchester

Sarum Rd SO22 5QE

☎ 01962 852462

🖹 01962 865048

e-mail: manager@royalwinchestergolfclub.com

web: royalwinchestergolfclub.com

The Royal Winchester course is a sporting downland course centred on a rolling valley, so the course is hilly in places with fine views over the surrounding countryside. Built on chalk downs, the course drains extremely well and offers an excellent playing surface.

18 holes, 6216yds, Par 71, SSS 70, Course record 65. Club membership 800.

Visitors Mon-Fri except BHs. Booking required. Handicap certificate. Dress code. **Societies** Booking required.

continued

Green Fees £60 per day, £40 per round. **Prof** Steven Hunter **Course Designer** J H Taylor
Facilities ⓦ ⦿ by prior arrangement ⓑ 🖵 🖵 ⛳ 🏌 ⚬
Conf Corporate Hospitality Days **Location** 1.5m W off A3090
Hotel ★★★★ HL Lainston House Hotel, Sparsholt,
WINCHESTER ☎ 01962 863588 50 en suite

HEREFORDSHIRE

KINGTON

Kington
Bradnor Hill HR5 3RE
☎ 01544 230340 (club) & 231320 (pro shop)
📄 01544 230340 /231320 (pro)
e-mail: kingtongolf@ukonline.co.uk
The highest 18-hole course in England, with magnificent views over seven counties. A natural heathland course with easy walking on mountain turf cropped by sheep. There is bracken to catch any really bad shots but no sand traps. The greens play true and fast and are generally acknowledged as some of the best in the west Midlands.
18 holes, 5980yds, Par 70, SSS 69, Course record 63. Club membership 510.
Visitors Mon-Sun & BHs. Booking required. Handicap certificate. Dress code. **Societies** Welcome. **Green Fees** £26 per day, £20 per round (£32/£26 Sat, Sun & BHs). ⊛ **Prof** Andy Gealy **Course Designer** Major C K Hutchison **Facilities** ⓦ ⦿ ⓑ 🖵
🖵 ⛳ 🏌 ⚬ ⚬ Ⓕ **Location** 0.5m N of Kington off B4355
Hotel ★★★ 72% HL Best Western Talbot Hotel, West St,
LEOMINSTER ☎ 01568 616347 20 en suite

ROSS-ON-WYE

Ross-on-Wye
Two Park, Gorsley HR9 7UT
☎ 01989 720267
📄 01989 720212
e-mail: admin@therossonwyegolfclub.co.uk
web: www.therossonwyegolfclub.co.uk
This undulating, parkland course has been cut out of a silver birch forest. The fairways are well-screened from each other and tight, the greens good and the bunkers have been restructured.
18 holes, 6451yds, Par 72, SSS 71, Course record 68. Club membership 730.
Visitors Wed-Sun & BHs. Booking required. Handicap certificate. Dress code. **Societies** Booking required. **Green Fees** £50 per 36 holes; £46 per 27 holes; £40 per round. **Prof** Paul Middleton **Course Designer** Mr C K Cotton **Facilities** ⓦ ⦿ ⓑ 🖵 ⛳ 🏌 ⚬ ⚬ Ⓕ **Leisure** snooker. **Conf** Corporate Hospitality Days **Location** M50 junct 3, on B4221 N

Hotel ★★★ 80% HL Best Western Pengethley Manor,
Pengethley Park, ROSS-ON-WYE ☎ 01989 730211 11 en suite
14 annexe en suite

South Herefordshire
Twin Lakes HR9 7UA
☎ 01989 780535
📄 01989 780535
e-mail: info@herefordshiregolf.co.uk
web: www.herefordshiregolf.co.uk
Impressive 6672yd parkland course fast maturing into one of Herefordshire's finest. Magnificent panoramic views of the Welsh mountains and countryside. Drains well and is playable in any weather. The landscape has enabled the architect to design 18 individual and varied holes.
Twin Lakes: 18 holes, 6672yds, Par 71, SSS 72, Course record 71. Club membership 400.
Visitors Mon-Sun & BHs. Dress code. **Societies** Welcome. **Green Fees** £20 per 18 holes (£25 Sat & Sun). **Prof** Leo Tarrant **Course Designer** John Day **Facilities** ⓦ ⦿ ⓑ 🖵 🖵 ⛳ 🏌 ⚬ ⚬ Ⓕ
Conf Corporate Hospitality Days **Location** M50 junct 4, to Upton Bishop, right onto B4224, 1m left
Hotel ★★★ 70% CHH Pencraig Court Country House Hotel, Pencraig, ROSS-ON-WYE ☎ 01989 770306 11 en suite

HERTFORDSHIRE

BERKHAMSTED

Berkhamsted
The Common HP4 2QB
☎ 01442 865832
📄 01442 863730
e-mail: barryh@berkhamstedgc.co.uk
web: www.berkhamstedgolfclub.co.uk
There are no sand bunkers on this Championship heathland course but this does not make it any easier to play. The natural hazards will test the skill of the most able players, with a particularly testing hole at the 11th, 568yds, Par 5. Fine greens, long carries and heather and gorse.
18 holes, 6605yds, Par 71, SSS 72, Course record 65. Club membership 700.
Visitors Mon-Sun & BHs. Handicap certificate. Dress code. **Societies** Booking required. **Green Fees** £55 per day, £40 per 18 holes (£50 per 18 holes Sat, Sun & BHs). **Prof** John Clarke
continued

CHAMPIONSHIP COURSE
HERTFORDSHIRE — WARE

MARRIOTT HANBURY MANOR

SG12 0SD
☎ **01920 487722** 📄 **01920 487692**
e-mail: golf.hanburymanor@
marriotthotels.co.uk
web: www.hanbury-manor.com
18 holes, 7052yds, Par 72, SSS 74,
Course record 61.
Club membership 850.
Visitors Mon-Sun & BHs. Booking required.
Handicap certificate. Must be hotel resident.
Societies welcome. **Green Fees** Phone.
Course Designer Jack Nicklaus II
Facilities ⑪ ⑩ 🍴 🛒 ♨ 🏠 ⛳ ☂ ♦ 🚗 🏌
Leisure hard tennis courts, heated indoor
swimming pool, sauna, solarium, gymnasium,
Health spa. **Conf** facs Corporate Hospitality
Days **Location** M25 junct 25, 12m N on A10

There can be few golf venues that combine the old and the new so successfully. The old is the site itself, dominated since the 19th century by Hanbury Manor, a Jacobean-style mansion; the wonderful grounds included a nine-hole parkland course designed by the legendary Harry Vardon. The new is the conversion of the estate into the golf and country club; the manor now offers a five-star country house hotel, while Jack Nicklaus II redesigned the grounds for an 18-hole course. The American-style design took the best of Vardon's original and added meadowland to produce a course that looks beautiful and plays superbly. Hanbury Manor has hosted a number of professional events, including the Women's European Open in 1996 and the Men's European Tour's English Open from 1997 to 1999, won respectively by Per Ulrik Johannson, Lee Westwood and Darren Clarke.

Course Designer Colt/Braid **Facilities** ⓘ ▱ ⌘ ⚒ 🏌️ 🍴 ✦
Location 1.5m E
Hotel ★★★★ 76% HL Pendley Manor Hotel, Cow Ln, TRING
☎ 01442 891891 73 en suite

BROOKMANS PARK

Brookmans Park
Golf Club Rd AL9 7AT
☎ 01707 652487
📄 01707 661851
e-mail: info@bpgc.co.uk
web: www.bpgc.co.uk
Undulating parkland with several cleverly
constructed holes. But it is a fair course, although it can
play long. The 11th, Par 3, is a testing hole which plays
across a lake.
18 holes, 6249yds, Par 71, SSS 71, Course record 65.
Club membership 750.
Visitors Mon, Wed-Fri except BHs. Booking required. Handicap
certificate. Dress code. **Societies** Booking required. **Green
Fees** £45 per day; £32 per round. ⊛ **Prof** Ian Jelley **Course
Designer** Hawtree/Taylor **Facilities** ⓘ ⌂ ⚑ ▱ ⌘ ⚒ 🍴 ✦ 🏌️
✦ **Location** N of village off A1000
Hotel ★★★ 75% HL Bush Hall, Mill Green, HATFIELD
☎ 01707 271251 25 en suite

BROXBOURNE

Hertfordshire
Broxbournebury Mansion, White Stubbs Ln EN10 7PY
☎ 01992 466666 & 441268 (pro shop)
📄 01992 470326
e-mail: hertfordshire@crowngolf.co.uk
web: www.crowngolf.co.uk
An 18 hole course of a 'Nicklaus' design set around a
Grade II listed clubhouse to full USGA specifications.
Considered to be one of the best private courses to
appear in recent years.
18 holes, 6388yds, Par 70, SSS 70, Course record 62.
Club membership 600.
Visitors Mon-Sun & BHs. Dress code. **Societies** Booking
required. **Green Fees** £35 (£40 Sat & Sun). **Prof** Mark Payne
Course Designer Jack Nicklaus II **Facilities** ⓘ ⌂ ⚑ ▱ ⌘
🏌️ 🍴 🏌️ ✦ 🏌️ **Leisure** hard tennis courts, heated indoor
swimming pool, fishing, sauna, solarium, gymnasium, jacuzzis.
Conf facs Corporate Hospitality Days **Location** Off A10 for
Broxbourne, signs for Paradise Wildlife Park, left at Bell Ln over
A10, on right
Hotel ★★★★ 76% HL Cheshunt Marriott Hotel, Halfhide Ln,
Turnford, BROXBOURNE ☎ 01992 451245 143 en suite

LETCHWORTH

Letchworth
Letchworth Ln SG6 3NQ
☎ 01462 683203
📄 01462 484567
e-mail: secretary@letchworthgolfclub.com
web: www.letchworthgolfclub.com
Planned more than 100 years ago by Harry Vardon,
this is an adventurous parkland course. To its variety of
natural and artificial hazards is added an unpredictable
wind.
18 holes, 6459yds, Par 71, SSS 71, Course record 66.
Club membership 950.
Visitors Mon-Fri. Dress code. **Societies** Booking required.
Green Fees Phone. ⊛ **Prof** Karl Teschner **Course Designer**
Harry Vardon **Facilities** ⓘ ⌂ ⚑ ⚑ ▱ ⌘ ⚒ 🍴 🏌️ ✦ 🏌️ ✦ 🏌️
Leisure 9 hole Par 3 course. **Conf** Corporate Hospitality Days
Location S side of town centre off A505
Hotel ★★★★ 70% HL Cromwell Hotel, High St,
Old Town, STEVENAGE ☎ 01438 779954 & 775859
📄 01438 742169 76 en suite

RADLETT

Porters Park
Shenley Hill WD7 7AZ
☎ 01923 854127
📄 01923 855475
e-mail: info@porterspark.fsnet.co.uk
web: www.porterspark.com
18 holes, 6313yds, Par 70, SSS 70, Course record 64.
Course Designer Braid **Location** NE of village off A5183
Telephone for further details
Hotel BUD Innkeeper's Lodge London Borehamwood, Studio
Way, BOREHAM WOOD ☎ 0845 112 6120 55 en suite

RICKMANSWORTH

Moor Park
WD3 1QN
☎ 01923 773146
📄 01923 777109
e-mail: enquiries@moorparkgc.co.uk
web: www.moorparkgc.co.uk
Two parkland courses with rolling fairways - High
Course is challenging and will test the best golfer and
West Course demands a high degree of accuracy. The
clubhouse is a grade 1 listed mansion.

Moor Park

High Golf Course: 18 holes, 6713yds, Par 72, SSS 72, Course record 63.
West Golf Course: 18 holes, 5815yds, Par 69, SSS 68, Course record 60. Club membership 1700.
Visitors Mon-Sun & BHs. Booking required Sat, Sun & BHs. Handicap certificate. Dress code. **Societies** Booking required. **Green Fees** High: £80 per round. West: £50 per round (£120/£80 Sat, Sun & BHs). **Prof** Lawrence Farmer **Course Designer** H S Colt **Facilities** ⑨🍴🍴🍔🍺🎱🏌️🚩🚶🎯🍺🏌️ **Leisure** hard and grass tennis courts, chipping green snooker room. **Conf** facs Corporate Hospitality Days **Location** M25 junct 17/18, off A404 to Northwood
Hotel ★★★ 75% HL The Bedford Arms Hotel, CHENIES ☎ 01923 283301 10 en suite 8 annexe en suite

WATFORD

West Herts
Cassiobury Park WD3 3GG
☎ 01923 236484
🖹 01923 222300
Set in parkland, the course is close to Watford but its tree-lined setting is beautiful and tranquil. Set out on a plateau the course is exceedingly dry. It also has a very severe finish with the 17th, a hole of 378yds, the toughest on the course. The last hole measures over 480yds.
18 holes, 6620yds, Par 72, SSS 72, Course record 65. Club membership 700.
Visitors Mon-Sun & BHs. Booking required. Dress code. **Societies** Booking required. **Green Fees** £40 per 18 holes (£50 weekends). **Prof** Charles Gough **Course Designer** Tom Morris **Facilities** ⑨🍴🍴🍔🍺🎱🏌️🚩🚶🎯🍺 **Leisure** indoor teaching facility. **Conf** Corporate Hospitality Days **Location** W of town centre off A412
Hotel ★★★ 71% HL Best Western The White House, Upton Rd, WATFORD ☎ 01923 237316 57 en suite

KENT

BROADSTAIRS

North Foreland
Convent Rd, Kingsgate CT10 3PU
☎ 01843 862140
🖹 01843 862663
e-mail: office@northforeland.co.uk
web: www.northforeland.co.uk
A picturesque cliff top course situated where the Thames Estuary widens towards the sea. One of the few courses where the sea can be seen from every hole. Walking is easy and the wind is deceptive. The 8th and 17th, both Par 4, are testing holes. There is also an 18-hole approach and putting course.
18 holes, 6430yds, Par 71, SSS 71, Course record 63. Club membership 1100.
Visitors Mon-Fri except BHs. Sat & Sun pm only. Handicap certificate. Dress code. **Societies** Booking required. **Green Fees** £51 per day; £34 per round (£76/51 Sat & Sun). Par 3 course £8 (£9.50 Sat & Sun). **Prof** Darren Parris **Course Designer** Fowler & Simpson **Facilities** ⑨🍴🍴🍔🍺🎱🏌️🚩🚶🎯🍺 **Leisure** hard tennis courts, 18 hole Par 3 course. **Conf** Corporate Hospitality Days **Location** 1.5m N off B2052

DEAL

Royal Cinque Ports
Golf Rd CT14 6RF
☎ 01304 374007
🖹 01304 379530
e-mail: rcpgcsec@aol.com
web: www.royalcinqueports.com
18 holes, 6899yds, Par 72, SSS 73.
Course Designer James Braid **Location** On seafront at N end of Deal
Telephone for further details
Hotel ★★★ 82% HL Wallett's Court Country House Hotel & Spa, West Cliffe, St Margarets-at-Cliffe, DOVER ☎ 01304 852424 & 0800 0351628 🖹 01304 853430 3 en suite 13 annexe en suite

FAVERSHAM

Faversham
Belmont Park ME13 0HB
☎ 01795 890561
🖹 01795 890760
e-mail: themanager@favershamgolf.co.uk
web: www.favershamgolf.co.uk
A beautiful inland course laid out over part of a large estate with pheasants walking the fairways quite tamely. Play follows two heavily wooded valleys but the trees affect only the loose shots going out of bounds. Fine views.

continued

ROYAL ST GEORGE'S

CT13 9PB
☎ 01304 613090 📠 01304 611245
e-mail: secretary@royalstgeorges.com
web: www.royalstgeorges.com
18 holes, 7102yds, Par 70, SSS 74,
Course record 67.
Club membership 750.
Visitors Mon, Tue, Thu except BHs.
Booking required. Handicap certificate. Dress
code. **Societies** booking required.
Green Fees £150 per 36 holes, £120
per 18 holes. Reduced winter rates.
Prof A Brooks **Course Designer** Dr Laidlaw
Purves **Facilities** ⑨ by prior arrangement
▭ ▯ ⚒ ▤ ⛳ ◇ ✦ ✦ **Conf** Corporate
Hospitality Days **Location** 1.5m E of
Sandwich. Enter town for golf courses

Consistently ranked among the leading golf courses in the world, Royal St George's occupies a unique place in the history of golf, playing host in 1894 to the first Open Championship outside Scotland. Set among the dunes of Sandwich Bay, the links provide a severe test for the greatest of golfers. Only three Open winners (Bill Rogers in 1981, Greg Norman in 1993 and Ben Curtis in 2003) have managed to under Par after 72 holes. The undulating fairways, the borrows on the greens, the strategically placed bunkers, and the prevailing winds that blow on all but the rarest of occasions; these all soon reveal any weakness in the player. There are few over the years who have mastered all the vagaries in one round. It hosted its thirteenth Open Championship in 2003, won dramatically by outsider Ben Curtis.

18 holes, 5978yds, Par 70, SSS 69, Course record 62. Club membership 800.
Visitors Mon-Fri & BHs. Booking required. Dress code.
Societies Welcome. **Green Fees** £35 per round. ☺ **Prof** Stuart Rokes **Course Designer** J H Taylor/D Steel **Facilities** ⊕ⓘ◗ ⊾ ⤶ ⓣ⌂ ⎙ ⚞ ✝ **Conf** Corporate Hospitality Days
Location 3.5m S on Belmont road
Hotel ★★★★ HL Eastwell Manor, Eastwell Park, Boughton Lees, ASHFORD ☎ 01233 213000 23 en suite 39 annexe en suite

GRAVESEND

Mid Kent
Singlewell Rd DA11 7RB
☎ 01474 568035
🖩 01474 564218
e-mail: secretary@mkgc.co.uk
web: www.mkgc.co.uk
A well-maintained downland course with some easy walking and some excellent greens. The first hole is short, but nonetheless a real challenge. The slightest hook and the ball is out of bounds or lost.
18 holes, 6106yds, Par 70, SSS 69, Course record 60. Club membership 900.
Visitors Mon-Fri except BHs. Handicap certificate. Dress code. **Societies** Welcome. **Green Fees** £50 per day; £35 per round. ☺ **Prof** Mark Foreman **Course Designer** Frank Pennick **Facilities** ⊕ ⓘ◗ ⊾ by prior arrangement ⊾ ⤶ ⓣ⌂ ⎙ ⚞ ✝ ✝ **Leisure** snooker. **Location** S of town centre off A227
Hotel BUD Premier Travel Inn Gravesend, Wrotham Rd, GRAVESEND ☎ 08701 977118 36 en suite

KINGSDOWN

Walmer & Kingsdown
The Leas CT14 8EP
☎ 01304 373256
🖩 01304 382336
e-mail: info@kingsdowngolf.co.uk
web: www.kingsdowngolf.co.uk
This beautiful downland site is situated near Deal and, being situated on top of the famous White Cliffs, offers breathtaking views of the Channel from every hole.

18 holes, 6471yds, Par 72, SSS 71, Course record 66. Club membership 640.
Visitors Mon-Fri. Sat, Sun & BHs pm only. Booking required. Handicap certificate. Dress code. **Societies** Welcome. **Green Fees** £40 per day; £32 per round (£40 per round Sat, Sun & BHs). **Prof** Jude Read **Course Designer** James Braid **Facilities** ⊕ⓘ◗ ⊾ ⤶ ⓣ⌂ ⎙ ⚞ ✝ **Conf** Corporate Hospitality Days
Location 1.5m E of Ringwould off A258 Dover-Deal road
Hotel ★★★ 74% HL Dunkerleys Hotel & Restaurant, 19 Beach St, DEAL ☎ 01304 375016 16 en suite

LITTLESTONE

Littlestone
St Andrew's Rd TN28 8RB
☎ 01797 363355
🖩 01797 362740
e-mail: secretary@littlestonegolfclub.org.uk
web: www.littlestonegolfclub.org.uk
Located in the Romney Marshes, this fairly flat seaside links course calls for every variety of shot. The 8th, 15th, 16th and 17th are regarded as classics by international golfers. Fast running fairways and faster greens.
18 holes, 6486yds, Par 71, SSS 72, Course record 66. Club membership 550.
Visitors Mon-Fri. Booking required. Handicap certificate. Dress code. **Societies** booking required. **Green Fees** not confirmed. **Prof** Andrew Jones **Course Designer** Laidlaw Purves **Facilities** ⊕ ⊾ ⤶ ⓣ⌂ ⎙ ⚞ ✝ ⚞ ✝ ⚑ **Leisure** hard tennis courts. **Conf** Corporate Hospitality Days **Location** 1m from New Romney off Littlestone road B2070
Hotel ★★★★ 75% HL The Hythe Imperial, Princes Pde, HYTHE ☎ 01303 267441 100 en suite

RAMSGATE

St Augustine's

Cottington Rd, Cliffsend CT12 5JN

☎ 01843 590333

🖹 01843 590444

e-mail: sagc@ic24.net

web: www.staugustines.co.uk

A comfortably flat course in this famous bracing championship area of Kent. Neither as long nor as difficult as its lordly neighbours, St Augustine's will nonetheless extend most golfers. Dykes run across the course.

18 holes, 5254yds, Par 69, SSS 66, Course record 61. Club membership 670.

Visitors Mon-Sun & BHs. Booking required Sat & Sun. Dress code. **Societies** Booking required. **Green Fees** Phone. **Prof** Derek Scott **Course Designer** Tom Vardon **Facilities** ⑪ ⓘ ⬚ ⬚ 🖇 ⬚ 🖓 🛇 🍴 ✍ **Location** Off A256 Ramsgate-Sandwich

ROCHESTER

Rochester & Cobham Park

Park Pale ME2 3UL

☎ 01474 823411

🖹 01474 824446

e-mail: rcpgc@talk21.com

web: www.rochesterandcobhamgc.co.uk

A first-rate course of challenging dimensions in undulating parkland. All holes differ and each requires accurate drive placing to derive the best advantage. Open Championship regional qualifying course.

18 holes, 6597yds, Par 71, SSS 72, Course record 64. Club membership 730.

Visitors Mon-Fri except BHs. Handicap certificate. Dress code. **Societies** booking required. **Green Fees** not confirmed. **Prof** Iain Higgins **Course Designer** Donald Steel **Facilities** ⑪ ⓘ ⬚ ⬚ 🖓 🛇 🖇 ⬚ 🍴 ✍ 🏌 **Conf** Corporate Hospitality Days **Location** 2.5m W on A2

Hotel ★★★★ 74% HL Bridgewood Manor, Bridgewood Roundabout, Walderslade Woods, CHATHAM ☎ 01634 201333 100 en suite

SANDWICH

Prince's

Prince's Dr, Sandwich Bay CT13 9QB

☎ 01304 611118

🖹 01304 612000

e-mail: office@princesgolfclub.co.uk

web: www.princesgolfclub.co.uk

With 27 championship holes, Prince's Golf Club has a world-wide reputation as a traditional links of the finest quality and is a venue that provides all that is best in modern links golf. One of only 14 courses to be selected to host the Open Championship.

Dunes: 9 holes, 3425yds, Par 36, SSS 36.
Himalayas: 9 holes, 3163yds, Par 35, SSS 35.
Shore: 9 holes, 3347yds, Par 36, SSS 36.
Club membership 310.

Visitors Mon-Sun & BHs. Booking required. Dress code. **Societies** booking required. **Green Fees** not confirmed. **Prof** Derek Barbour **Course Designer** Sir Guy Campbell & J S F Morrison **Facilities** ⑪ ⓘ by prior arrangement ⬚ ⬚ 🖓 🛇 ⬚ ⬚ 🦅 ✍ ⬚ ✍ 🏌 **Leisure** private beach area. **Conf** facs Corporate Hospitality Days **Location** 2m E via toll road, signs from Sandwich

Hotel ★★★ 74% HL Dunkerleys Hotel & Restaurant, 19 Beach St, DEAL ☎ 01304 375016 16 en suite

SEVENOAKS

Knole Park

Seal Hollow Rd TN15 0HJ

☎ 01732 452150

🖹 01732 463159

e-mail: secretary@knoleparkgolfclub.co.uk

web: www.knoleparkgolfclub.co.uk

The course is laid out within the grounds of the Knole Estate and can rightfully be described as a natural layout. The course designer has used the contours of the land to produce a challenging course in all weather conditions and throughout all seasons. While, for most of the year, it may appear benign, in summer, when the bracken is high, Knole Park represents a considerable challenge but always remains a fair test of golf.

18 holes, 6246yds, Par 70, SSS 70, Course record 62. Club membership 750.

Visitors Mon-Fri except BHs. Booking required. Handicap certificate. Dress code. **Societies** Welcome. **Green Fees** £50 per day, £39 per round. **Prof** Phil Sykes **Course Designer** J A Abercromby **Facilities** ⓘ ⦿ 🏌 ♿ 🍴 🎯 🛒 ✔ **Leisure** squash. **Conf** Corporate Hospitality Days **Location** NE of town centre off B2019

Hotel ★★★ 75% HL Best Western Donnington Manor, London Rd, Dunton Green, SEVENOAKS ☎ 01732 462681 60 en suite

---

TUNBRIDGE WELLS (ROYAL)

Nevill
Benhall Mill Rd TN2 5JW
☎ 01892 525818
🖨 01892 517861
e-mail: manager@nevillgolfclub.co.uk
web: www.nevillgolfclub.co.uk
The Kent-Sussex border forms the northern perimeter of the course. Open undulating ground, well-wooded with some heather and gorse for the first half. The second nine holes slope away from the clubhouse to a valley where a narrow stream hazards two holes.
18 holes, 6349yds, Par 71, SSS 70, Course record 64. Club membership 800.
Visitors Mon-Fri except BHs. Booking required. Handicap certificate. Dress code. **Societies** booking required. **Green Fees** not confirmed. ☜ **Prof** Paul Huggett **Course Designer** Henry Cotton **Facilities** ⓘ 🏌 ♿ 🍴 🛒 ✔ **Location** S of Tunbridge Wells

Hotel ★★★★ 74% HL The Spa Hotel, Mount Ephraim, TUNBRIDGE WELLS ☎ 01892 520331 69 en suite

Tunbridge Wells
Langton Rd TN4 8XH
☎ 01892 523034
🖨 01892 536918
e-mail: info@tunbridgewellsgolfclub.co.uk
web: www.tunbridgewellsgolfclub.co.uk
Somewhat hilly, well-bunkered parkland course with lake; trees form natural hazards.
9 holes, 4725yds, Par 65, SSS 62, Course record 59. Club membership 470.
Visitors Mon-Sun & BHs. Booking required. Dress code. **Societies** booking required. **Green Fees** not confirmed. **Facilities** ⓘ ⦿ 🏌 ♿ 🍴 🛒 ✔ **Location** 1m W on A264

Hotel ★★★★ 74% HL The Spa Hotel, Mount Ephraim, TUNBRIDGE WELLS ☎ 01892 520331 69 en suite

LANCASHIRE

CHORLEY

Chorley
Hall o' th' Hill, Heath Charnock PR6 9HX
☎ 01257 480263
🖨 01257 480722
e-mail: secretary@chorleygolfclub.freeserve.co.uk
web: www.chorleygolfclub.co.uk
18 holes, 6269yds, Par 71, SSS 70, Course record 62.
Course Designer J A Steer **Location** 2.5m SE on A673

Telephone for further details
Hotel ★★★ 78% HL Pines Hotel, 570 Preston Rd, Clayton-Le-Woods, CHORLEY ☎ 01772 338551 37 en suite

Shaw Hill Hotel Golf & Country Club
Preston Rd, Whittle-Le-Woods PR6 7PP
☎ 01257 269221
🖨 01257 261223
e-mail: info@shaw-hill.co.uk
web: www.shaw-hill.co.uk
A fine heavily wooded parkland course designed by one of Europe's most prominent golf architects and offering a considerable challenge as well as tranquillity and scenic charm. Six holes are protected by water and signature holes are the 8th and the closing 18th played slightly up hill to the imposing club house.
18 holes, 6283yds, Par 72, SSS 71, Course record 65. Club membership 500.
Visitors Mon-Sat & BHs. Booking required. Handicap certificate. Dress code. **Societies** Booking required. **Green Fees** Mon- Thu £35 per 18 holes, Fri, Sat & BHs £45. **Prof** David Clark **Course Designer** Harry Vardon **Facilities** ⓘ ⦿ 🏌 ♿ 🍴 🎯 🛒 🛒 ◇ 🛒 ✔ **Leisure** heated indoor swimming pool, sauna, solarium, gymnasium, snooker. **Conf** facs Corporate Hospitality Days **Location** 1.5m N on A6

Hotel ★★★ 74% HL Best Western Park Hall Hotel, Park Hall Rd, Charnock Richard, CHORLEY ☎ 01257 455000 56 en suite 84 annexe en suite

---

CLITHEROE

Clitheroe
Whalley Rd, Pendleton BB7 1PP
☎ 01200 422292
🖨 01200 422292
e-mail: secretary@clitheroegolfclub.com
web: www.clitheroegolfclub.com
One of the best inland courses in the country. Clitheroe is a parkland-type course with water hazards and good scenic views, particularly towards Longridge and Pendle Hill.

18 holes, 6326yds, Par 71, SSS 71, Course record 63. Club membership 700.
Visitors Mon-Wed & Fri except BHs. Booking required. Handicap certificate. Dress code. **Societies** Booking required. **Green Fees** Mon-Thu £45 per day, £35 per 18 holes, Fri £45/£38. ☜ **Prof** Paul McEvoy **Course Designer** James Braid **Facilities** ⓘ ⦿ 🏌 ♿ 🍴 🛒 🎯 ✔ ☞ **Conf** Corporate Hospitality Days **Location** 2m S of Clitheroe

Hotel ★★★ 71% HL Shireburn Arms Hotel, Whalley Rd, Hurst Green, CLITHEROE ☎ 01254 826518 22 en suite

FLEETWOOD

Fleetwood
Princes Way FY7 8AF
☎ 01253 873661 & 773573
📄 01253 773573
e-mail: fleetwoodgc@aol.com
web: www.fleetwoodgolfclub.org.uk
Championship length, flat seaside links where the player must always be alert to changes of direction or strength of the wind.

18 holes, 6723yds, Par 72, SSS 72.
Club membership 600.
Visitors Mon-Sun & BHs. Booking required. Handicap certificate. Dress code. **Societies** Booking required. **Green Fees** Phone.
@ **Prof** S McLaughlin **Course Designer** J A Steer **Facilities** ⊕ ⊙ 🛍 ⌷ 🍴 ⟁ 🏌 ✔ **Conf** facs Corporate Hospitality Days **Location** W of town centre
Hotel BUD Premier Travel Inn Blackpool (Bispham), Devonshire Rd, Bispham, BLACKPOOL ☎ 08701 977033 39 en suite

LANCASTER

Lancaster Golf Club
Ashton Hall, Ashton-with-Stodday LA2 0AJ
☎ 01524 751247
📄 01524 752742
e-mail: office@lancastergc.co.uk
web: www.lancastergc.co.uk
This parkland course is unusual as it is exposed to winds from the Irish Sea. It is situated on the Lune estuary and has some natural hazards and easy walking. There are several fine holes among woods near the old clubhouse. Fine views towards the Lake District.
18 holes, 6282yds, Par 71, SSS 71, Course record 66.
Club membership 925.
Visitors Mon-Fri except BHs. Booking required. Handicap certificate. Dress code. **Societies** Welcome. **Green Fees** £50 per day, £40 per round. **Prof** David Sutcliffe **Course Designer** James Braid **Facilities** ⊕ ⊙ 🛍 ⌷ 🍴 ⟁ 🏌 ✔ ✔ 🏌 ✔ **Conf** Corporate Hospitality Days **Location** 3m S on A588
Hotel ★★★★ 73% HL Best Western Lancaster House Hotel, Green Ln, Ellel, LANCASTER ☎ 01524 844822 99 en suite

MORECAMBE

Morecambe
Bare LA4 6AJ
☎ 01524 412841
📄 01524 400088
e-mail: secretary@morecambegolfclub.com
web: www.morecambegolfclub.com
Holiday golf at its most enjoyable. The well-maintained, wind-affected seaside parkland course is not long but full of character. Even so the panoramic views of Morecambe Bay, the Lake District and the Pennines make concentration difficult. The 4th is a testing hole.
18 holes, 5750yds, Par 67, SSS 69, Course record 69.
Club membership 850.
Visitors Mon-Sun & BHs. Booking required. Handicap certificate. Dress code. **Societies** booking required. **Green Fees** not confirmed. **Prof** Simon Fletcher **Course Designer** Dr Alister Mackenzie **Facilities** ⊕ ⊙ 🛍 ⌷ 🍴 ⟁ 🏌 ✔ **Location** N of town centre on A5105
Hotel ★★★ 72% HL Elms Hotel, Bare Village, MORECAMBE ☎ 01524 411501 39 en suite

ORMSKIRK

Ormskirk
Cranes Ln, Lathom L40 5UJ
☎ 01695 572227
📄 01695 572227
e-mail: ormskirk@ukgolfer.org
web: www.ukgolfer.org
Pleasantly secluded, fairly flat parkland with much heath and silver birch. Accuracy from the tees will provide an interesting variety of second shots.
18 holes, 6358yds, Par 70, SSS 71, Course record 63.
Club membership 300.
Visitors Mon, Wed-Fri, Sun & BHs. Tue & Sat pm only. Booking required. Dress code. **Societies** booking required. **Green Fees** not confirmed. @ **Prof** Jack Hammond **Course Designer** Harold Hilton **Facilities** ⊕ ⊙ 🛍 ⌷ 🍴 ⟁ 🏌 ✔ **Conf** Corporate Hospitality Days **Location** 1.5m NE

PLEASINGTON

Pleasington
BB2 5JF
☎ 01254 202177
📄 01254 201028
e-mail: secretary-manager@pleasington-golf.co.uk
web: www.pleasington-golf.co.uk
Plunging and rising across lovely parkland and heathland turf, this course tests judgement of distance through the air to greens of widely differing levels. The 11th and 4th are testing holes. A regular regional qualifying course for the Open Championship.
18 holes, 6402yds, Par 71, SSS 71, Course record 65.
Club membership 700.

continued

CHAMPIONSHIP COURSE

LANCASHIRE — LYTHAM ST ANNES

ROYAL LYTHAM & ST ANNES

Links Gate FY8 3LQ
☎ 01253 724206 📄 01253 780946
e-mail: bookings@royallytham.org
web: www.royallytham.org
18 holes, 6882yds, Par 71, SSS 74,
Course record 64.
Club membership 850.
Visitors Mon-Fri & Sun. Booking required.
Handicap certificate. Dress code.
Societies Booking required.
Green Fees £180 per 36 holes, £120
per 18 holes (limited play Sun £180
per 18 holes). All prices including lunch. **Prof**
Eddie Birchenough **Course Designer** George
Lowe **Facilities** 🍴🍽🛍🛒🏌🚶🏪🔹🏌🏌
Leisure caddies available. **Conf** Corporate
Hospitality Days **Location** 0.5m E of St Annes

Founded in 1886, this huge links course can be difficult, especially in windy conditions. Unusually for a championship course, it starts with a Par 3, the nearby railway line and red-brick houses creating distractions that add to the challenge. The course has hosted 10 Open Championships with some memorable victories: amateur Bobby Jones famously won the first here in 1926; Bobby Charles of New Zealand became the only left-hander to win the title; in 1969 Tony Jacklin helped to revive British golf with his win; and the most recent in 2001 was won by David Duval.

Visitors Mon-Fri & BHs. Booking required. Dress code.
Societies Booking required. **Green Fees** £45 per round ◉
Prof Ged Furey **Course Designer** George Lowe **Facilities** ⑪
🍴① 🍺 ♫ ⛟ ♨ ⚲ ♥ 🏌
Conf facs Corporate Hospitality Days **Location** M65 junct 3,
signed for Blackburn
Hotel ★★ 85% HL The Millstone at Mellor, Church Ln, Mellor,
BLACKBURN ☎ 01254 813333   17 en suite   6 annexe en suite

PRESTON

Penwortham
Blundell Ln, Penwortham PR1 0AX
☎ 01772 744630
🖨 01772 740172
e-mail: penworthamgolfclub@supanet.com
web: www.ukgolfer.org/clubs/penwortham
18 holes, 5877yds, Par 69, SSS 69, Course record 65.
Location 1.5m W of town centre off A59
Telephone for further details
Hotel ★★★ 75% HL Macdonald Tickled Trout, Preston New Rd,
Samlesbury, PRESTON ☎ 0870 1942120   102 en suite

UPHOLLAND

Dean Wood
Lafford Ln WN8 0QZ
☎ 01695 622219
🖨 01695 622245
web: www.deanwoodgolfclub.co.uk
This parkland course has a varied terrain - flat front
nine, undulating back nine. Beware the Par 4 11th
and 17th holes, which have ruined many a card. If
there were a prize for the best maintained course in
Lancashire, Dean Wood would be a strong contender.
18 holes, 6148yds, Par 71, SSS 70, Course record 65.
Club membership 730.
Visitors Mon-Fri. Booking required Tue & Wed. Handicap
certificate. Dress code. **Societies** booking required. **Green
Fees** not confirmed. ◉ **Prof** Stuart Danchin **Course Designer**
James Braid **Facilities** ⑪ 🍴① 🍺 ♫ ⛟ ♨ ⚲ ♥ **Conf** Corporate
Hospitality Days **Location** M6 junct 26, 1m on A577

LEICESTERSHIRE

LOUGHBOROUGH

Longcliffe
Snell's Nook Ln, Nanpantan LE11 3YA
☎ 01509 239129
🖨 01509 231286
e-mail: longcliffegolf@btconnect.com
web: www.longcliffegolf.co.uk

18 holes, 6625yds, Par 72, SSS 73, Course record 65.
Course Designer Williamson **Location** 1.5m from M1 junct 23
off A512
Telephone for further details
Hotel ★★★ 71% HL Quality Hotel & Suites Loughborough, New
Ashby Rd, LOUGHBOROUGH ☎ 01509 211800   94 en suite

LINCOLNSHIRE

SKEGNESS

Seacroft
Drummond Rd, Seacroft PE25 3AU
☎ 01754 763020
🖨 01754 763020
e-mail: enquiries@seacroft-golfclub.co.uk
web: www.seacroft-golfclub.co.uk
A championship seaside links traditionally laid out with
tight undulations and hogsback fairways. Adjacent to
Gibraltar Point Nature Reserve, overlooking the Wash.

18 holes, 6492yds, Par 71, SSS 71, Course record 65.
Club membership 590.

continued

CHAMPIONSHIP COURSE

LINCOLNSHIRE — WOODHALL SPA

THE NATIONAL GOLF CENTRE

The Broadway LN10 6PU
☎ 01526 352511 📠 01526 351817
e-mail: booking@englishgolfunion.org
web: www.woodhallspagolf.com
The Hotchkin: 18 holes, 7080yds, Par 73,
SSS 75, Course record 66.
The Bracken: 18 holes, 6735yds, Par 72,
SSS 74, Course record 68.
Club membership 520.
Visitors Mon-Sun & BHs. Booking required.
Handicap certificate. Dress code. **Societies**
Booking required. **Green Fees** Hotchkin £100
per day, £65 per round. Bracken £75 per
day, £50 round. £90 per day playing both
courses. **Prof** A Hare **Course Designer** Col S V
Hotchkin **Facilities** ⑨ ⑩ 🛏 🖵 🛅 ⤴ 🏠 ◇ 🚍
✂ ⛳ **Leisure** pitch & putt 9 hole course. **Conf**
Corporate Hospitality Days **Location** Exit A1
onto B6403 to Ancaster. Turn right onto A153 to
Coningsby and then left onto B1192.

The Championship Course at Woodhall Spa, now known as the Hotchkin, is considered to be the best inland course in the UK . This classic course has cavernous bunkers and heather-lined fairways. Golf has been played here for over a century and the Hotchkin has hosted most of the top national and international amateur events. The English Golf Union acquired Woodhall Spa in 1995 to create a centre of excellence. A second course, the Bracken, has been built, along with extensive practice facilities including one of Europe's finest short-game practice areas. The English Golf Union actively encourages visitors to the National Golf Centre throughout the year, to experience the facilities and to enjoy the unique ambience.

Visitors Mon-Sun & BHs. Booking required. Handicap certificate. Dress code. **Societies** Booking required. **Green Fees** Phone. **Prof** Robin Lawie **Course Designer** Tom Dunn/Willie Fernie **Facilities** ⊕ ⓒ 🏌 🖫 🖭 🛆 🛢 ℓ ℐ **Conf** Corporate Hospitality Days **Location** S of town centre towards Gibralter Point Nature Reserve

Hotel ★★★ 68% HL Crown Hotel, Drummond Rd, SKEGNESS ☎ 01754 610760 29 en suite

LONDON

N20 WHETSTONE

South Herts
Links Dr, Totteridge N20 8QU
☎ 020 8445 2035
📄 020 8445 7569
e-mail: secretary@southhertsgolfclub.co.uk
web: www.southhertsgolfclub.co.uk

An open undulating parkland course perhaps most famous for the fact that two of the greatest of all British professionals, Harry Vardon and Dai Rees CBE, were professionals at the club. The course is testing, over rolling fairways, especially in the prevailing south-west wind.

18 holes, 6432yds, Par 72, SSS 71, Course record 63.
Club membership 850.

Visitors may play Mon-Fri. Advance booking required. Handicap certificate required. Dress code. **Societies** advance booking required. **Green Fees** not confirmed. ⊛ **Prof** Bobby Mitchell **Course Designer** Harry Vardon **Facilities** ⊕ ⓒ by prior arrangement 🏌 🖫 🖭 🛆 🛢 ℐ 🛒 ℓ ℐ **Conf** Corporate Hospitality Days **Location** 2m E of A1 at Apex Corner

Hotel BUD Innkeeper's Lodge London Southgate, 22 The Green, Southgate, LONDON ☎ 0845 112 6123 19 en suite

SE9 ELTHAM

Royal Blackheath
Court Rd SE9 5AF
☎ 020 8850 1795
📄 020 8859 0150
e-mail: info@rbgc.com
web: www.royalblackheath.com

A pleasant, parkland course of great character, with many great trees and two ponds. The 18th requires a pitch to the green over a thick clipped hedge, which also crosses the front of the 1st tee. The clubhouse dates from the 17th century, and you may wish to visit the club's fine museum of golf.

18 holes, 6147yds, Par 70, SSS 70, Course record 65.
Club membership 720.

Visitors Mon-Fri except BHs. Handicap certificate. Dress code. **Societies** Booking required. **Green Fees** £70 per day; £50 per round. **Prof** Richard Harrison **Course Designer** James Braid **Facilities** ⊕ ⓒ 🏌 🖫 🖭 🛆 🛢 ℓ 🛒 ℓ **Leisure** golf museum.

Conf facs Corporate Hospitality Days **Location** M25 junct 3, A20 towards London, 2nd lights right, club 500yds on right

Hotel ★★★ 77% HL Best Western Bromley Court Hotel, Bromley Hill, BROMLEY ☎ 020 8461 8600 114 en suite

SW15 PUTNEY

Richmond Park
Roehampton Gate, Priory Ln SW15 5JR
☎ 020 8876 1795
📄 020 8878 1354
e-mail: richmondpark@glendale-services.co.uk
web: www.gcmgolf.com

Two public parkland courses.

Princes Course: 18 holes, 5868yds, Par 69, SSS 67.
Dukes Course: 18 holes, 6036yds, Par 69, SSS 68.

Visitors Mon-Sun & BHs. Booking required Sat, Sun & BHs. Dress code. **Societies** Booking required. **Green Fees** £19 per 18 holes; (£23 weekends). **Prof** Stuart Hill & David Bown **Course Designer** Fred Hawtree **Facilities** ⊕ 🏌 🖫 🖭 🛆 🛢 ℓ 🛒 ℓ 🛒 **Conf** Corporate Hospitality Days **Location** Inside Richmond Park, entrance via Roehampton Gate

Hotel ★★★★ 71% HL Richmond Hill Hotel, Richmond Hill, RICHMOND UPON THAMES ☎ 020 8940 2247 138 en suite

SW19 WIMBLEDON

Royal Wimbledon
29 Camp Rd SW19 4UW
☎ 020 8946 2125
📄 020 8944 8652
e-mail: secretary@rwgc.co.uk
web: www.rwgc.co.uk

The third-oldest club in England, established in 1865 and steeped in the history of the game. Mainly heathland with trees and heather, a good test of golf with many fine holes, the 12th being rated as the best.

18 holes, 6350yds, Par 70, SSS 71, Course record 66.
Club membership 1050.

Visitors may play Mon-Thu except BHs. Advance booking required. Handicap certificate. Dress code. **Societies** Booking required.

Green Fees £95 per day, £70 per round. **Prof** David Jones **Course Designer** H Colt **Facilities** ⊕ 🏌 🖫 🖭 🛆 🛢 ℓ 🛒 ℓ 🛒 **Conf** Corporate Hospitality Days **Location** 1m from Tibbatt's Corner roundabout on A3 off Wimbledon Park before war memorial in village

Hotel BUD Premier Travel Inn London Wimbledon South, Merantum Way, Merton, LONDON POSTAL DISTRICTS ☎ 0870 990 6342

MERSEYSIDE

BLUNDELLSANDS

West Lancashire
Hall Rd West L23 8SZ
☎ 0151 924 1076
📄 0151 931 4448
e-mail: golf@westlancashiregolf.co.uk
web: www.westlancashiregolf.co.uk
Challenging, traditional links with sandy subsoil overlooking the Mersey estuary. The course provides excellent golf throughout the year. The four short holes are very fine.
18 holes, 6763yds, Par 72, SSS 73, Course record 66. Club membership 650.
Visitors Mon, Wed-Fri, Sun & BHs. Booking required. Dress code. **Societies** Booking required. **Green Fees** £80 per day; £65 per round (£100/£85 Sun). **Prof** Gary Edge **Course Designer** C K Cotton **Facilities** ⑪ ⑩ ⓛ ⊑ ⑪ ⌁ 🏠 ✈ ⚡ ⚶ **Conf** Corporate Hospitality Days **Location** N of village, next to Hall Road station

CALDY

Caldy
Links Hey Rd CH48 1NB
☎ 0151 625 5660
📄 0151 625 7394
e-mail: secretarycaldygc@btconnect.com
web: www.caldygolfclub.co.uk
A heathland and clifftop links course situated on the estuary of the River Dee with many of the fairways running parallel to the river. Of championship length, the course offers excellent golf all year, but is subject to variable winds that noticeably alter the day-to-day playing of each hole. There are excellent views of the Welsh Hills
18 holes, 6133metres, Par 72, SSS 72, Course record 65. Club membership 900.
Visitors Mon & Thu-Fri. Booking required. Handicap certificate. Dress code. **Societies** Booking required. **Green Fees** £70 per day, £60 per round. 🅮 **Prof** A Gibbons **Course Designer** J Braid **Facilities** ⑪ ⑩ ⓛ ⊑ ⑪ ⌁ 🏠 🛁 ⚡ **Leisure** ball hire & collection. **Conf** Corporate Hospitality Days **Location** Signed from Caldy A540 rdbt to Caldy
Hotel ★★★★ 77% HL Thornton Hall Hotel and Health Club, Neston Rd, THORNTON HOUGH ☎ 0151 336 3938   63 en suite

FORMBY

Formby
Golf Rd L37 1LQ
☎ 01704 872164
📄 01704 833028
e-mail: info@formbygolfclub.co.uk
web: www.formbygolfclub.co.uk
Championship seaside links through sandhills and pine trees. Partly sheltered from the wind by high dunes it features firm, springy turf, fast seaside greens and natural sandy bunkers. Well drained it plays well throughout the year.

18 holes, 6701yds, Par 72, SSS 72, Course record 65. Club membership 700.
Visitors Booking required. Handicap certificate. Dress code **Societies** Booking required. **Green Fees** £95 per day/round (£105 Sat & Sun). **Prof** Gary Butler **Course Designer** Park/Colt **Facilities** ⑪ ⑩ ⓛ ⊑ ⑪ ⌁ 🏠 ◇ ⚡ ⚶ **Conf** facs Corporate Hospitality Days **Location** N of town next to Freshfield railway station

HESWALL

Heswall
Cottage Ln CH60 8PB
☎ 0151 342 1237
📄 0151 342 6140
e-mail: dawn@heswallgolfclub.com
web: www.heswallgolfclub.com
Pleasant parkland in soft undulating country overlooking the Dee estuary. There are excellent views of the Welsh hills and coastline, and a good test of golf.

continued

CHAMPIONSHIP COURSE

MERSEYSIDE — SOUTHPORT

ROYAL BIRKDALE

Waterloo Rd, Birkdale PR8 2LX
☎ **01704 567920** 📠 **01704 562327**
e-mail: secretary@royalbirkdale.com
web: www.royalbirkdale.com
18 holes, 6726yds, Par 72, SSS 73.
Club membership 800.
Visitors Mon-Fri, Sun except BHs. Booking
required. Handicap certificate. Dress
code. **Societies** Booking required.
Green Fees May-Sep £165 per round (£195
per round Sun). Oct/Nov £120 per round
including soup and sandwiches (£150 Sun).
Dec-Feb £80 per round soup and sandwiches
(£105 Sun). **Prof** Brian Hodgkinson
Course Designer Hawtree **Facilities** 🍴 🍽 by
prior arrangement 🏌 🖥 🍸 🍴 🏖 🏕 🎯 ⛳ ⛳
Conf Corporate Hospitality Days
Location 1.75m S of town centre on A565

Founded in 1889, the Royal Birkdale is
considered by many to be the ultimate
championship venue, having hosted every
major event in the game including eight Open
Championships, two Ryder Cup matches, the
Walker Cup, the Curtis Cup and many amateur
events. The 1st hole provides an immediate
taste of what is to come, requiring a well-placed
drive to avoid a bunker, water hazard and out-
of-bounds and leave a reasonably clear view of
the green. The 10th, the first of the inward nine
is unique in that it is the only hole to display
the significant fairway undulations one would
expect from a classic links course. The 12th is
the most spectacular of the short holes on the
course, and is considered by Tom Watson to
be one of the best Par 3s in the world; tucked
away in the sand hills it continues to claim its
fair share of disasters. The approach on the
final hole is arguably the most recognisable in
golf with the distinctive clubhouse designed to
appear like an ocean cruise liner rising out of
the sand hills. It's a Par 5 for mere mortals, and
played as a Par 4 in the Open, but it will provide
a memorable finish to any round of golf.

CHAMPIONSHIP COURSE

MERSEYSIDE — HOYLAKE

ROYAL LIVERPOOL

Meols Dr CH47 4AL
☎ 0151 632 3101 & 632 3102
🖷 0151 632 6737
e-mail: secretary@royal-liverpool-golf.com
web: www.royal-liverpool-golf.com
18 holes, 6440yds, Par 72, SSS 71.
Club membership 950.
Visitors Mon-Fri except BHs. Booking required. Handicap certificate. Dress code.
Societies Booking required. **Green Fees** £135 per round inc lunch. **Prof** John Heggarty
Course Designer R Chambers/G Morris/D Steel **Facilities** ⑪ ⓑ ⬜ ⬛ 🏌 🛒 ⛳ ✎ ✦
Conf Corporate Hospitality Days **Location** SW side of town on A540

Built in 1869 on the site of a former racecourse, this world-famous championship course was one of the first seaside courses to be established in England. In 1921 Hoylake was the scene of the first international match between the US and Britain, now known as the Walker Cup. Over the years, golfing enthusiasts have come to Hoylake to witness 18 amateur championships and 11 Open Championships, which the club hosted again in 2006. Visitors playing on this historic course can expect a challenging match, with crosswinds, deep bunkers and hollows, all set against the backdrop of stunning Welsh hills. Watch out for the 8th hole, which saw the great Bobby Jones take an 8 on this Par 5 on the way to his famous Grand Slam in 1930.

18 holes, 6556yds, Par 72, SSS 72, Course record 62.
Club membership 940.

Visitors Mon, Wed, Fri, Sun except BHs. Booking required.
Handicap certificate. Dress code. **Societies** booking required.
Green Fees not confirmed. **Prof** Alan Thompson **Course**
Designer McKenzie/Ebert **Facilities** ⓦ ⓑ ⓛ ⛳ ⓟ 🏊 🎯 ✦ **Conf**
Corporate Hospitality Days **Location** 1m S off A540
Hotel ★★★★ 77% HL Thornton Hall Hotel and Health Club,
Neston Rd, THORNTON HOUGH ☎ 0151 336 3938 63 en suite

LIVERPOOL

The Childwall
Naylors Rd, Gateacre L27 2YB
☎ 0151 487 0654
🖷 0151 487 0654
e-mail: office@childwallgolfclub.co.uk
web: www.childwallgolfclub.co.uk
Parkland golf is played here over a testing course, where
accuracy from the tee is well-rewarded. The course is
very popular with visiting societies for the clubhouse has
many amenities. Course designed by James Braid.
18 holes, 6425yds, Par 72, SSS 71, Course record 66.
Club membership 650.
Visitors Mon, Wed-Sun except BHs. Booking required. Handicap
certificate. Dress code. **Societies** booking required. **Green Fees**
not confirmed. **Prof** Nigel M Parr **Course Designer** James
Braid **Facilities** ⓦ ⓘ by prior arrangement ⓛ ⛳ ⓟ 🏊 🎯 ✦
✦ **Conf** facs Corporate Hospitality Days **Location** 7m E of city
centre off B5178
Hotel BUD Premier Travel Inn Liverpool (Roby), Roby Rd,
Huyton, LIVERPOOL ☎ 0870 9906596 53 en suite

West Derby
Yew Tree Ln, West Derby L12 9HQ
☎ 0151 254 1034
🖷 0151 259 0505
e-mail: pmilne@westderbygc.freeserve.co.uk
A parkland course always in first-class condition, and so
giving easy walking. The fairways are well-wooded. Care
must be taken on the first nine holes to avoid the brook
which guards many of the greens.
18 holes, 6275yds, Par 72, SSS 70, Course record 65.
Club membership 550.
Visitors Mon, Wed-Fri except BHs. Booking required. Dress
code. **Societies** Booking required. **Green Fees** £35 per day. 🞄
Prof Andrew Witherup **Facilities** ⓦ ⓘ ⓛ ⛳ ⓟ 🏊 🎯 ✦ **Conf**
facs Corporate Hospitality Days **Location** 4.5m E of city centre
off A57
Hotel ★★★ 80% HL The Royal Hotel, Marine Ter, Waterloo,
LIVERPOOL ☎ 0151 928 2332 25 en suite

NEWTON-LE-WILLOWS

Haydock Park
Newton Ln WA12 0HX
☎ 01925 228525
🖷 01925 224984
e-mail: secretary@haydockparkgc.co.uk
web: www.haydockparkgc.co.uk
A well-wooded parkland course, close to the well-known
racecourse, and always in excellent condition. The
pleasant undulating fairways offer some very interesting
golf and the 6th, 9th, 11th and 13th holes are particularly
testing.
18 holes, 6058yds, Par 70, SSS 69, Course record 65.
Club membership 630.
Visitors Mon-Sun except BHs. Booking required. Handicap
certificate. Dress code. **Societies** Booking required. **Green**
Fees £35 per day, £30 per round. 🞄 **Prof** Peter Kenwright
Course Designer James Braid **Facilities** ⓦ ⓘ ⓛ ⛳ ⓟ 🏊 🎯
✦ **Location** 0.75m NE off A49
Hotel ★★ 62% HL Kirkfield Hotel, 2/4 Church St, NEWTON LE
WILLOWS ☎ 01925 228196 17 en suite

ST HELENS

Grange Park
Prescot Rd WA10 3AD
☎ 01744 26318
🖷 01744 26318
e-mail: secretary@grangeparkgolfclub.co.uk
web: www.grangeparkgolfclub.co.uk
Possibly one of the finest tests of inland golf in the
northwest, set in 150 acres only a short distance from
the centre of town. While not too long, the contours of
the fairways, small greens and penal rough demand
the best from players. A wide shot making repertoire is
required to gain the best score possible.

Grange Park

18 holes, 6446yds, Par 72, SSS 71, Course record 65.
Club membership 730.
Visitors Mon, Wed-Fri, Sun & BHs. Booking required. Handicap
certificate. Dress code. **Societies** booking required. **Green Fees**
not confirmed. 🞄 **Prof** Paul Roberts **Course Designer** James
Braid **Facilities** ⓦ ⓘ ⓛ ⛳ ⓟ 🏊 🎯 ✦ **Conf** facs Corporate
Hospitality Days **Location** 1.5m SW on A58

Hotel ★★ 62% HL Kirkfield Hotel, 2/4 Church St, NEWTON LE WILLOWS ☎ 01925 228196 17 en suite

---

SOUTHPORT

The Hesketh
Cockle Dick's Ln, off Cambridge Rd PR9 9QQ
☎ 01704 536897
🖹 01704 539250
e-mail: secretary@heskethgolfclub.co.uk
web: www.heskethgolfclub.co.uk
The Hesketh is the oldest of the six clubs in Southport, founded in 1885. Set at the northern end of south-west Lancashire's dune system, the course sets a unique challenge with half of the holes threaded through tall dunes while the other holes border the Ribble estuary. The course is next to a renowned bird reserve and across the estuary are fine views of the mountains of Lancashire, Cumbria and Yorkshire. Used as a final qualifying course for the Open Championship.
18 holes, 6655yds, Par 72, SSS 72, Course record 67. Club membership 600.
Visitors Mon, Wed-Fri, Sun & BHs. Tue & Sat pm only. Booking required. Handicap certificate. Dress code. **Societies** Welcome. **Green Fees** £70 per day; £55 per round (£70 per round Sat, Sun & BHs). **Prof** Scott Astin **Course Designer** J F Morris **Facilities** ⊕ ⏣ 🖫 ⌨ ⛳ ⚒ ☂ ✦ **Leisure** snooker. **Conf** Corporate Hospitality Days **Location** 1m NE of town centre off A565
Hotel ★★★ 75% HL Best Western Stutelea Hotel & Leisure Club, Alexandra Rd, SOUTHPORT ☎ 01704 544220 22 en suite

Hillside
Hastings Rd, Hillside PR8 2LU
☎ 01704 567169
🖹 01704 563192
e-mail: secretary@hillside-golfclub.co.uk
web: www.hillside-golfclub.co.uk
Championship links course with natural hazards open to strong wind.
18 holes, 6850yds, Par 72, SSS 74, Course record 65. Club membership 700.
Visitors Contact club for details. **Societies** Welcome. **Green Fees** £95 per day, £75 per round (£95 per round Sun). **Prof** Brian Seddon
Course Designer Hawtree/Steel **Facilities** ⊕ ⏣ 🖫 ⌨ ⛳ ⚒ ☂ **Conf** Corporate Hospitality Days **Location** 3m S of town centre on A565

Hotel ★★★ 77% HL Scarisbrick Hotel, Lord St, SOUTHPORT ☎ 01704 543000 88 en suite

Southport & Ainsdale
Bradshaws Ln, Ainsdale PR8 3LG
☎ 01704 578000
🖹 01704 570896
e-mail: secretary@sandagolfclub.co.uk
web: www.sandagolfclub.co.uk
S and A, as it is known in the north, is another of the fine championship courses for which this part of the country is famed. The club has staged many important events and offers golf of the highest order.
18 holes, 6705yds, Par 72, SSS 73, Course record 62. Club membership 815.
Visitors Mon-Sun & BHs. Booking required. Handicap certificate. Dress code. **Societies** Booking required. **Green Fees** £65 per 18 holes; £90 per 36 holes (£90 per 18 holes weekends). **Prof** Jim Payne
Course Designer James Braid **Facilities** ⊕ ⏣ 🖫 ⌨ ⛳ ☂ 🖐 **Conf** facs Corporate Hospitality Days **Location** 3m S off A565
Hotel ★★★ 73% HL Best Western Royal Clifton Hotel, Promenade, SOUTHPORT ☎ 01704 533771 120 en suite

Wallasey
Bayswater Rd CH45 8LA
☎ 0151 691 1024
🖹 0151 638 8988
e-mail: wallaseygc@aol.com
web: wallaseygolf.com
A well-established links course, adjacent to the Irish Sea. A true test of golf due in part to the prevailing westerly winds and the natural undulating terrain. Spectacular views across Liverpool Bay and the Welsh hills.
18 holes, 6503yds, Par 72, SSS 72, Course record 65. Club membership 650.
Visitors Mon-Fri & Sun. Restricted Sat & BHs. Booking required. Dress code. **Societies** Welcome. **Green Fees** £80 per day, £70 per round (£95/£85 Sun & BHs). **Prof** Mike Adams **Course Designer** Tom Morris **Facilities** ⊕ ⏣ by prior arrangement 🖫 ⌨ ⛳ ☂ ✦ **Location** N of town centre off A554
Hotel ★★★ 78% HL Grove House Hotel, Grove Rd, WALLASEY ☎ 0151 639 3947 & 0151 630 4558 🖹 0151 639 0028 14 en suite

ENGLAND

NORFOLK

BARNHAM BROOM

Barnham Broom Hotel, Golf, Conference, Leisure
Honingham Rd NR9 4DD
☎ 01603 759552 & 759393
🖷 01603 758224
e-mail: golfmanager@barnham-broom.co.uk
web: www.barnham-broom.co.uk
Course meanders through the Yare valley, parkland
and mature trees. Hill course has wide fairways, heavily
guarded greens and spectacular views.
Valley Course: 18 holes, 6483yds, Par 72, SSS 71.
Hill Course: 18 holes, 6495yds, Par 71, SSS 71.
Club membership 500.
Visitors Contact club for details. Handicap certificate. Dress
code. **Societies** Welcome. **Green Fees** Valley £40, Hill £35.
Prof Ian Rollett **Course Designer** Frank Pennink **Facilities**
⑪ ⑩ ⬡ ⬜ ⬠ ⬡ ⬢ ⬣ ◇ ✔ 🏌 ✔ 🏌 **Leisure** hard tennis
courts, heated indoor swimming pool, squash, sauna, solarium,
gymnasium, 3 academy holes. Golf school. Squash tuition.
Conf facs Corporate Hospitality Days **Location** Off A47 at
Honingham
Hotel ★★★ 83% HL Barnham Broom Hotel, Golf & Restaurant,
BARNHAM BROOM ☎ 01603 759393 52 en suite

BRANCASTER

Royal West Norfolk
PE31 8AX
☎ 01485 210223
🖷 01485 210087
A fine links laid out in grand manner characterised
by sleepered greens, superb cross bunkers and salt
marshes. The tranquil surroundings include a harbour,
the sea, farmland and marshland, inhabited by many
rare birds. A great part of the year the club is cut off by
tidal flooding that restricts the amount of play.
18 holes, 6428yds, Par 71, SSS 71, Course record 65.
Club membership 898.
Visitors Mon-Sun except BHs. Booking required. Handicap
certificate. **Societies** Booking required. **Green Fees** Phone. **Prof**
S Rayner
Course Designer Holcombe-Ingleby **Facilities** ⑪ ⑩ by
prior arrangement ⬡ ⬜ ⬠ ⬡ ⬢ ⬣ ✔ **Location** Off A149 in
Brancaster 1m to seafront
Hotel ★★ 82% HL The White Horse, BRANCASTER STAITHE
☎ 01485 210262 7 en suite 8 annexe en suite

CROMER

Royal Cromer
145 Overstrand Rd NR27 0JH
☎ 01263 512884
🖷 01263 512430
e-mail: general.manager@royal-cromer.com
web: www.royalcromergolfclub.com
Challenging course with spectacular views out to sea
and overlooking the town. Strong sea breezes affect
the clifftop holes, the most famous being the 14th (the
Lighthouse) which has a green in the shadow of a
lighthouse.
18 holes, 6508yds, Par 72, SSS 72, Course record 67.
Club membership 700.
Visitors Mon-Sun & BHs. Booking required. Handicap certificate.
Dress code. **Societies** Booking required. **Green Fees** £45 per
day (£55 Sat, Sun & BHs). **Prof** Lee Patterson **Course Designer**
J H Taylor
Facilities ⑪ ⑩ ⬡ ⬜ ⬠ ⬡ ⬢ ⬣ ✔ 🏌 ✔ **Conf** Corporate
Hospitality Days **Location** 1m E on B1159
Hotel ★★ 76% HL Red Lion, Brook St, CROMER ☎ 01263 514964
12 en suite

GREAT YARMOUTH

Great Yarmouth & Caister
Beach House, Caister-on-Sea NR30 5TD
☎ 01493 728699
🖷 01493 728831
e-mail: office@caistergolf.co.uk
web: www.caistergolf.co.uk
A traditional links-style course played over tight and
undulating fairways and partly set amongst sand
dunes with gorse and marram grass. Well drained with
excellent greens. A challenge for golfers of all abilities.
18 holes, 6330yds, Par 70, SSS 70, Course record 65.
Club membership 720.
Visitors Mon-Fri except BHs. Handicap certificate. Dress code.
Societies Booking required. **Green Fees** £35 per day; £25 after
noon. **Prof** Martyn Clarke **Course Designer** H Colt **Facilities**
⑪ ⑩ ⬡ ⬜ ⬠ ⬡ ⬢ ⬣ ✔ **Leisure** snooker. **Location** 0.5m N off
A149, at S end of Caister
Hotel ★★ 72% HL Burlington Palm Court Hotel, 11
North Dr, GREAT YARMOUTH ☎ 01493 844568 & 842095
🖷 01493 331848 70 en suite

HUNSTANTON

Hunstanton
Golf Course Rd PE36 6JQ
☎ 01485 532811
🖷 01485 532319
e-mail: hunstanton.golf@eidosnet.co.uk
web: www.hunstantongolfclub.com
A championship links course set among some of the
natural golfing country in East Anglia. Keep out of the
numerous bunkers and master the fast greens to play to
your handicap - then you only have the wind to contend
with. Good playing conditions all year round.
18 holes, 6759yds, Par 72, SSS 73.
Club membership 675.
Visitors Mon-Sun except BHs. Booking required. Handicap
certificate. Dress code. **Societies** welcome. **Green Fees** not
confirmed. **Prof** James Dodds **Course Designer** James Braid
Facilities ⑪ ⓑ ⌷ ⓣ ⌂ ⓕ ⌻ ⚑ ⚑ **Location** Off A149 in Old
Hunstanton, signed
Hotel ★★★ 81% HL Best Western Le Strange Arms Hotel, Golf
Course Rd, Old Hunstanton, HUNSTANTON ☎ 01485 534411
36 en suite

SHERINGHAM

Sheringham
Weybourne Rd NR26 8HG
☎ 01263 823488
🖷 01263 826129
e-mail: info@sheringhamgolfclub.co.uk
web: www.sheringhamgolfclub.co.uk
The course is laid out along a rolling, gorse-clad cliff
top from where the sea is visible on every hole. The
Par 4 holes are outstanding with a fine view along the
cliffs from the 5th tee.
18 holes, 6456yds, Par 70, SSS 71, Course record 64.
Club membership 760.
Visitors Mon-Sun & BHs. Booking required. Handicap certificate.
Dress code. **Societies** booking required **Green Fees** not
confirmed. ⊜ **Prof** M W Jubb **Course Designer** Tom Dunn
Facilities ⑪ ⓞ ⓑ ⌷ ⓣ ⌂ ⚑ ⚑ **Conf** Corporate Hospitality
Days **Location** W of town centre on A149
Hotel ★★ 75% HL Beaumaris Hotel, South St, SHERINGHAM
☎ 01263 822370 21 en suite

THETFORD

Thetford
Brandon Rd IP24 3NE
☎ 01842 752169
🖷 01842 766212
e-mail: sally@thetfordgolfclub.co.uk
web: www.club-noticeboard.co.uk
18 holes, 6849yds, Par 72, SSS 73, Course record 66.
Course Designer James Braid **Location** 2m W of Thetford on
B1107
Telephone for further details

Hotel ★★ 68% HL The Thomas Paine Hotel, White Hart St,
THETFORD ☎ 01842 755631 13 en suite

NORTHAMPTONSHIRE

COLLINGTREE

Collingtree Park
Windingbrook Ln NN4 0XN
☎ 01604 700000 & 701202
🖷 01604 702600
e-mail: info@collingtreeparkgolf.com
web: www.collingtreeparkgolf.com
An 18-hole resort course designed by former US and
British Open champion Johnny Miller. The American-
style course has water hazards on 10 holes with a
spectacular Par 5 18th Island Green.

18 holes, 6776yds, Par 72, SSS 72, Course record 66.
Club membership 660.
Visitors Mon-Sun & BHs. Booking required. Handicap certificate.
Dress code. **Societies** welcome. **Green Fees** not confirmed.
Prof G.Pook/A.Carter **Course Designer** Johnny Miller
Facilities ⑪ ⓞ ⓑ ⌷ ⓣ ⌂ ⚑ ⓕ ⚑ **Leisure** fishing, Golf
Academy. **Conf** facs Corporate Hospitality Days **Location** M1
junct 15, on A508 to Northampton
Hotel ★★★★ 73% HL Northampton Marriott Hotel, Eagle Dr,
NORTHAMPTON ☎ 01604 768700 120 en suite

NORTHUMBERLAND

BAMBURGH

Bamburgh Castle
The Club House, 40 The Wynding NE69 7DE
☎ 01668 214378 (club) & 214321 (sec)
🖷 01668 214607
e-mail: sec@bamburghcastlegolfclub.co.uk
web: www.bamburghcastlegolfclub.co.uk
Superb coastal course with excellent greens that are
both fast and true; natural hazards of heather and whin
bushes abound. Magnificent views of the Farne Islands,
Holy Island, Lindisfarne Castle, Bamburgh Castle and the
Cheviot Hills.
18 holes, 5621yds, Par 68, SSS 67, Course record 64.
Club membership 785.
continued

55

Visitors Mon-Fri & Sun except BHs. Booking required. Handicap certificate. Dress code. **Societies** Booking required. **Green Fees** £45 per day, £33 per round (£50/£38 Sun). **Course Designer** George Rochester **Facilities** ⑪ ⑩ ⓵ ⓵ ⓷ ⓵ ⓶ ⓵ **Conf** Corporate Hospitality Days **Location** 6m E of A1 via B1341 or B1342

Hotel ★★ 72% HL The Lord Crewe, Front St, BAMBURGH ☎ 01668 214243 18 rms (17 en suite)

BERWICK-UPON-TWEED

Berwick-upon-Tweed (Goswick)
Goswick TD15 2RW
☎ 01289 387256
📄 01289 387334
e-mail: goswickgc@btconnect.com
web: www.goswicklinksgc.co.uk
Natural seaside links course, with undulating fairways, elevated tees and good greens. Qualifying course for the Open Championship from 2008.
18 holes, 6686yds, Par 72, SSS 72, Course record 69. Club membership 700.
Visitors Mon-Sun & BHs. Booking required. Dress code. **Societies** Booking required. **Green Fees** contact for details. **Prof** Paul Terras **Course Designer** James Braid **Facilities** ⑪ ⑩ⓘ ⓵ ⓵ ⓵ ⓵ ⓶ ⓵ ⓵ ⓵ **Conf** Corporate Hospitality Days **Location** 6m S of Berwick off A1
Hotel ★★★ 72% HL Marshall Meadows Country House Hotel, BERWICK-UPON-TWEED ☎ 01289 331133 19 en suite

HEXHAM

Hexham
Spital Park NE46 3RZ
☎ 01434 603072
📄 01434 601865
e-mail: info@hexhamgolf.co.uk
web: www.hexhamgolf.co.uk
A very pretty, well-drained course with interesting natural contours. Exquisite views from parts of the course of the Tyne valley below. As good a parkland course as any in the north of England.
18 holes, 6294yds, Par 70, SSS 70, Course record 61. Club membership 700.
Visitors Mon-Sun & BHs. Booking required. Dress code. **Societies** Booking required. **Green Fees** £30 per round (£40 Sat, Sun & BHs). **Prof** Ben West **Course Designer** Vardon/Caird **Facilities** ⑪ ⑩ⓘ ⓵ ⓵ ⓵ ⓵ ⓶ ⓵ ⓵ **Leisure** squash, squash courts. **Conf** facs Corporate Hospitality Days **Location** 1m NW on B6531
Hotel ★★★ 75% HL Best Western Beaumont Hotel, Beaumont St, HEXHAM ☎ 01434 602331 25 en suite

NOTTINGHAMSHIRE

KIRKBY IN ASHFIELD

Notts
Derby Rd NG17 7QR
☎ 01623 753225
📄 01623 753655
e-mail: office@nottsgolfclub.co.uk
web: www.nottsgolfclub.co.uk
Undulating heathland championship course.
18 holes, 7213yds, Par 72, SSS 75, Course record 64. Club membership 450.
Visitors Mon-Fri except BHs. Booking required. Handicap certificate. **Societies** Welcome. **Green Fees** £99 per day; £66 per round. **Prof** Mike Bradley **Course Designer** Willie Park **Facilities** ⑪ ⑩ⓘ ⓵ ⓵ ⓵ ⓵ ⓶ ⓵ ⓵ ⓵ **Conf** facs **Location** 2m SE of Mansfield off A611
Hotel ★★★★ 77% HL Renaissance Derby/Nottingham Hotel, Carter Ln East, SOUTH NORMANTON ☎ 01773 812000 & 0870 4007262 📄 01773 580032 & 0870 4007362 158 en suite

MANSFIELD

Sherwood Forest
Eakring Rd NG18 3EW
☎ 01623 627403
📄 01623 420412
e-mail: sherwood@forest43.freeserve.co.uk
As the name suggests, the forest is the main feature of this natural heathland course with its heather, silver birch and pine trees. The homeward nine holes are particularly testing. The 11th to the 14th are notable Par 4 holes on this well-bunkered course.
18 holes, 6289yds, Par 71, SSS 71. Club membership 750.
Visitors Mon, Wed-Fri except BHs, Tue pm only. Booking required. Handicap certificate. Dress code. **Societies** booking required. **Green Fees** not confirmed. **Prof** Ken Hall **Course Designer** H S Colt/James Braid **Facilities** ⑪ ⑩ⓘ ⓵ ⓵ ⓵ ⓵ **Leisure** snooker. **Conf** facs Corporate Hospitality Days **Location** E of Mansfield
Hotel ★★ 69% HL Pine Lodge Hotel, 281-283 Nottingham Rd, MANSFIELD ☎ 01623 622308 20 en suite

NOTTINGHAM

Wollaton Park
Limetree Av, Wollaton Park NG8 1BT
☎ 0115 978 7574
📄 0115 970 0736
e-mail: wollatonparkgc@aol.com
web: www.wollatonparkgolfclub.com
A traditional parkland course on slightly undulating land, winding through historic woodland and set in a historic deer park. Fine views of 16th-century Wollaton Hall.
18 holes, 6445yds, Par 71, SSS 71, Course record 64. Club membership 700.

Visitors Mon, Tue, Thu, Fri, Sun & BHs. Dress code. **Societies** Booking required. **Green Fees** £48 per day; £35 per round (£55/£40 Sun & BHs). **Prof** John Lower **Course Designer** T Williamson **Facilities** ⑨ ⑩↑ ⑬ ⑬ ♥️↑ ☒ 🝙 ✓ **Conf** Corporate Hospitality Days **Location** 2.5m W of city centre off ring road junct A52

Hotel ★★★ 68% HL Swans Hotel & Restaurant, 84-90 Radcliffe Rd, West Bridgford, NOTTINGHAM ☎ 0115 981 4042 30 en suite

SUTTON IN ASHFIELD

Coxmoor

Coxmoor Rd NG17 5LF
☎ 01623 557359
🖨 01623 557435
e-mail: coxmoorgc@btconnect.com
web: www.coxmoor.freeuk.com
Undulating moorland and heathland course with easy walking and excellent views. The clubhouse is traditional with a well-equipped games room. The course lies adjacent to Forestry Commission land over which there are several footpaths and extensive views.
18 holes, 6577yds, Par 73, SSS 72, Course record 65. Club membership 700.
Visitors Mon, Wed-Fri except BHs. Booking required. Handicap certificate. Dress code. **Societies** Booking required. **Green Fees** £55 per day; £40 per round. **Prof** Craig Wright **Facilities** ⑨ ⑩↑ ⑬ ♥️↑ ☒ 🝙 ✓ **Leisure** snooker. **Conf** Corporate Hospitality Days **Location** 2m SE off A611

Hotel ★★★★ 77% HL Renaissance Derby/Nottingham Hotel, Carter Ln East, SOUTH NORMANTON ☎ 01773 812000 & 0870 4007262 🖨 01773 580032 & 0870 4007362 158 en suite

WORKSOP

Lindrick

Lindrick Common S81 8BH
☎ 01909 475282
🖨 01909 488685
e-mail: lgc@ansbronze.com
web: www.lindrickgolfclub.co.uk
Heathland course with some trees and masses of gorse which has hosted many major golf tournaments including the Ryder Cup.
18 holes, 6486yds, Par 71, SSS 71, Course record 63. Club membership 510.
Visitors Mon, Wed-Fr & Sun except BHs. Booking required. Handicap certificate. Dress code. **Societies** Booking required. **Green Fees** £65 per day, £50 per 18 holes. Reduced winter rate. **Prof** John R King **Facilities** ⑨ ⑩↑ ⑬ ♥️↑ ☒ 🝙 ✓ **Leisure** buggies for disabled only. **Conf** Corporate Hospitality Days **Location** M1 junct 31, 4m NW of Worksop on A57

Hotel ★★★ 78% HL Best Western Lion Hotel, 112 Bridge St, WORKSOP ☎ 01909 477925 45 en suite

OXFORDSHIRE

FRILFORD

Frilford Heath

OX13 5NW
☎ 01865 390864
🖨 01865 390823
e-mail: secretary@frilfordheath.co.uk
web: www.frilfordheath.co.uk
Fifty-four holes in three layouts of differing character. The Green course is a fully mature heathland course of some 6006yds. The Red Course is of championship length at 6884yds with a parkland flavour and a marked degree of challenge. The Blue Course is of modern design, and at 6728yds, it incorporates water hazards and large shallow sand traps.
Red Course: 18 holes, 6884yds, Par 73, SSS 73, Course record 66.
Green Course: 18 holes, 6006yds, Par 69, SSS 69, Course record 67.
Blue Course: 18 holes, 6728yds, Par 72, SSS 72, Course record 63. Club membership 1300.
Visitors may play Mon-Sun & BHs. Handicap certificate. Dress code. **Societies** Booking required. **Green Fees** £65 per day (£80 Sat & Sun). **Prof** Derek Craik **Course Designer** J Taylor/D Cotton/S Gidman **Facilities** ⑨ ⑩↑ ⑬ ♥️↑ ☒ 🝙 ✓ 🝙 ✓ **Conf** facs Corporate Hospitality Days **Location** 0.5m N of Frilford off A338

Hotel ★★★ 74% HL Abingdon Four Pillars Hotel, Marcham Rd, ABINGDON ☎ 0800 374 692 & 01235 553456 🖨 01235 554117 63 en suite

MILTON COMMON

The Oxfordshire

Rycote Ln OX9 2PU
☎ 01844 278300
🖨 01844 278003
e-mail: info@theoxfordshiregolfclub.com
web: www.theoxfordshiregolfclub.com
Designed by Rees Jones, The Oxfordshire is considered to be one of the most exciting courses in the country. The strategically contoured holes blend naturally into the surrounding countryside to provide a challenging game of golf. With four lakes and 135 bunkers, the course makes full use of the terrain and the natural elements to provide characteristics similar to those of a links course.

continued

Huntercombe

18 holes, 7192yds, Par 72, SSS 75, Course record 64. Club membership 456.
Visitors Mon-Fri. Sat, Sun & BHs pm only. Booking required. Handicap certificate. Dress code. **Societies** Booking required. **Green Fees** Summer: £90 per 18 holes (£110 Sat, Sun & BHs). Winter: £65/£75. **Prof** Stephen Gibson **Course Designer** Rees Jones **Facilities** ⊕ ⏅ by prior arrangement 🏌 ⏅ 🍴 ⏅ 🏪 ⏅ ✦ 🏌 ✦ **Leisure** Japanese ofuro baths, halfway house. **Conf** facs Corporate Hospitality Days **Location** M40 junct 7, 1.5m on A329 **Hotel** ★★★ 82% HL Spread Eagle Hotel, Cornmarket, THAME ☎ 01844 213661 33 en suite

NUFFIELD

Huntercombe
RG9 5SL
☎ 01491 641207
🖻 01491 642060
e-mail: office@huntercombegolfclub.co.uk
web: www.huntercombegolfclub.co.uk
This heathland and woodland course overlooks the Oxfordshire plain and has many attractive and interesting fairways and fair true greens. Walking is easy after the 3rd which is a notable hole. The course is subject to wind and grass pot bunkers are interesting hazards.

18 holes, 6271yds, Par 70, SSS 70, Course record 63. Club membership 800.

Visitors Mon-Sun & BHs. **Societies** Welcome. **Green Fees** £60 per day; £45 per round (£75/£60 per round Sat, Sun & BHs). **Prof** Ian Roberts **Course Designer** Willie Park jnr **Facilities** ⊕ ⏅ 🏌 ⏅ 🍴 🏪 ⏅ 🏪 ✦ 🏌 ✦ **Location** Off A4130 at Nuffield **Hotel** ★★★ 74% HL Shillingford Bridge Hotel, Shillingford, WALLINGFORD ☎ 01865 858567 32 en suite 8 annexe en suite

OXFORD

Southfield
Hill Top Rd OX4 1PF
☎ 01865 242158
🖻 01865 250023
e-mail: sgcltd@btopenworld.com
web: www.southfieldgolf.com
Home of the City, University and Ladies Clubs, and well-known to graduates throughout the world. A challenging course, in a varied parkland setting, providing a real test for players.

18 holes, 6325yds, Par 70, SSS 70, Course record 61. Club membership 740.
Visitors Mon-Sun & BHs. Booking required Sat, Sun & BHs. Dress code. **Societies** Welcome. **Green Fees** £40 per day/ round. **Prof** Tony Rees **Course Designer** H S Colt **Facilities** ⊕ ⏅ 🏌 ⏅ 🍴 🏪 ⏅ 🏪 ✦ 🏌 ✦ **Conf** Corporate Hospitality Days **Location** 1.5m SE of city centre off B480

Hotel ★★★ 77% HL Westwood Country Hotel, Hinksey Hill, Boars Hill, OXFORD ☎ 01865 735408 23 en suite

Southfield

is downhill over a tangle of mounds and studded with tricky bunkers.

18 holes, 6563yds, Par 70, SSS 72, Course record 64. Club membership 550.
Visitors Mon, Wed-Sun & BHs. Booking required Sat, Sun & BHs. Handicap certificate. Dress code. **Societies** Booking required. **Green Fees** Phone. **Prof** Ian Burnett **Course Designer** James Braid **Facilities** ⊕ ⏺ ▯ ☐ ☑ ▯ ⬚ 🛒 ⚡ **Conf** Corporate Hospitality Days **Location** 1.5m SW of Ketton on A6121 by Foster's Bridge
Hotel ★★★ 85% HL The George of Stamford, 71 St Martins, STAMFORD ☎ 01780 750750 & 750700 (Res) ▤ 01780 750701 47 en suite

TADMARTON

Tadmarton Heath
OX15 5HL
☎ 01608 737278
▤ 01608 730548
e-mail: thgc@btinternet.com
web: ww.thgc.btinternet.co.uk
A mixture of heath and sandy land on a plateau in the Cotswolds. The course opens gently before reaching the scenic 7th hole across a trout stream close to the clubhouse. The course then progressively tightens through the gorse before a challenging 430yd dog-leg completes the round.
18 holes, 5936yds, Par 69, SSS 69, Course record 62. Club membership 650.
Visitors Mon-Wed, Fri-Sun & BHs. Booking required. Handicap certificate. Dress code. **Societies** Booking required. **Green Fees** £45 per day, £40 after 10am (£50 Sat & Sun, £40 after 12pm). Reduced winter rates. **Prof** Tom Jones **Course Designer** Col C K Hutchison **Facilities** ⊕ ⏺ by prior arrangement ▯ ☐ ☑ ▯ ⬚ 🛒 ⚡ **Leisure** fishing.
Conf facs Corporate Hospitality Days **Location** 1m SW of Lower Tadmarton off B4035, 6m from Banbury
Hotel ★★★ 77% HL Best Western Banbury House, Oxford Rd, BANBURY ☎ 01295 259361 64 en suite

RUTLAND

KETTON

Luffenham Heath
PE9 3UU
☎ 01780 720205
▤ 01780 722146
e-mail: jringleby@theluffenhamheathgc.co.uk
web: www.luffenhamheath.co.uk
A James Braid course with firm driving fairways framed by swaying fescue, cross bunkers, grassy wastes and subtly undulating greens, hemmed in by sculpted traps. Many outstanding and challenging holes, placing a premium on accuracy. The 17th Par 3 signature hole

SHROPSHIRE

WESTON-UNDER-REDCASTLE

Hawkstone Park Hotel
SY4 5UY
☎ 01939 200611
▤ 01939 200335
e-mail: info@hawkstone.co.uk
web: www.hawkstone.co.uk
Hawkstone Course: 18 holes, 6491yds, Par 72, SSS 71, Course record 65.
Windmill Course: 18 holes, 6476yds, Par 72, SSS 72, Course record 64.
Academy Course: 6 holes, 741yds, Par 18, SSS 18.
Course Designer J Braid **Location** Off A49/A442
Telephone for further details

WHITCHURCH

Hill Valley
Terrick Rd SY13 4JZ
☎ 01948 663584 & 667788
▤ 01948 665927
e-mail: info@hillvalley.co.uk
web: www.hill-valley.co.uk
Emerald: 18 holes, 6628yds, Par 73, SSS 72, Course record 64.
Sapphire: 18 holes, 4800yds, Par 66, SSS 64.
Course Designer Peter Alliss/Dave Thomas **Location** 1m N. Follow signs from Bypass

continued

Telephone for further details
Hotel ★★ 71% HL Best Western Crown Hotel & Restaurant, High St, NANTWICH ☎ 01270 625283 18 en suite

SOMERSET

BATH

Bath
Sham Castle, North Rd BA2 6JG
☎ 01225 463834
📄 01225 331027
e-mail: enquiries@bathgolfclub.org.uk
web: www.bathgolfclub.org.uk
Considered to be one of the finest courses in the west, this is the site of Bath's oldest golf club. Situated on high ground overlooking the city and with splendid views over the surrounding countryside. The rocky ground supports good quality turf and there are many good holes. The 17th is a dog-leg right past, or over the corner of an out of bounds wall, and then on to an undulating green.
18 holes, 6442yds, Par 71, SSS 71, Course record 66. Club membership 750.
Visitors Mon-Sun & BHs. Handicap certificate. Dress code. **Societies** Booking required. **Green Fees** £36 per 18 holes (£40 Sat, Sun & BHs). **Prof** Peter J Hancox **Course Designer** Colt & others **Facilities** ⊕ ⑩ ⌷ ▙ ⌷ ⅋ ⚘ ⚐ ✦ ⚮ ⚘ **Conf** Corporate Hospitality Days **Location** 1.5m SE city centre off A36
Hotel ★★★ 72% HL Mercure Francis Hotel, Queen Square, BATH ☎ 0870 400 8223 95 en suite

BURNHAM-ON-SEA

Burnham & Berrow
St Christopher's Way TA8 2PE
☎ 01278 785760
📄 01278 795440
e-mail: secretary@burnhamandberrow.plus.com
web: www.burnhamandberrowgolfclub.co.uk
Natural championship links course with panoramic views of the Somerset hills and the Bristol Channel. A true test of golf suitable only for players with a handicap of 22 or better.

Burnham & Berrow

Championship Course: 18 holes, 6393yds, Par 71, SSS 71, Course record 64.
Channel Course: 9 holes, 6120yds, Par 70, SSS 69. Club membership 900.
Visitors Mon-Fri & Sun except BHs. Handicap certificate required. Dress code. **Societies** Booking required. **Green Fees** Championship Course: £63 per day, £50 per round (£63 per round Sat, Sun & BHs). **Prof** Mark Crowther-Smith **Course Designer** H S Colt **Facilities** ⊕ ⑩ ⌷ ▙ ⌷ ⅋ ⚘ ✦ ⚮ ⚘ **Location** 1m N of town on B3140

CLEVEDON

Clevedon
Castle Rd, Walton St Mary BS21 7AA
☎ 01275 874057
📄 01275 341228
e-mail: secretary@clevedongolfclub.co.uk
web: clevedongolfclub.co.uk
Situated on the cliff overlooking the Severn estuary with distant views of the Welsh coast. Excellent parkland course in first-class condition. Magnificent scenery and some tremendous drop holes.
18 holes, 6557yds, Par 72, SSS 72, Course record 68. Club membership 750.
Visitors Mon-Sun & BHs. Booking required. Handicap certificate. Dress code. **Societies** Booking required. **Green Fees** £32 per day (£40 Sat & Sun). ⊕ **Prof** Robert Scanlan **Course Designer** S Herd **Facilities** ⊕ ⑩ ⌷ ▙ ⌷ ⅋ ⚘ ✦ ⚘ **Conf** facs Corporate Hospitality Days **Location** M5 junct 20, 1m NE of town centre
Hotel ★★★ 71% HL Best Western Walton Park Hotel, Wellington Ter, CLEVEDON ☎ 01275 874253 40 en suite

MINEHEAD

Minehead & West Somerset
The Warren TA24 5SJ
☎ 01643 702057
📄 01643 705095
e-mail: secretary@mineheadgolf.co.uk
web: www.mineheadgolf.co.uk
Flat seaside links, very exposed to wind, with good turf set on a shingle bank. The last five holes adjacent to the beach are testing. The 215yd 18th is wedged between the beach and the club buildings and provides a good finish.
18 holes, 6228yds, Par 71, SSS 69, Course record 65. Club membership 620.
Visitors Mon-Sun & BHs. Dress code. **Societies** Booking required. **Green Fees** £35 per day (£40 Sat & Sun). **Prof** Ian Read **Facilities** ⊕ ⑩ ⌷ ▙ ⌷ ⅋ ⚘ ✦ ⚘ **Conf** Corporate Hospitality Days **Location** E end of esplanade
Hotel ★★ 80% HL Channel House Hotel, Church Path, MINEHEAD ☎ 01643 703229 8 en suite

WESTON-SUPER-MARE

Weston-Super-Mare
Uphill Rd North BS23 4NQ
☎ 01934 626968 & 633360(pro)
🖹 01934 621360
e-mail: wsmgolfclub@eurotelbroadband.com
web: www.westonsupermaregolfclub.com
A compact and interesting layout with the opening hole adjacent to the beach. The sandy, links-type course is slightly undulating and has beautifully maintained turf and greens. The 15th is a testing 455yd Par 4. Superb views across the Bristol Channel to Cardiff.

18 holes, 6245yds, Par 70, SSS 70, Course record 65. Club membership 750.
Visitors Mon-Sun & BHs. Handicap certificate. Dress code. **Societies** Booking required. **Green Fees** £48 per day, £36 per round. **Prof** Mike Laband **Course Designer** T Dunne/Dr Mackenzie
Facilities ⑨ ⓑ ☐ ⌻ ⚲ 🖴 ✎ ➴ **Location** S of town centre off A370
Hotel ★★★ 70% HL Beachlands Hotel, 17 Uphill Rd North, WESTON-SUPER-MARE ☎ 01934 621401 23 en suite

YEOVIL

Yeovil
Sherborne Rd BA21 5BW
☎ 01935 422965
🖹 01935 411283
e-mail: office@yeovilgolfclub.com
web: www. yeovilgolfclub.com
On the Old Course the opener lies by the River Yeo before the gentle climb to high downs with good views. The outstanding 14th and 15th holes present a challenge, being below the player with a deep railway cutting on the left of the green. The 1st on the Newton Course is played over the river which then leads to a challenging but scenic course.
Old Course: 18 holes, 6150yds, Par 71, SSS 70, Course record 64.
Newton Course: 9 holes, 4905yds, Par 68, SSS 65, Course record 63. Club membership 1000.
Visitors Mon-Sun & BHs. Booking required. Handicap certificate for Old Course. Dress code. **Societies** Booking required. **Green Fees** Old Course Apr-Oct: £35 (£45 Sat, Sun & BHs) Nov-Mar: £25 (£30). Newton Course £20. **Prof** Geoff Kite **Course Designer** Fowler & Allison **Facilities** ⑨ ⓑ ☐ ⌻ ⚲ 🖴 ⚲ ✎ 🖴
✎ ➴ **Location** 1m E on A30
Hotel ★★★ 75% HL The Yeovil Court Hotel & Restaurant, West Coker Rd, YEOVIL ☎ 01935 863746 18 en suite 12 annexe en suite

STAFFORDSHIRE

LICHFIELD

Whittington Heath
Tamworth Rd WS14 9PW
☎ 01543 432317
🖹 01543 433962
e-mail: info@whittingtonheathgc.co.uk
web: www.whittingtonheathgc.co.uk
The 18 magnificent holes wind through heathland and trees, presenting a good test for the serious golfer. Leaving the fairway can be severely punished. The dog-legs are most tempting, inviting the golfer to chance his arm. Local knowledge is a definite advantage. Clear views of the famous three spires of Lichfield Cathedral.
18 holes, 6490yds, Par 70, SSS 71, Course record 64. Club membership 660.
Visitors Mon-Fri except BHs. Booking required. Handicap certificate. Dress code. **Societies** Booking required. **Green Fees** £55 per 36
holes; £48 per 27 holes; £40 per 18 holes. **Prof** Adrian Sadler **Course Designer** Colt **Facilities** ⑨ ⓘ ◎! ⓑ ☐ ⌻ ⚲ 🖴
Conf Corporate Hospitality Days **Location** 2.5m SE on A51
Hotel ★★★ 74% HL Little Barrow Hotel, 62 Beacon St, LICHFIELD ☎ 01543 414500 32 en suite

SUFFOLK

ALDEBURGH

Aldeburgh
Saxmundham Rd IP15 5PE
☎ 01728 452890
🖹 01728 452937
e-mail: info@aldeburghgolfclub.co.uk
web: www.aldeburghgolfclub.co.uk
Good natural drainage provides year round golf in links-type conditions. Accuracy is the first challenge on well-bunkered, gorse-lined holes. Fine views over an Area of Outstanding Natural Beauty.
18 holes, 6349yds, Par 68, SSS 71, Course record 65. River Course: 9 holes, 4228yds, Par 64, SSS 61, Course record 62. Club membership 900.
Visitors Contact club for details. Handicap certificate. Dress code. **Societies** Booking required. **Green Fees** £55 per day; £45 after 12 noon (weekends £60/£50). **Prof** Keith Preston **Course Designer** Thompson, Fernie, Taylor, Park. **Facilities** ⓣ
🔄 ♨ 📇 🖥 ☎ ⛳ ✔ **Location** 1m W on A1094
Hotel ★★★ 86% HL Wentworth Hotel, Wentworth Rd, ALDEBURGH ☎ 01728 452312 28 en suite 7 annexe en suite

HINTLESHAM

Hintlesham
IP8 3JG
☎ 01473 652761
🖹 01473 652750
e-mail: office@hintleshamgolfclub.com
web: www.hintleshamgolfclub.com
Magnificent championship length course blending harmoniously with the ancient parkland surrounding the hotel. Opened in 1991 but seeded two years beforehand, this parkland course has reached a level maturity that allows it to be rivalled in the area only by a few ancient courses. The signature holes are the 4th and 17th, both featuring water at very inconvenient interludes.
18 holes, 6638yds, Par 72, SSS 72, Course record 63. Club membership 470.
Visitors Mon-Sun & BHs. Booking required. Dress code. **Societies** Welcome. **Green Fees** £36 per round (£44 Sat, Sun & BHs). **Prof** Henry Roblin **Course Designer** Hawtree & Sons **Facilities** ⓣ 🔄 ♨ 📇 🖥 ☎ ⛳ ✔ ♦ ✔ 🚗 ✔ **Leisure** hard tennis

courts, heated outdoor swimming pool, sauna, gymnasium, spa bath. **Conf** Corporate Hospitality Days **Location** In village on A1071
Hotel ★★★★ HL Hintlesham Hall Hotel, George St, HINTLESHAM ☎ 01473 652334 33 en suite

IPSWICH

Ipswich
Purdis Heath IP3 8UQ
☎ 01473 728941
🖹 01473 715236
e-mail: neill@ipswichgolfclub.com
web: www.ipswichgolfclub.com
Many golfers are surprised when they hear that Ipswich has, at Purdis Heath, a first-class course. In some ways it resembles some of Surrey's better courses; a beautiful heathland course with two lakes and easy walking.
Purdis Heath: 18 holes, 6439yds, Par 71, SSS 71, Course record 64. 9 holes, 1930yds, Par 31. Club membership 885.
Visitors Mon-Sun except BHs. Booking required for main course. Handicap certificate.for main course. Dress code. **Societies** Booking required. **Green Fees** 18 hole course £45 per day; £35 per round pm (£50/£40 Sat, Sun & BHs), 9 hole course £10 per day (£12.50 Sat, Sun & BHs). **Course Designer** James Braid **Facilities** ⓣ 🍽 🔄 ♨ 📇 🖥 ⛏ 🖨 ✔ **Location** 3m E of town centre off A1156

RAYDON

Brett Vale
Noakes Rd IP7 5LR
☎ 01473 310718
e-mail: info@brettvalegolf.co.uk
web: www.brettvalegolf.co.uk
Brett Vale course takes you through a nature reserve and on lakeside walks, affording views over Dedham Vale. The excellent fairways demand an accurate tee and good approach shots; 1, 2, 3, 8, 10 and 15 are all affected by crosswinds, but once in the valley it is much more sheltered. Although only 5864yds the course is testing and interesting at all levels of golf.
18 holes, 5864yds, Par 70, SSS 69, Course record 65. Club membership 600.
Visitors Mon-Sun & BHs. Dress code. **Societies** Booking required. **Green Fees** £22.50 per 18 holes (£28 Sat, Sun & BHs). **Prof** Paul Bate **Course Designer** Howard Swan **Facilities** ⓣ 🍽 🔄 ♨ 🖥 ⛏ 🖨 ☎ ⛳ ✔ 🚗 ✔ 🍴 **Leisure** fishing, gymnasium. **Conf** facs Corporate Hospitality Days **Location** A12 onto B1070 towards Hadleigh, left at Raydon, by water tower
Hotel ★★★ CHH Maison Talbooth, Stratford Rd, DEDHAM ☎ 01206 322367 10 en suite

THORPENESS

Thorpeness Golf Club & Hotel
Lakeside Av IP16 4NH
☎ 01728 452176
🖹 01728 453868
e-mail: info@thorpeness.co.uk
web: www.thorpeness.co.uk
A 6271yd coastal heathland course, designed in 1923 by
James Braid. The quality of his design combined with
modern green keeping techniques has resulted in an
extremely challenging course for golfers at all levels. It is
also one of the driest courses in the region.

Thorpeness Golf Club & Hotel
18 holes, 6271yds, Par 69, SSS 71, Course record 66.
Club membership 700.
Visitors Mon-Sun & BHs. Booking required. Handicap certificate.
Dress code. **Societies** Booking required. **Green Fees** £37 per
day/round (£42 Sat, Sun & BHs), £25 after 3pm. **Prof** Frank Hill
Course Designer James Braid **Facilities** ⑪ ⑩ 🍴 🖥 🗗 🎏 🛠 🛒
🔌 🛏 ✍ **Leisure** hard and grass tennis courts, fishing, snooker
room. **Conf** facs Corporate Hospitality Days **Location** Off
A1094 to Aldeburgh, signed
Hotel ★★★ 77% HL Thorpeness Hotel, Lakeside Av,
THORPENESS ☎ 01728 452176 30 annexe en suite

WOODBRIDGE

Woodbridge
Bromeswell Heath IP12 2PF
☎ 01394 382038
🖹 01394 382392
e-mail: woodbridgegc@anglianet.co.uk
web: www.woodbridgegolfclub.com
Main Course: 18 holes, 6299yds, Par 70, SSS 70,
Course record 64.
Forest Course: 9 holes, 3191yds, Par 70, SSS 70.
Course Designer Davie Grant **Location** 2.5m NE off A1152
Telephone for further details
Hotel ★★★ 78% CHH Seckford Hall Hotel, WOODBRIDGE
☎ 01394 385678 22 en suite 10 annexe en suite

WORLINGTON

Royal Worlington & Newmarket
Golf Links Rd IP28 8SD
☎ 01638 712216 & 717787
🖹 01638 717787
web: www.royalworlington.co.uk
Inland links course, renowned as one of the best nine-
hole courses in the world. Well drained, giving excellent
winter playing conditions.
9 holes, 3123yds, Par 35, SSS 70, Course record 65.
Club membership 325.
Visitors Mon-Sun & BHs. Booking required. Handicap certificate.
Dress code. **Societies** Booking required. **Green Fees** £60 per
day (reductions after 2 pm). ⊕ **Prof** Steve Barker **Course
Designer** Tom Dunn **Facilities** ⑪ by prior arrangement 🍴 🗗 🛠🗒
🛏 🛒 🎏 ✍ **Location** 0.5m SE of Worlington near Mildenhall
Hotel ★★★★ 80% HL Bedford Lodge Hotel, Bury Rd,
NEWMARKET ☎ 01638 663175 55 en suite

SURREY

ADDLESTONE

New Zealand
Woodham Ln KT15 3QD
☎ 01932 345049
🖹 01932 342891
e-mail: roger.marrett@nzgc.org
18 holes, 6073yds, Par 68, SSS 69, Course record 66.
Course Designer Muir Fergusson/Simpson **Location** 1.5m E
of Woking
Telephone for further details
Hotel ★★★ 71% HL The Ship Hotel, Monument Green,
WEYBRIDGE ☎ 01932 848364 77 en suite

BROOKWOOD

West Hill
Bagshot Rd GU24 0BH
☎ 01483 474365
🖹 01483 474252
e-mail: secretary@westhill-golfclub.co.uk
web: www.westhill-golfclub.co.uk
A challenging course with fairways lined with heather
and tall pines, one of Surrey's finest courses. Demands
every club in the bag to be played.
18 holes, 6343yds, Par 69, SSS 70, Course record 62.
Club membership 500.
Visitors Mon-Fri except BHs. Booking required. Handicap
certificate. Dress code. **Societies** Booking required. **Green Fees**
£85 per day, £65 per round. £45 per round winter. **Prof** Guy
Shoesmith **Course Designer** C Butchart/W Parke **Facilities**
⑪ ⑩ by prior arrangement 🍴 🗗 🗒 🛏 🛒 🎏 🛠 ✍ **Leisure**
halfway hut.
Conf facs Corporate Hospitality Days **Location** E of village on
A322
Hotel ★★★★★ HL Pennyhill Park Hotel & The Spa, London Rd,
BAGSHOT ☎ 01276 471774 26 en suite 97 annexe en suite

CHAMPIONSHIP COURSE

WENTWORTH

Wentworth Dr GU25 4LS
☎ 01344 842201 📄 01344 842804
e-mail: reception@wentworthclub.com
web: www.wentworthclub.com
West Course: 18 holes, 7301yds, Par 73,
SSS 74, Course record 63.
East Course: 18 holes, 6201yds, Par 68,
SSS 70, Course record 62.
Edinburgh Course: 18 holes, 7004yds,
Par 72, SSS 74, Course record 67.
Visitors Mon-Fri except BHs. Booking
required. Handicap certificate. Dress code.
Societies booking required. **Green Fees** West
Course: from £100-£285; Edinburgh Course:
from £80-£160; East Course: from £75-£130.
Prof Jason Macniven **Course Designer** Colt/
Jacobs/Gallacher/Player **Facilities** ⑨ ⑩ ⓛ
⬜ ⑨ ⬛ ⬛ ⑨ ⬛ ⬛ **Leisure** hard
and grass tennis courts, outdoor and indoor
heated pools, fishing, sauna, solarium, gym,
spa with 6 treatment rooms. **Conf** Corporate
Hospitality Days **Location** Main gate directly
opposite turning for A329 on A30

Wentworth Club, the home of the PGA and World Match Play championships, is a very special venue for any sporting, business or social occasion. The West Course is familiar to millions of television viewers who have followed the championships here. There are two other courses, the East Course and the Edinburgh Course, and a nine-hole Par 3 executive course. The courses cross Surrey heathland with woods of pine, oak and birch. The Club is renowned for its fine food, and the health and leisure facilities include a holistic spa, 13 outdoor tennis courts (with four different playing surfaces) and a 25-metre indoor swimming pool.

WALTON HEATH

Deans Ln, Walton-on-the-Hill KT20 7TP
☎ **01737 812380** 🖷 **01737 814225**
e-mail: secretary@whgc.co.uk
web: www.whgc.co.uk
Old Course: 18 holes, 6836yds, Par 72, SSS 73, Course record 65.
New Course: 18 holes, 6613yds, Par 72, SSS 72, Course record 67.
Club membership 1000.
Visitors Mon-Fri. Booking required. Sat, Sun & BHs by arrangement. Handicap certificate. Dress code. **Societies** Booking required.
Green Fees Old Course £100; New Course £90. Both courses £120 (Old Course £120: New Course £100 weekends). **Prof** Ken Macpherson **Course Designer** Herbert Fowler **Facilities** ⑨ ⮝ ⯊ ⯎ ⯄ ⯅ ⯆ ⯇ ✐
Conf Corporate Hospitality Days **Location** SE of village off B2032

Walton Heath, a traditional member club, has two extremely challenging courses. Enjoying an enviable international reputation, the club was founded in 1903. It has played host to over 60 major amateur and professional championships, including the 1981 Ryder Cup and five European Open Tournaments (1991, 1989, 1987, 1980 and 1977); among the many prestigious amateur events, Walton Heath hosted the English Amateur in 2002. In recent years the club has hosted the European qualification for the U.S. Open Championship. The Old Course is popular with visitors, while the New Course is very challenging, requiring subtle shots to get the ball near the hole. Straying from the fairway brings gorse, bracken and heather to test the golfer.

CAMBERLEY

Camberley Heath
Golf Dr GU15 1JG
☎ 01276 23258
📄 01276 692505
e-mail: info@camberleyheathgolfclub.co.uk
web: www.camberleyheathgolfclub.co.uk
Set in attractive Surrey countryside, a challenging golf course that features an abundance of pine and heather. A true classic heathland course with many assets, including the mature fairways.

18 holes, 6147yds, Par 72, SSS 70, Course record 65. Club membership 600.
Visitors Mon-Thu except BHs. Booking required. Handicap certificate. Dress code. **Societies** Booking required. **Green Fees** £74 per 36 holes, £57 per 18 holes. **Prof** Glenn Ralph **Course Designer** Harry S Colt **Facilities** ⑪ 🕪 🛒 🖵 🍴 🏌 ⛳ 🛅 ✦ 🛒 ✦ **Conf** facs Corporate Hospitality Days **Location** 1.25m SE of town centre off A325
Hotel ★★★★★ HL Pennyhill Park Hotel & The Spa, London Rd, BAGSHOT ☎ 01276 471774 26 en suite 97 annexe en suite

EFFINGHAM

Effingham
Guildford Rd KT24 5PZ
☎ 01372 452203
📄 01372 459959
e-mail: secretary@effinghamgolfclub.com
web: www.effinghamgolfclub.com
Easy-walking downland course laid out on 270 acres with tree-lined fairways. It is one of the longest of the Surrey courses with wide subtle greens that provide a provocative but by no means exhausting challenge. Fine views of the London skyline.
18 holes, 6554yds, Par 71, SSS 71, Course record 64. Club membership 800.
Visitors may play Mon-Sun except BHs. Handicap certificate. Dress code. **Societies** Booking required. **Green Fees** £60 per day, £45 per round, £25 after 3.30pm. ⛳ **Prof** Steve Hoatson **Course Designer** H S Colt **Facilities** ⑪ 🕪 by prior arrangement 🛒 🖵 🍴 🏌 🛅 ⛳ ✦ 🛒 ✦ 🏌 **Leisure** hard tennis courts, snooker table. **Conf** facs Corporate Hospitality Days **Location** W of village on A246

Hotel ★★ 67% HL Bookham Grange Hotel, Little Bookham Common, Bookham, LEATHERHEAD ☎ 01372 452742 27 en suite

ENTON GREEN

West Surrey
GU8 5AF
☎ 01483 421275
📄 01483 415419
e-mail: office@wsgc.co.uk
web: www.wsgc.co.uk
An attractive course with tree-lined fairways and contrasting views of the Surrey landscape. The course winds slowly upwards towards its highest point 440ft above sea level.
18 holes, 6482yds, Par 71, SSS 71, Course record 65. Club membership 600.
Visitors Mon-Sun & BHs. Booking required. Handicap certificate. Dress code. **Societies** Booking required. **Green Fees** £60 per day; £40 per round (£70/£50 Sat, Sun & BHs). ⛳ **Prof** Alister Tawse
Course Designer Herbert Fowler **Facilities** ⑪ 🕪 🛒 🖵 🍴 🏌 🛅 ✦ 🛒 ✦ 🏌 **Leisure** hard tennis courts. **Conf** Corporate Hospitality Days **Location** S of village
Hotel ★★★ 78% HL Mercure Bush Hotel, The Borough, FARNHAM ☎ 0870 400 8225 & 01252 715237 📄 01252 733530 83 en suite

FARNHAM

Farnham
The Sands GU10 1PX
☎ 01252 782109
📄 01252 781185
e-mail: farnhamgolfclub@tiscali.co.uk
web: www.farnhamgolfclub.co.uk
A mixture of meadowland and heath with quick drying sandy subsoil. Several of the earlier holes have interesting features.
18 holes, 6447yds, Par 72, SSS 71, Course record 66. Club membership 700.
Visitors Mon-Fri except BHs. Handicap certificate. Dress code **Societies** Welcome. **Green Fees** £50 per day; £45 per round. **Prof** Grahame Cowlishaw **Course Designer** Donald Steel **Facilities** ⑪ 🕪 by prior arrangement 🛒 🖵 🍴 🛅 ✦ ✦ **Conf** Corporate Hospitality Days **Location** 3m E off A31
Hotel ★★★ 78% HL Mercure Bush Hotel, The Borough, FARNHAM ☎ 0870 400 8225 & 01252 715237 📄 01252 733530 83 en suite

GUILDFORD

Guildford

High Path Rd, Merrow GU1 2HL
☎ 01483 563941
🖹 01483 453228
e-mail: secretary@guildfordgolfclub.co.uk
web: www.guildfordgolfclub.co.uk

The course is on Surrey downland bordered by attractive woodlands. Situated on chalk, it is acknowledged to be one of the best all-weather courses in the area, and the oldest course in Surrey. Although not a long course, the prevailing winds across the open downs make low scoring difficult. It is possible to see four counties on a clear day.

18 holes, 6090yds, Par 69, SSS 69, Course record 64. Club membership 700.

Visitors Mon, Tue, Thu, Fri except BHs. Wed pm only.
Societies welcome. **Green Fees** not confirmed. ⊕ **Prof** P G Hollington **Course Designer** J H Taylor/Hawtree **Facilities** ⚲ 🖼 ✐ ✐ **Conf** facs Corporate Hospitality Days **Location** E of town centre off A246

HINDHEAD

Hindhead

Churt Rd GU26 6HX
☎ 01428 604614
🖹 01428 608508
e-mail: secretary@the-hindhead-golf-club.co.uk
web: www.hindhead-golfclub.co.uk

A picturesque Surrey heathland course. The front nine holes follow heather lined valleys which give the players a very remote and secluded feel. For the back nine play moves on to a plateau which offers a more traditional game before the tough challenge of the final two finishing holes.

18 holes, 6356yds, Par 70, SSS 70, Course record 63. Club membership 610.

Visitors Mon-Sun & BHs. Booking required. Handicap certificate. Dress code. **Societies** Booking required. **Green Fees** £60 per day; £50 per round (£70/£60 Sat, Sun & BHs). **Prof** Ian Benson **Course Designer** J H Taylor **Facilities** ⊕ 🖼 ✐ 🍴 ⚲ 🖼 ⚓ ✐ ✈ **Leisure** snooker. **Conf** Corporate Hospitality Days **Location** 1.5m NW of Hindhead on A287

Hotel ★★★★ 77% HL Lythe Hill Hotel & Spa, Petworth Rd, HASLEMERE ☎ 01428 651251 41 en suite

OTTERSHAW

Foxhills Club and Resort

Stonehill Rd KT16 0EL
☎ 01932 872050
🖹 01932 875200
e-mail: events@foxhills.co.uk
web: www.foxhills.co.uk

The Bernard Hunt Course: 18 holes, 6770yds, Par 73, SSS 72, Course record 65.
Longcross Course: 18 holes, 6453yds, Par 72, SSS 71, Course record 70.

Course Designer F W Hawtree **Location** 1m NW of Ottershaw
Telephone for further details
Hotel ★★★★ 79% HL Foxhills Club & Resort, Stonehill Rd, OTTERSHAW ☎ 01932 872050 70 en suite

TANDRIDGE

Tandridge

RH8 9NQ
☎ 01883 712274
🖹 01883 730537
e-mail: secretary@tandridgegolfclub.com
web: www.tandridgegolfclub.com

A parkland course with two loops of nine holes from the clubhouse. The first nine are relatively flat. The second nine undulate with outstanding views of the North Downs.

18 holes, 6277yds, Par 70, SSS 70, Course record 66. Club membership 750.

Visitors Mon, Wed & Thu except BHs. Booking required. Handicap certificate. Dress code. **Societies** Booking required. **Green Fees** £65 per day, £45 after noon. Winter:£35 per round. **Prof** Chris Evans **Course Designer** H S Colt **Facilities** ⊕ 🖼 ✐ 🍴 ⚲ 🖼 ⚓ ✐ **Conf** Corporate Hospitality Days **Location** M25 junct 6, 2m SE on A25
Hotel ★★★★ 80% HL Nutfield Priory, Nutfield, REDHILL ☎ 01737 824400 60 en suite

TILFORD

Hankley Common

The Club House GU10 2DD
☎ 01252 792493
🖹 01252 795699
web: hankley.co.uk

A natural heathland course subject to wind. Greens are first rate. The 18th, a long Par 4, is most challenging, the green being beyond a deep chasm which traps any but the perfect second shot. The 7th is a spectacular one-shotter.

18 holes, 6702yds, Par 72, SSS 72, Course record 62. Club membership 700.

continued

ENGLAND

Visitors Mon-Sun except BHs. Booking required. Handicap certificate. Dress code. **Societies** Booking required. **Green Fees** £85 per day, £70 per round (£85 per round Sat & Sun). **Prof** Peter Stow **Course Designer** James Braid **Facilities** ⊕ ⅃ ⌂ ⚐ ⛳
⚲ ⌂⛳ ✔ **Location** 0.75m SE of Tilford
Hotel ★★★ 78% HL Mercure Bush Hotel, The Borough, FARNHAM ☎ 0870 400 8225 & 01252 715237
▤ 01252 733530 83 en suite

WALTON-ON-THAMES

Burhill

Burwood Rd KT12 4BL
☎ 01932 227345
▤ 01932 267159
e-mail: info@burhillgolf-club.co.uk
web: www.burhillgolf-club.co.uk
The Old Course is a mature tree-lined parkland course with some of the finest greens in Surrey. The New Course, opened in 2001, is a modern course built to USGA specifications has many bunkers and water hazards, including the River Mole.
Old Course: 18 holes, 6479yds, Par 70, SSS 71, Course record 65. New Course: 18 holes, 6597yds, Par 72, SSS 71. Club membership 1100.
Visitors Mon-Fri except Bhs. Booking required. Dress code. **Societies** Booking required. **Green Fees** £85 per day, £65 per 18 holes. **Course Designer** Willie Park/Simon Gidman **Facilities** ⊕ ⌂ ⅃ ⌂ ⚐ ⛳
⚲ ⌂⛳ ✔ ⛟ ⌂ ✔ ⌖ **Conf** facs Corporate Hospitality Days **Location** M25 junct 10 on to A3 towards London, 1st exit(Painshill junct
Hotel ★★★ 71% HL The Ship Hotel, Monument Green, WEYBRIDGE ☎ 01932 848364 77 en suite

WEST BYFLEET

West Byfleet

Sheerwater Rd KT14 6AA
☎ 01932 343433
▤ 01932 340667
e-mail: secretary@wbgc.co.uk
web: www.wbgc.co.uk
An attractive course set against a background of woodland and gorse. The 13th is the famous pond shot with a water hazard and two bunkers fronting the green. No less than six holes of 420yds or more.
18 holes, 6211yds, Par 70, SSS 70.
Club membership 622.
Visitors Contact club for details. **Societies** Welcome.
Green Fees £70 per day, £50 per round. **Prof** David Regan **Course Designer** C S Butchart **Facilities** ⊕ ⌂ ⅃ ⌂ ⚐ ⚲ ⌂
⛳ ✔ ⌂ ✔ ⌖ **Conf** Corporate Hospitality Days **Location** W of village on A245

St George's Hill

Golf Club Rd, St George's Hill KT13 0NL
☎ 01932 847758
▤ 01932 821564
e-mail: admin@stgeorgeshillgolfclub.co.uk
web: stgeorgeshillgolfclub.co.uk
Comparable and similar to Wentworth, a feature of this course is the number of long and difficult Par 4s. To score well it is necessary to place the drive - and long driving pays handsomely. Walking is hard on this undulating, heavily wooded course with plentiful heather and rhododendrons.
Red & Blue: 18 holes, 6513yds, Par 70, SSS 71, Course record 64.
Green: 9 holes, 2897yds, Par 35.
Club membership 600.
Visitors Wed-Fri except BHs. Booking required. Handicap certificate. Dress code. **Societies** booking required. **Green Fees** not confirmed. **Prof** A C Rattue **Course Designer** H S Colt **Facilities** ⚲ ⌂⛳ ✔ **Conf** Corporate Hospitality Days **Location** 2m S off B374
Hotel ★★★ 71% HL The Ship Hotel, Monument Green, WEYBRIDGE ☎ 01932 848364 77 en suite

WOKING

Woking

Pond Rd, Hook Heath GU22 0JZ
☎ 01483 760053
▤ 01483 772441
e-mail: woking.golf@btconnect.com
web: www.wokinggolfclub.co.uk
An 18-hole course on Surrey heathland with few changes from the original course designed in 1892 by Tom Dunn. Bernard Darwin, a past captain and president, has written 'the beauty of Woking is that there is something distinctive about every hole'.
18 holes, 6340yds, Par 70, SSS 70, Course record 65. Club membership 600.
Visitors Mon-Fri except BHs. Handicap certificate. Dress code. **Societies** booking required. **Green Fees** not confirmed. **Prof** Carl Bianco
Course Designer Tom Dunn **Facilities** ⊕ ⌂ ⅃ ⌂ ⚐ ⛳ ⚲ ⌂⛳
⛟ ⌂ ✔ **Conf** Corporate Hospitality Days **Location** W of town centre in area of St Johns Heath
Hotel ★★★★★ HL Pennyhill Park Hotel & The Spa, London Rd, BAGSHOT ☎ 01276 471774 26 en suite 97 annexe en suite

Worplesdon

Heath House Rd GU22 0RA
☎ 01483 472277
e-mail: office@worplesdongc.co.uk
The scene of the celebrated mixed-foursomes competition. Accurate driving is essential on this heathland course. The short 10th across a lake from

tee to green is a notable hole, and the 18th provides a wonderfully challenging Par 4 finish.

18 holes, 6431yds, Par 71, SSS 71, Course record 66. Club membership 610.
Visitors Mon-Fri except BHs. Booking required. Handicap certificate. Dress code. **Societies** booking required. **Green Fees** not confirmed. **Prof** J Christine **Course Designer** J F Abercromby **Facilities** ⛳🏌️‍♂️🏊⛽🍴🏌️ **Location** 1.5m N of village off A322 **Hotel** ★★★★★ HL Pennyhill Park Hotel & The Spa, London Rd, BAGSHOT ☎ 01276 471774 26 en suite 97 annexe en suite

SUSSEX, EAST

BEXHILL

Cooden Beach
Cooden Sea Rd TN39 4TR
☎ 01424 842040 & 843938 (Pro Shop)
🖹 01424 842040
e-mail: enquiries@coodenbeachgc.com
web: www.coodenbeachgc.com
The course is close by the sea, but is not real links. Despite that, it is dry and plays well throughout the year. There are some excellent holes such as the 4th, played to a built-up green, the short 12th, and three good holes to finish. There are added ponds which make the player think more about tee shots and shots to the green.

Cooden Beach

18 holes, 6504yds, Par 72, SSS 71, Course record 67. Club membership 850.
Visitors Mon-Fri excep& BHs. Sat after 1pm, Sun after 11am. Booking required. Handicap certificate. Dress code. **Societies** Booking required. **Green Fees** £43 per day, £37 per round (£46/£49 weekends). **Prof** Jeffrey Sim **Course Designer** W Herbert Fowler **Facilities** ⛳🏌️‍♂️🏊🍴⛽🏌️ **Leisure** indoor practice facility. **Conf** facs Corporate Hospitality Days **Location** 2m W on A259
Hotel ★★★ 79% HL Powder Mills Hotel, Powdermill Ln, BATTLE ☎ 01424 775511 30 en suite 10 annexe en suite

BRIGHTON & HOVE

Dyke
Devils Dyke, Dyke Rd BN1 8YJ
☎ 01273 857296(office) & 857260(pro shop)
🖹 01273 857078
e-mail: dykegolfclub@btconnect.com
web: www.dykegolf.com
Easy drasining downland course has some glorious views both towards the sea and inland. The signature hole on the course is probably the 17th; it is one of those tough Par 3s of just over 200yds, and is played across a gully to a well protected green. Greens are small,fast and true.

18 holes, 6627yds, Par 72, SSS 72, Course record 66. Club membership 800.
Visitors Mon, Wed-Sun & BHs. Booking required. Dress code. **Societies** Booking required. **Green Fees** £35 per round (£45 Sat & Sun). **Prof** Richard Arnold **Course Designer** Fred Hawtree
Facilities ⛳🏌️‍♂️🏊🍴⛽🏌️🏌️‍♀️ **Conf** facs Corporate Hospitality Days **Location** 4m N of Brighton, between A23 & A27
Hotel ★★★ 72% HL Best Western Old Tollgate Restaurant & Hotel, The Street, BRAMBER ☎ 01903 879494 12 en suite 28 annexe en suite

CROWBOROUGH

Crowborough Beacon
Beacon Rd TN6 1UJ
☎ 01892 661511
🖹 01892 611988
e-mail: secretary@cbgc.co.uk
web: www.cbgc.co.uk
Standing some 800ft above sea level, this is a testing heathland course where accuracy off the tee rather than distance is paramount. Panoramic views of the South Downs, Eastbourne and even the sea on a clear day.

18 holes, 6031yds, Par 71, SSS 69, Course record 66. Club membership 700.
Visitors Mon-Fri. Sat, Sun & BHs after 2.30pm. Booking required. Handicap certificate. Dress code. **Societies** Booking required. **Green Fees** £50 per round, £60 per day (£60 per round Sat, Sun & BHs). **Prof** Mr D C Newnham **Facilities** ⛳🏌️ by prior arrangement ⛳🍴⛽🏊⛽🏌️🏌️‍♀️

continued

Conf Corporate Hospitality Days **Location** 9m S of Tunbridge Wells on A26
Hotel ★★★★ 74% HL The Spa Hotel, Mount Ephraim, TUNBRIDGE WELLS ☎ 01892 520331 69 en suite

EASTBOURNE

Royal Eastbourne
Paradise Dr BN20 8BP
☎ 01323 729738
🖷 01323 744048
e-mail: sec@regc.co.uk
web: www.regc.co.uk
A famous club which celebrated its centenary in 1987. The course plays longer than it measures. Testing holes are the 8th, a Par 3 played to a high green and the 16th, a Par 5 righthand dog-leg.
Devonshire Course: 18 holes, 6077yds, Par 70, SSS 69, Course record 62.
Hartington Course: 9 holes, 2147yds, Par 64, SSS 61. Club membership 800.
Visitors Mon-Sun & BHs. Booking required Mon, Sat, Sun & BHs. Handicap certificate. Dress code. **Societies** Booking required.
Green Fees Devonshire £33 per round (£39 Sat, Sun & BHs), Hartington £19 per day. **Prof** Alan Harrison **Course Designer** Arthur Mayhewe **Facilities** ⑪ ⭗ by prior arrangement ⓑ ⌂ ⑂
⚐ ⌂ ⚐ ◇ ⚞ ⛟ ⚟ **Leisure** snooker table. **Conf** facs Corporate Hospitality Days **Location** 0.5m W of town centre

FOREST ROW

Royal Ashdown Forest
Chapel Ln RH18 5LR
☎ 01342 822018
🖷 01342 825211
e-mail: office@royalashdown.co.uk
web: www.royalashdown.co.uk
Old Course is on undulating heathland with no bunkers. Long carries off the tees and magnificent views over the Forest. Not a course for the high handicapper. West Course on natural heathland with no bunkers. Less demanding than Old Course although accuracy is at a premium.

Old Course: 18 holes, 6502yds, Par 72, SSS 71, Course record 67.

West Course: 18 holes, 5606yds, Par 68, SSS 67, Course record 65. Club membership 450.
Visitors Mon-Sun & BHs. Booking required. Dress code.
Societies Booking required. **Green Fees** Old Course £55 per round (£75 Sat & Sun). West Course £28 per round (£33 Sat & Sun). Reduced winter rates. **Prof** Martyn Landsborough
Course Designer Archdeacon Scott **Facilities** ⑪ ⭗ by prior arrangement ⓑ ⌂ ⑂ ⚐ ⌂ ⚐ ⚞ ⛟ ⚟ **Location** On B2110 in Forest Row
Hotel ★★★★ HL Ashdown Park Hotel and Country Club, Wych Cross, FOREST ROW ☎ 01342 824988 106 en suite

RYE

Rye
New Lydd Rd, Camber TN31 7QS
☎ 01797 225241
🖷 01797 225460
e-mail: links@ryegolfclub.co.uk
web: www.ryegolfclub.co.uk
Unique links course with superb undulating greens set among ridges of sand dunes alongside Rye Harbour. Fine views over Romney Marsh and towards Fairlight and Dungeness.
Old Course: 18 holes, 6317yds, Par 68, SSS 71, Course record 64.
Jubilee Course: 18 holes, 5848yds, Par 69, SSS 69, Course record 71. Club membership 1200.
Visitors Mon-Sun & BHs. Booking required. Handicap certificate. Dress code. **Green Fees** Phone. **Prof** Michael Lee
Course Designer H S Colt **Facilities** ⑪ ⓑ ⌂ ⑂ ⚐ ⌂ ⚐ ◇ ⚞
Location 2.75m SE off A259
Hotel ★★★★ 80% HL The George in Rye, 98 High St, RYE
☎ 01797 222114 24 en suite

SEAFORD

Seaford
Firle Rd BN25 2JD
☎ 01323 892442
🖷 01323 894113
e-mail: secretary@seafordgolfclub.co.uk
web: www.seafordgolfclub.co.uk
The great H Taylor did not perhaps design as many courses as his friend and rival, James Braid, but Seaford's original design was Taylor's. It is a splendid downland course with magnificent views and some fine holes.
18 holes, 6546yds, Par 69, SSS 71. Club membership 600.
Visitors Mon-Sat except BHs. Handicap certificate. Dress code.
Societies Booking required. **Green Fees** £40 per 18 holes (£30 winter). **Prof** David Mills/Clay Morris **Course Designer** J H Taylor **Facilities** ⑪ ⭗ by prior arrangement ⓑ ⌂ ⑂ ⚐ ⌂ ⚐ ◇ ⚟
⚞ ⚟ ⛟ **Conf** Corporate Hospitality Days **Location** Turn inland off A259 at war memorial
Hotel ★★★ 70% HL The Star Inn, ALFRISTON ☎ 01323 870495
37 en suite

CHAMPIONSHIP COURSE

EAST SUSSEX NATIONAL GOLF RESORT AND SPA

Little Horsted TN22 5ES
☎ **01825 880088** 📄 **01825 880066**
e-mail: golf@eastsussexnational.co.uk
web: www.eastsussexnational.co.uk
East Course: 18 holes, 7138yds, Par 72,
SSS 74, Course record 63.
West Course: 18 holes, 7154yds, Par 72,
SSS 74. **Club membership 650.**
Visitors Mon-Sun & BHs. Booking required.
Dress code. **Societies** booking required.
Green Fees £50 per 18 holes (£60 weekends).
Prof Sarah Maclennan/Mike Clark
Course Designer Bob Cupp **Facilities** ⑨ 🍴 🄻
🖵 🍴 ⛱ 🏠 ⛳ ◇ ✦ 🛒 ✦ ✦ **Leisure** hard
tennis courts, heated indoor swimming pool,
fishing, sauna, solarium, health club and
spa, gymnasium, golf academy shop. **Conf**
Corporate Hospitality Days **Location** 2m S of
Uckfield on A22

East Sussex National offers two huge courses ideal for big-hitting professionals. The European Open has been staged here and it is home to the European Headquarters of the David Leadbetter Golf Academy, with indoor and outdoor video analysis. Bob Cupp designed the courses using 'bent' grass from tee to green, resulting in an American-style course to test everyone. The greens on both courses are immaculately maintained. The West Course, with stadium design and chosen for major events, is reserved for members and their guests; visitors are welcome on the East Course, also with stadium design, and which was the venue for the 1993 and 1994 European Open. The complex features a new 104-bedroom hotel and a bespoke conference centre capable of seating up to 600 delegates.

ENGLAND

TICEHURST

Dale Hill Hotel & Golf Club
TN5 7DQ
☎ 01580 200112
🖹 01580 201249
e-mail: info@dalehill.co.uk
web: www.dalehill.co.uk
Dale Hill is set in over 350 acres, high on the Weald
in an Area of Outstanding Natural Beauty. Offering
two 18-hole courses, one of which has been designed by
Ian Woosnam to USGA specifications.

Dale Hill: 18 holes, 6106yds, Par 70, SSS 69.
Ian Woosnam: 18 holes, 6512yds, Par 71, SSS 71,
Course record 64. Club membership 850.
Visitors Mon-Sun & BHs. Dress code. **Societies** Welcome.
Green Fees Dale Hill: £25 (£35 weekends). Ian Woosnam
(including buggy) £60 (£70 Sat & Sun). **Prof** Mark Wood **Course
Designer** Ian Woosnam **Facilities** ⑪ 🍴 🍺 ⬜ 🏐 🎿 🍸 🛍 🦅 ◇
🦅 🛥 🦅 🏹
Leisure heated indoor swimming pool, sauna, gymnasium.
Conf facs Corporate Hospitality Days **Location** M25
junct 5,A21, B2087 left after 1 mile
Hotel ★★★★ 80% HL Dale Hill Hotel & Golf Club, TICEHURST
☎ 01580 200112 35 en suite

SUSSEX, WEST

ANGMERING

Ham Manor
West Dr BN16 4JE
☎ 01903 783288
🖹 01903 850886
e-mail: secretary@hammanor.co.uk
web: www.hammanor.co.uk
Two miles from the sea, this parkland course has fine
springy turf and provides an interesting test in two loops
of nine holes each.
18 holes, 6267yds, Par 70, SSS 70, Course record 64.
Club membership 780.
Visitors Mon-Sun & BHs. Handicap certificate. Dress code.
Societies Welcome. **Green Fees** £35 (£50 Sat & Sun). **Prof**
Simon Buckley **Course Designer** Harry Colt **Facilities** ⑪ 🍴 🍺
⬜ 🏐 🎿 🛍 🛥 🦅 **Conf** Corporate Hospitality Days **Location**
Off A259

Guesthouse ★★★★ GA Kenmore Guest House, Claigmar Rd,
RUSTINGTON ☎ 01903 784634 7 rms (6 en suite)

BOGNOR REGIS

Bognor Regis
Downview Rd, Felpham PO22 8JD
☎ 01243 821929 (Secretary)
🖹 01243 860719
e-mail: sec@bognorgolfclub.co.uk
web: www.bognorgolfclub.co.uk
This flattish, well tree-lined, parkland course has more
variety than is to be found on some other south coast
courses. The course is open
to the prevailing wind and the River Rife and many water
ditches
need negotiation.
18 holes, 6238yds, Par 70, SSS 70, Course record 64.
Club membership 700.
Visitors Mon, Wed-Fri except BHs. Tue pm only. Handicap
certificate. Dress code. **Societies** Booking required. **Green
Fees** £30. ⊛ **Prof** Matthew Kirby **Course Designer** James
Braid **Facilities** ⑪ 🍴 🍺 ⬜ 🏐 🎿 🛍 🦅 🛥 🦅 **Conf** facs
Location 0.5m N at Felpham lights on A259
Hotel ★★ 71% HL Beachcroft Hotel, Clyde Rd, Felpham Village,
BOGNOR REGIS ☎ 01243 827142 35 en suite

COPTHORNE

Copthorne
Borers Arms Rd RH10 3LL
☎ 01342 712033 & 712508
🖹 01342 717682
e-mail: info@copthornegolfclub.co.uk
web: www.copthornegolfclub.co.uk
Despite it having been in existence since 1892, this club
remains one of the lesser known Sussex courses. It is
hard to know why because it is most attractive with
plenty of trees and much variety.
18 holes, 6435yds, Par 71, SSS 71, Course record 66.
Club membership 550.
Visitors Mon-Fri except BHs. Handicap certificate. Dress code.
Societies
Welcome. **Green Fees** £38. **Prof** Joe Burrell **Course Designer**
James Braid **Facilities** 🎿 🛥 🦅 🛍 🦅 **Conf** Corporate Hospitality
Days **Location** M23 junct 10, E of village off A264
Hotel ★★★★ 71% HL Copthorne Hotel London Gatwick,
Copthorne Way, COPTHORNE ☎ 01342 348800 & 348888
🖹 01342 348833 227 en suite

LITTLEHAMPTON

Littlehampton
170 Rope Walk, Riverside West BN17 5DL
☎ 01903 717170
📄 01903 726629
e-mail: lgc@talk21.com
web: www.littlehamptongolf.co.uk
A delightful seaside links in an equally delightful setting -
and the only links course in the area.

18 holes, 6226yds, Par 70, SSS 70, Course record 61.
Club membership 600.
Visitors Mon-Sun & BHs. Dress code. **Societies** Booking
required.
Green Fees Phone. **Prof** Stuart Fallow **Course Designer**
Hawtree **Facilities** ⑪ ⑩ 🖐 ⛳ 🍴 🏌 🛆 🏠 🏤 ⚅ **Conf** facs
Corporate Hospitality Days **Location** 1m W off A259
Hotel BUD Travelodge Littlehampton Rustington, Worthing Rd,
RUSTINGTON ☎ 08700 850 950 36 en suite

MANNINGS HEATH

Mannings Heath
Fullers, Hammerpond Rd RH13 6PG
☎ 01403 210228
📄 01403 270974
e-mail: enquiries@manningsheath.com
web: www.manningsheath.com
The Waterfall is a downhill, parkland, part heathland,
championship course with streams and trees in
abundance. It has three spectacular Par 3s but all
the holes are memorably unique. The Kingfisher
course is a modern design with a lake which comes
into play. It is more open and forgiving but not to be
underestimated.
Waterfall: 18 holes, 6483yds, Par 72, SSS 71,
Course record 63.
Kingfisher: 18 holes, 6217yds, Par 70, SSS 70,
Course record 66. Club membership 700.
Visitors Mon-Sun & BHs. Booking required Fri-Sun & BHs. Dress
code. **Societies** welcome. **Green Fees** not confirmed. **Prof** Neil
Darnell **Course Designer** David Williams **Facilities** ⑪ ⑩ 🖐 ⛳
🍴 🛆 🏠 🏤 ⚅ 🏌 **Leisure** hard tennis courts, fishing, sauna,
chipping practice area. **Conf** facs Corporate Hospitality Days
Location Off A281 on N side of village

Hotel ★★★★ CHH South Lodge Hotel, Brighton Rd, LOWER
BEEDING ☎ 01403 891711 45 en suite

PULBOROUGH

West Sussex
Golf Club Ln, Wiggonholt RH20 2EN
☎ 01798 872563
📄 01798 872033
e-mail: secretary@westsussexgolf.co.uk
web: www.westsussexgolf.co.uk
An outstanding beautiful heathland course occupying
an oasis of sand, heather and pine in the middle of
attractive countryside, which is predominately clay and
marsh. The 6th and 13th holes are particularly notable.
18 holes, 6264yds, Par 68, SSS 70, Course record 61.
Club membership 850.
Visitors Mon, Wed, Thu. Tue pm only. Sat & Sun by
arrangement. Booking required. Handicap certificate. Dress
code. **Societies** Booking required. **Green Fees** £75 per
day (£80 Sat & Sun). **Prof** Tim Packham **Course Designer**
Campbell/Hutcheson/Hotchkin **Facilities** ⑪ 🖐 ⛳ 🍴 🛆 🏠 🏤 🏦
⚅ 🏌 **Location** 1.5m E of Pulborough off A283
Hotel ★★★ 75% HL Best Western Roundabout Hotel,
Monkmead Ln, WEST CHILTINGTON ☎ 01798 813838 23 en suite

WORTHING

Worthing
Links Rd BN14 9QZ
☎ 01903 260801
📄 01903 694664
e-mail: enquiries@worthinggolf.com
web: www.worthinggolf.co.uk
The Upper Course, short and tricky with entrancing
views, will provide good entertainment. Lower Course
is considered to be one of the best downland courses in
the country.
Lower Course: 18 holes, 6505yds, Par 71, SSS 71,
Course record 62.
Upper Course: 18 holes, 5211yds, Par 66, SSS 65.
Club membership 1200.
Visitors Mon, Thu & Fri. Booking required. Handicap certificate.
Dress code. **Societies** Booking required. **Green Fees** Phone. ⚄
Prof Stephen Rolley **Course Designer** H S Colt **Facilities** ⑪ 🖐
⛳ 🍴 🛆 🏠 🏤 ⚅ 🏌 **Location** N of town centre off A27
Hotel ★★★ 77% HL Ardington Hotel, Steyne Gardens,
WORTHING ☎ 01903 230451 45 en suite

THE BELFRY

Wishaw B76 9PR
☎ **01675 470301** 🖹 **01675 470178**
e-mail: **enquiries@thebelfry.com**
web: **www.devereonline.co.uk**
The Brabazon: 18 holes, 6724yds, Par 72,
SSS 71. **PGA National:** 18 holes, 6639yds,
Par 71, SSS 70. **The Derby:** 18 holes, 6057yds,
Par 69, SSS 69. **Club membership 450.**
Visitors booking required for non-residents.
Handicap certificate. **Societies** booking
required. **Green Fees** Brabazon: £140, PGA:
£75, Derby: £40. Reduced winter rates. **Prof**
Simon Wordsworth **Course Designer** Dave
Thomas/Peter Alliss **Facilities** ⑪ 🍽 🏋 🖵 🖫
🛋 🖾 ⛾ ◇ ✓ 🛏 ✓ 🏆 **Leisure** hard tennis
courts, heated indoor swimming pool, squash,
sauna, solarium, gymnasium, PGA National
Golf Academy. **Conf** facs Corporate Hospitality
Days **Location** M42 junct 9, 4m E on A446

The Belfry is unique as the only venue
to have staged the biggest golf event
in the world, the Ryder Cup matches,
an unprecedented four times, most
recently in 2002. The Brabazon is
regarded throughout the world as a great
championship course with some of the
most demanding holes in golf; the 10th
(Ballesteros's Hole) and the 18th, with
its dangerous lakes and its amphitheatre
around the final green, are world famous.
Alternatively, you can pit your wits against
a new legend in the making, the PGA
National Course. The Dave Thomas and
Peter Alliss designed course has been used
for professional competition and is one of
Britain's leading courses. For those who like
their golf a little easier or like to get back
into the swing gently, the Derby is ideal and
can be played by golfers of any standard.

CHAMPIONSHIP COURSE

WEST MIDLANDS — MERIDEN

MARRIOTT FOREST OF ARDEN

Maxstoke Ln CV7 7HR
☎ **0870 400 7272** 🖨 **0870 400 7372**
web: www.marriotthotels.com/cvtgs
Arden Course: 18 holes, 6707yds, Par 72, SSS 73, Course record 63.
Aylesford Course: 18 holes, 5801yds, Par 69, SSS 68.
Club membership 800.
Visitors Mon-Sun & BHs. Booking required. Handicap certificate. Dress code.
Societies booking required. **Green Fees** Arden £100 (£110 Fri-Sun). Aylesford £45/£55. **Prof** Philip Hoye **Course Designer** Donald Steele **Facilities** ⚒ 🏠 🏌 ◇ ✓ 🛒 ✂
🏊 **Leisure** hard tennis courts, heated indoor pool, fishing, sauna, solarium, gym, croquet lawn, steam room, jacuzzi, aerobics studio.
Conf Corporate Hospitality Days
Location 1m SW on B4102

This is one of the finest golf destinations in the UK, with a range of facilities to impress every golfer. The jewel in the crown is the Arden championship parkland course, set in 10,000 acres of the Packington Estate. Designed by Donald Steel, it presents one of the country's most spectacular challenges and has hosted a succession of international tournaments, including the British Masters and English Open. Beware the 18th hole, which is enough to stretch the nerves of any golfer. The shorter Aylesford Course offers a varied and enjoyable challenge, which golfers of all abilities will find rewarding. Golf events are a speciality, and there is a golf academy and extensive leisure facilities.

TYNE & WEAR

NEWCASTLE UPON TYNE

Northumberland
High Gosforth Park NE3 5HT
☎ 0191 236 2498
🖹 0191 236 2036
e-mail: sec@thengc.co.uk
Predominatly a level heathland style course, the firm, fast greens are a particular feature.
18 holes, 6683yds, Par 72, SSS 72, Course record 65. Club membership 580.
Visitors Mon-Sun & BHs. Booking required Sat/Sun & BHs. Handicap certificate. Dress code. **Societies** booking required. **Green Fees** not confirmed. ◉ **Course Designer** Colt/Braid **Facilities** ⊕ ⏣ ⎁ ⌨ ⚑ ⚒ ✓ **Conf** Corporate Hospitality Days **Location** 4m N of city centre off A1
Hotel ★★★★ 76% HL Newcastle Marriott Hotel Gosforth Park, High Gosforth Park, Gosforth, NEWCASTLE UPON TYNE ☎ 0191 236 4111   178 en suite

SUNDERLAND

Wearside
Coxgreen SR4 9JT
☎ 0191 534 2518
🖹 0191 534 6186
web: wearsidegolfclub.com
Open, undulating parkland rolling down to the River Wear beneath the shadow of the famous Penshaw Monument. Built on the lines of a Greek temple it is a well-known landmark. Two ravines cross the course presenting a variety of challenging holes.
18 holes, 6373yds, Par 71, SSS 74, Course record 63. Club membership 648.
Visitors Contact club for details. **Societies** Welcome. **Green Fees** Phone. ◉ **Prof** Doug Brolls **Facilities** ⊕ ⏣ ⎁ ⌨ ⚑ ⚒ ⏢ **Conf** Corporate Hospitality Days **Location** 3.5m W off A183
Hotel ★★★★ 75% HL Sunderland Marriott Hotel, Queen's Pde, Seaburn, SUNDERLAND ☎ 0191 529 2041   82 en suite

WEST MIDLANDS

BIRMINGHAM

Edgbaston
Church Rd, Edgbaston B15 3TB
☎ 0121 454 1736
🖹 0121 454 2395
e-mail: secretary@edgbastongc.co.uk
web: www.edgbastongc.co.uk
Set in 144 acres of woodland, lake and parkland, 2m from the centre of Birmingham, this delightful course utilises the wealth of natural features to provide a series of testing and adventurous holes set in the traditional double loop that starts directly in front of the clubhouse, an imposing Georgian mansion.

18 holes, 6106yds, Par 69, SSS 69, Course record 63. Club membership 970.
Visitors Mon-Sun except BHs. Booking required Sat & Sun. Handicap certificate. Dress code. **Societies** Booking required **Green Fees** Phone. **Prof** Jamie Cundy **Course Designer** H S Colt **Facilities** ⊕ ⏣ ⎁ ⌨ ⚑ ⚒ ⏢ ✓ ⚒ ✓ **Conf** facs Corporate Hospitality Days **Location** 2m S of city centre on B4217, off A38
Hotel ★★★ 73% HL Thistle Birmingham Edgbaston, 225 Hagley Rd, Edgbaston, BIRMINGHAM ☎ 0870 333 9127   151 en suite

COVENTRY

Coventry
St Martins Rd, Finham Park CV3 6RJ
☎ 024 7641 4152
🖹 024 7669 0131
e-mail: coventrygolfclub@hotmail.com
web: www.coventrygolfcourse.co.uk
The scene of several major professional events, this undulating parkland course has a great deal of quality. More than that, it usually plays its length, and thus scoring is never easy, as many professionals have found to their cost.
18 holes, 6601yds, Par 73, SSS 73, Course record 66. Club membership 500.
Visitors Mon-Fri except BHs. Handicap certificate. Dress code. **Societies** Booking required **Green Fees** £40 per day. **Prof** Philip Weaver **Course Designer** Vardon Bros/ Hawtree **Facilities** ⊕ ⏣ ⎁ ⌨ ⚑ ⚒ ⏢ ✓ **Conf** Corporate Hospitality Days **Location** 3m S of city centre on B4113
Hotel ★★★ 66% HL Hylands Hotel, Warwick Rd, COVENTRY ☎ 024 7650 1600   61 en suite

WEST BROMWICH

Sandwell Park
Birmingham Rd B71 4JJ
☎ 0121 553 4637
🖹 0121 525 1651
e-mail: secretary@sandwellparkgolfclub.co.uk
web: www.sandwellparkgolfclub.co.uk
A picturesque course wandering over wooded heathland and utilising natural features. Each hole is entirely separate, shielded from the others by either natural banks or lines of trees. A course that demands careful placing of shots that have been given a great deal of thought. Natural undulating fairways create difficult and testing approach shots to the greens.

18 holes, 6204yds, Par 71, SSS 71, Course record 65. Club membership 550.

Visitors Mon-Fri except BHs. Booking required. Handicap certificate. Dress code. **Societies** booking required. **Green Fees** not confirmed. ⊜ **Prof** Nigel Wylie **Course Designer** H S Colt **Facilities** ⑪ ⎸◎⎹ 🍴 ⌷ 🍴 ⚲ 🍴 ⚱ ✔ **Leisure** practice chipping area. **Conf** facs Corporate Hospitality Days **Location** M5 junct 1, 200yds on A41

Hotel ★★★ 68% HL Great Barr Hotel & Conference Centre, Pear Tree Dr, Newton Rd, Great Barr, BIRMINGHAM ☎ 0121 357 1141 105 en suite

WILTSHIRE

CASTLE COMBE

Manor House
SN14 7HR
☎ 01249 782206
🖷 01249 782992
e-mail: enquiries@manorhousegolfclub.com
web: www.exclusivehotels.co.uk
Set in a wonderful location within the wooded estate of the 14th-century Manor House, this course includes five Par 5s and some spectacular Par 3s. Manicured fairways and hand-cut greens, together with the River Bybrook meandering through the middle make for a picturesque and dramatic course.
The Manor House Golf Club at Castle Combe: 18 holes, 6500yds, Par 72. Club membership 450.

Visitors Mon-Sun & BHs. Booking required. Handicap certificate. Dress code. **Societies** Booking required. **Green Fees** £75 per round (£90 Fri-Sun). Spring/Autumn: £65/£80. Winter £40/$40. **Prof** Peter Green **Course Designer** Peter Alliss/Clive Clark **Facilities** ⑪ ⎸◎⎹ 🍴 ⌷ 🍴 ⚲ 🍴 ⚱ ◇ ✔ 🚗 ✔ **Leisure** hard tennis courts, fishing, sauna, croquet. **Conf** facs Corporate Hospitality Days **Location** 5m NW of Chippenham on B4039

Hotel ★★★★ CHH Manor House Hotel and Golf Club, CASTLE COMBE ☎ 01249 782206 22 en suite 26 annexe en suite

GREAT DURNFORD

High Post
SP4 6AT
☎ 01722 782356
🖷 01722 782674
e-mail: admin@highpostgolfclub.co.uk
web: www.highpostgolfclub.co.uk
The free-draining, easy walking downland course offers summer tees and greens all year. The opening three holes, usually played with the wind, get you to off to a flying start, but the closing three provide a tough finish. Peter Alliss has rated the 9th among his dream holes. The club welcomes golfers of all abilities.

18 holes, 6305yds, Par 70, SSS 70, Course record 64. Club membership 625.

Visitors Mon-Sun & BHs. Dress code. **Societies** Booking required. **Green Fees** £50 per day; £32 per round (£50/£42 Sun & Sat). **Prof** Tony Isaacs **Course Designer** Hawtree & Ptrs **Facilities** ⑪ ⎸◎⎹ 🍴 ⌷ 🍴 ⚲ 🍴 ⚱ ✔ 🚩 **Conf** facs Corporate Hospitality Days **Location** On A345 between Sailsbury and Amesbury

Hotel ★★★ 63% HL Quality Hotel Andover, Micheldever Rd, ANDOVER ☎ 01264 369111 13 en suite 36 annexe en suite

TIDWORTH

Tidworth Garrison
Bulford Rd SP9 7AF
☎ 01980 842301
🖷 01980 842301
e-mail: tidworthgolfclub@btconnect.com
web: www.tidworthgolfclub.co.uk
A breezy, dry downland course with lovely turf, fine trees and views over Salisbury Plain and the surrounding area. The 4th and 12th holes are notable. The 565yd 14th, going down towards the clubhouse, gives the big hitter a chance to let fly.
18 holes, 6320yds, Par 70, SSS 70, Course record 63. Club membership 750.

Visitors Mon-Sun & BHs. Booking required. Handicap certificate. Dress code. **Societies** Booking required. **Green Fees** £47 per round/day. ⊜ **Prof** Terry Gosden **Course Designer** Donald Steel **Facilities** ⑪ ⎸◎⎹ 🍴 ⌷ 🍴 ⚲ 🍴 ⚱ 🚩 🚗 ✔ **Location** W of village off A338

continued

Hotel ★★★ 63% HL Quality Hotel Andover, Micheldever Rd, ANDOVER ☎ 01264 369111 13 en suite 36 annexe en suite

WARMINSTER

West Wilts
Elm Hill BA12 0AU
☎ 01985 213133
🖹 01985 219809
e-mail: sec@westwiltsgolfclub.co.uk
web: www.westwiltsgolfclub.co.uk
A hilltop chalk downland course among the Wiltshire downs. Free draining, short, but a very good test of accurate iron play. Excellent fairways and greens all year round.
18 holes, 5754yds, Par 70, SSS 68, Course record 60. Club membership 570.
Visitors Mon-Fri, Sun & BHs. Booking required Sun. Handicap certificate. Dress code. **Societies** Booking required. **Green Fees** £30 per day (£35 Sun & BHs). **Prof** Rob Morris **Course Designer** J H Taylor
Facilities ⊕ ⑨ by prior arrangement ⓛ ⊑ ⑰ ⚐ 🖭 ⚏ ⚒
Conf Corporate Hospitality Days **Location** N of town centre off A350
Hotel ★★★★ 79% HL Bishopstrow House, WARMINSTER ☎ 01985 212312 32 en suite

WORCESTERSHIRE

ALVECHURCH

Kings Norton
Brockhill Ln, Weatheroak B48 7ED
☎ 01564 826706 & 826789
🖹 01564 826955
e-mail: info@kingsnortongolfclub.co.uk
web: www.kingsnortongolfclub.co.uk
Parkland with water hazards. A 27-hole championship venue playing as three combinations of nine holes.
Weatheroak: 18 holes, 6729yds, Par 72, SSS 72, Course record 65.
Brockhill: 18 holes, 6645yds, Par 72, SSS 72.
Wythall: 18 holes, 6600yds, Par 72, SSS 72.
Club membership 1000.
Visitors Mon-Fri except BHs. Dress code. **Societies** Booking required. **Green Fees** Phone. **Prof** Kevin Hayward **Course Designer** F Hawtree **Facilities** ⊕ ⑨ ⓛ ⊑ ⑰ ⚐ 🖭 ⚏ ⚒
Leisure Par 3 course.
Conf facs Corporate Hospitality Days **Location** M42 junct 3, off A435
Hotel ★★★★ 71% HL The Bromsgrove Hotel, Kidderminster Rd, BROMSGROVE ☎ 01527 576600 109 en suite

YORKSHIRE, NORTH

GANTON

Ganton
YO12 4PA
☎ 01944 710329
🖹 01944 710922
e-mail: secretary@gantongolfclub.com
web: www.gantongolfclub.com
Championship course, heathland, gorse-lined fairways and heavily bunkered; variable winds. The opening holes make full use of the contours of the land and the approach to the second demands the finest touch. The 4th is considered one of the best holes on the outward half with its shot across a valley to a plateau green, the surrounding gorse punishing anything less than a perfect shot. The finest hole is possibly the 18th, requiring an accurately placed drive to give a clear shot to the sloping, well-bunkered green.
18 holes, 6753yds, Par 72, SSS 73, Course record 65. Club membership 500.
Visitors Mon-Sun & BHs. Booking required. Handicap certificate. Dress code. **Societies** Booking required. **Green Fees** £73 per day (£83 Sat, Sun & BHs). **Prof** Gary Brown **Course Designer** Dunn/Vardon/Braid/Colt **Facilities** ⊕ ⑨ ⓛ ⊑ ⑰ ⚐ 🖭 ⚏ ⚒ 🖭 ⚒ **Conf** Corporate Hospitality Days **Location** N of village off A64
Hotel ★★★ 68% HL East Ayton Lodge Country House, Moor Ln, Forge Valley, EAST AYTON ☎ 01723 864227 12 en suite 14 annexe en suite

HARROGATE

Harrogate
Forest Ln Head, Starbeck HG2 7TF
☎ 01423 862999
🖹 01423 860073
e-mail: secretary@harrogate-gc.co.uk
web: www.harrogate-gc.co.uk
Course on fairly flat terrain with MacKenzie-style greens and tree-lined fairways. While not a long course, the layout penalises the golfer who strays off the fairway. Subtly placed bunkers and copses of trees require the golfer to adopt careful thought and accuracy if Par is be bettered. The last six holes include five Par 4s, of which four exceed 400yds.
18 holes, 6241yds, Par 69, SSS 70, Course record 63. Club membership 700.
Visitors Mon, Wed-Fri, Sun & BHs. Tue pm only. Handicap certificate. Dress code. **Societies** Booking required. **Green Fees** £40 per day, £35 per round (£45 Sat & Sun). **Prof** Gary Stothard, Sam Evison
Course Designer Sandy Herd **Facilities** ⊕ ⑨ ⓛ ⊑ ⑰ ⚐ 🖭 ⚏ ⚒ **Leisure** snooker. **Conf** Corporate Hospitality Days **Location** 2.25m N on A59
Hotel ★★★ 79% HL Grants Hotel, 3-13 Swan Rd, HARROGATE ☎ 01423 560666 42 en suite

Oakdale
Oakdale Glen HG1 2LN
☎ 01423 567162
🖷 01423 536030
e-mail: sec@oakdale-golfclub.com
web: www.oakdale-golfclub.com
A pleasant, undulating parkland course which provides a good test of golf for the low handicap player without intimidating the less proficient. A special feature is an attractive stream which comes in to play on four holes. Excellent views from the clubhouse with good facilities.
18 holes, 6456yds, Par 71, SSS 71, Course record 61. Club membership 975.
Visitors Mon-Sun & BHs. Booking required Sat, Sun & BHs. Handicap certificate. Dress code. **Societies** Booking required. **Green Fees** £46 for 27 holes, £39 per round (£55 Sat, Sun & BHs). **Prof** Clive Dell
Course Designer Dr McKenzie **Facilities** ⑪ 🍴 🍺 ☕ 🏌 🏖 🏡 🛍 🐾 ✓ **Conf** Corporate Hospitality Days **Location** N of town centre off A61
Hotel ★★★★ 75% HL Paramount Majestic Hotel, Ripon Rd, HARROGATE ☎ 01423 700300 156 en suite

---

PANNAL

Pannal
Follifoot Rd HG3 1ES
☎ 01423 872628
🖷 01423 870043
e-mail: secretary@pannalgc.co.uk
web: www.pannalgc.co.uk
Fine championship course chosen as a regional qualifying venue for the Open Championship. Moorland turf but well-wooded with trees closely involved with play. Excellent views enhance the course.
18 holes, 6622yds, Par 72, SSS 72, Course record 62. Club membership 850.
Visitors Mon-Sun & BHs. Booking required. Handicap certificate. Dress code. **Societies** Booking required. **Green Fees** £55 per day, £45 per round (£60 Sat & Sun). **Prof** David Padgett **Course Designer** Sandy Herd **Facilities** ⑪ 🍴 🍺 ☕ 🏌 🏖 🏡 🛍 🐾 ✓ 🏌 **Leisure** snooker. **Conf** Corporate Hospitality Days **Location** E of village off A61

YORK

Fulford
Heslington Ln YO10 5DY
☎ 01904 413579
🖷 01904 416918
e-mail: gary@fulfordgolfclub.co.uk
web: www.fulfordgolfclub.co.uk
A flat, parkland and heathland course well-known for the superb quality of its turf, particularly the greens, and now famous as the venue for some of the best golf tournaments in the British Isles in past years.
18 holes, 6775yds, Par 72, SSS 72, Course record 62. Club membership 700.

Visitors Mon-Fri & Sun. Booking required. Handicap certificate. Dress code. **Societies** Booking required **Green Fees** £65 per day. **Prof** Guy Wills **Course Designer** C. MacKenzie **Facilities** ⑪ 🍴 🍺 ☕ 🏌 🏖 🏡 🐾 ✓ **Conf** Corporate Hospitality Days
Location 2m S of York off A19
Hotel ★★★★ 75% HL York Marriott Hotel, Tadcaster Rd, YORK ☎ 01904 701000 151 en suite
Hotel ★★★ 74% HL Best Western York Pavilion Hotel, 45 Main St, Fulford, YORK ☎ 01904 622099 Fax 01904 626939 57 en suite

Best Western York Pavilion Hotel

YORKSHIRE, SOUTH

SHEFFIELD

Hallamshire Golf Club Ltd
Sandygate S10 4LA
☎ 0114 230 2153
🖷 0114 230 5413
e-mail: secretary@hallamshiregolfclub.co.uk
web: www.hallamshiregolfclub.co.uk
Situated on a shelf of land at a height of 850ft. Magnificent views to the west. Moorland turf, long carries over ravine and small and quick greens.
18 holes, 6346yds, Par 71, SSS 71, Course record 65. Club membership 600.
Visitors Mon-Fri except BHs. Booking required. Handicap certificate. Dress code. **Societies** Booking required. **Green Fees** £45 per day. **Prof** G R Tickell **Course Designer** Various **Facilities** ⑪ 🍴 🍺 ☕ 🏌 🏖 🏡 🐾 ✓ **Conf** Corporate Hospitality Days **Location** Off A57 at Crosspool onto Sandygate Rd, clubhouse 0.75m on right
Hotel ★★★★ 76% HL Sheffield Marriott, Kenwood Rd, SHEFFIELD ☎ 0114 258 3811 114 en suite

YORKSHIRE, WEST

ALWOODLEY

Alwoodley
Wigton Ln LS17 8SA
☎ 0113 268 1680
e-mail: alwoodley@btconnect.com
web: www.alwoodley.co.uk
Natural moorland course with heather, whins and shrubs. Plentifully and cunningly bunkered with undulating and interesting greens.
18 holes, 6666yds, Par 72, SSS 72.
Club membership 460.
Visitors Mon-Sun except BHs. Booking required. Dress code. **Societies** Booking required **Green Fees** £70 per day (£85 Sat & Sun).
£40 after 4pm. **Prof** John R Green **Course Designer** Dr Alistair MacKenzie **Facilities** ⑪ ⦿ ⅙ ☐ ⅎ ⅄ ⛭ ⛶ ⌁ **Conf**
Corporate Hospitality Days **Location** 5m N off A61
Hotel ★★★ 72% HL The Merrion Hotel, Merrion Centre, LEEDS
☎ 0113 243 9191   109 en suite

LEEDS

Moor Allerton
Coal Rd, Wike LS17 9NH
☎ 0113 266 1154
▤ 0113 237 1124
e-mail: info@magc.co.uk
web: www.magc.co.uk
Lakes Course: 18 holes, 6470yds, Par 71, SSS 72.
Blackmoor Course: 18 holes, 6673yds, Par 71, SSS 73.
High Course: 18 holes, 6841yds, Par 72, SSS 74.
Course Designer Robert Trent Jones **Location** 5.5m N of city centre on A61
Telephone for further details
Hotel ★★★ 72% HL The Merrion Hotel, Merrion Centre, LEEDS
☎ 0113 243 9191   109 en suite

Moortown
Harrogate Rd, Alwoodley LS17 7DB
☎ 0113 268 6521
▤ 0113 268 0986
e-mail: secretary@moortown-gc.co.uk
web: www.moortown-gc.co.uk
Championship course, tough but fair. Springy moorland turf, natural hazards of heather, gorse and streams, cunningly placed bunkers and immaculate greens. No winter tees or greens. Original home of Ryder Cup in 1929.
18 holes, 6757yds, Par 72, SSS 73, Course record 64.
Club membership 585.
Visitors Mon-Sun & BHs. Booking required. Dress code.
Societies booking required. **Green Fees** not confirmed.
◉ **Prof** Martin Heggie **Course Designer** Alistair Mackenzie

Facilities ⑪ ⦿ ⅙ ☐ ⅎ ⅄ ⛭ ⛶ ⌁ **Conf** facs
Corporate Hospitality Days **Location** 6m N of city centre on A61
Hotel ★★★ 72% HL The Merrion Hotel, Merrion Centre, LEEDS
☎ 0113 243 9191   109 en suite

Sand Moor
Alwoodley Ln LS17 7DJ
☎ 0113 268 5180
▤ 0113 266 1105
e-mail: ian.kerr@sandmoorgolf.co.uk
web: www.sandmoorgolf.co.uk
A beautiful, inland course situated next to Eccup reservoir on the north side of Leeds. It has been described as the finest example of golfing paradise being created out of a barren moor. With magnificent views of the surrounding countryside, the course has sandy soil and drains exceptionally well.
18 holes, 6446yds, Par 71, SSS 71, Course record 63.
Club membership 600.
Visitors Mon-Fri, Sun & BHs. Booking required. Handicap certificate. Dress code. **Societies** Booking required. **Green Fees** £55 per day, £45 per round (£55 per round Sun). **Prof** Frank Houlgate **Course Designer** Dr A Mackenzie **Facilities** ⑪ ⦿ ⅙ ☐ ⅎ ⅄ ⛭ ⛶ ⌁ ⌁ **Conf** Corporate Hospitality Days **Location** 5m N of city centre off A61
Hotel ★★★★ 71% HL Cedar Court Hotel, Denby Dale Rd, WAKEFIELD ☎ 01924 276310   150 en suite

OTLEY

Otley
Off West Busk Ln LS21 3NG
☎ 01943 465329
▤ 01943 850387
e-mail: office@otley-golfclub.co.uk
web: www.otley-golfclub.co.uk
An expansive course with magnificent views across Wharfedale. It is well wooded with streams crossing the fairway. The 4th is a fine hole which generally needs two woods to reach the plateau green. The 17th is a good short hole. A test of golf as opposed to stamina.
18 holes, 6211yds, Par 70, SSS 70, Course record 62.
Club membership 700.
Visitors Mon, Wed-Fri, Sun & BHs. Booking required. Handicap certificate. Dress code. **Societies** Booking required. **Green Fees** £40 per day, £34 per 18/27 holes (£47/£40 Sun & BHs). **Prof** Steven Tomkinson
Facilities ⑪ ⦿ ⅙ ☐ ⅎ ⅄ ⛭ ⛶ ⌁ ⅊ **Leisure** practice bunker. **Conf** facs Corporate Hospitality Days **Location** 1m W of Otley off A6038
Hotel BUD Premier Travel Inn Leeds/Bradford Airport, Victoria Av, Yeadon, LEEDS ☎ 08701 977153   40 en suite

CHANNEL ISLANDS

GUERNSEY

L'ANCRESSE VALE

Royal Guernsey
GY3 5BY
☎ 01481 246523
🖹 01481 243960
e-mail: bob.rggc@cwgsy.net
web: www.royalguernseygolfclub.com
Not quite as old as its neighbour Royal Jersey, Royal
Guernsey is a sporting course which was redesigned
after World War II by Mackenzie Ross, who has many
fine courses to his credit. It is a pleasant links, well-
maintained, and administered by the States of Guernsey.
The 8th hole, a good Par 4, requires an accurate second
shot to the green set among the gorse and thick rough.
The 18th, with lively views, needs a strong shot to reach
the green well down below. The course is windy, with
hard walking.
18 holes, 6215yds, Par 70, SSS 70, Course record 64.
Club membership 934.
Visitors Mon-Wed, Fri & BHs. Thu & Sat am only. Booking
required. Handicap certificate. Dress code. **Green Fees** £45 per
day. **Prof** Norman Wood **Course Designer** Mackenzie Ross
Facilities ⓑ🍴🍺☕🍸⚒🏖💈✆🏌 **Location** 3m N of St
Peter Port
Hotel ★★★★ 77% HL St Pierre Park Hotel, Rohais, ST PETER
PORT ☎ 01481 728282 131 en suite

CASTEL

La Grande Mare Golf & Country Club
Vazon Bay GY5 7LL
☎ 01481 253544
🖹 01481 255197
e-mail: golf@lagrandemare.com
web: www.lgm.guernsey.net
This hotel and golf complex is set in over 120 acres of
grounds. The Hawtree designed parkland course opened
in 1994 and was originally designed around 14 holes
with four double greens. Water hazards on 15 holes.
18 holes, 4755yards, Par 64, SSS 64,
Course record 65. Club membership 800.
Visitors Mon-Sun & BHs. Dress code. **Societies** Booking
required. **Green Fees** £34 per 18 holes (£38 Sat & Sun). **Prof**
Matt Groves **Course Designer** Hawtree **Facilities** ⓑ🍴🍺☕
🍸⚒🏖💈◇✆🏌 **Leisure** hard tennis courts, outdoor and
indoor heated swimming pools, fishing, sauna, gymnasium,
sports massage. **Conf** facs Corporate Hospitality Days
Hotel ★★★ 72% HL Hotel Hougue du Pommier, Hougue du
Pommier Rd, CATEL ☎ 01481 256531 37 en suite 6 annexe
en suite

JERSEY

GROUVILLE

Royal Jersey
Le Chemin au Greves JE3 9BD
☎ 01534 854416
🖹 01534 854684
e-mail: thesecretary@royaljersey.com
web: www.royaljersey.com
18 holes, 6100yds, Par 70, SSS 70, Course record 63.
Location 4m E of St Helier off coast road
Telephone for further details
Hotel ★★★ 74% HL Old Court House Hotel, GOREY
☎ 01534 854444 58 en suite

LA MOYE

La Moye
La Route Orange JE3 8GQ
☎ 01534 743401
🖹 01534 747289
e-mail: secretary@lamoyegolfclub.co.uk
web: www.lamoyegolfclub.co.uk
Seaside championship links course (venue for the Jersey
Seniors Open) situated in an exposed position on the
south western corner of the island overlooking St Ouen's
Bay. Offers spectacular views, two start points, full
course all year - no temporary greens.
18 holes, 6664yds, Par 72, SSS 73, Course record 65.
Club membership 1300.
Visitors Mon-Sun & BHs. Booking required. Handicap certificate.
Dress code. **Societies** Booking required. **Green Fees** £55
per 18 holes (£60 Sat, Sun & BHs). **Prof** Mike Deeley **Course
Designer** James Braid **Facilities** ⓑ🍺☕🍸⚒🏖💈✆🏌
Location W of village off A13
Hotel ★★★★ HL The Atlantic Hotel, Le Mont de la Pulente, ST
BRELADE ☎ 01534 744101 50 en suite

ABERDEENSHIRE

CRUDEN BAY

Cruden Bay
Aulton Rd AB42 0NN
☎ 01779 812285
📄 01779 812945
e-mail: cbaygc@aol.com
web: www.crudenbaygolfclub.co.uk
A typical links course which epitomises the old fashioned style of rugged links golf. The drives require accuracy with bunkers and protecting greens, blind holes and undulating greens. The 10th provides a panoramic view of half the back nine down at beach level, and to the east can be seen the outline of the spectacular ruin of Slains Castle featured in Bram Stoker's Dracula. The figure eight design of the course is quite unusual.
Main Course: 18 holes, 6395yds, Par 70, SSS 72, Course record 65.
St Olaf Course: 9 holes, 5106yds, Par 64, SSS 65.
Club membership 1100.
Visitors Mon-Sun & BHs. Booking required. Handicap certificate. Dress code. **Societies** Booking required. **Green Fees** £60 per round/£80 per day (£70 per round Sat & Sun). **Prof** Robbie Stewart **Course Designer** Thomas Simpson **Facilities** ⑪ ⽕🍴 ⬟ ⌷🛈⬡ 🏊 🖇🏌⚒⚐ **Conf** Corporate Hospitality Days **Location** SW side of village on A975
Hotel ★★ 69% HL Red House Hotel, Aulton Rd, CRUDEN BAY ☎ 01779 812215 6 rms (5 en suite)

ANGUS

BARRY

Panmure
Burnside Rd DD7 7RT
☎ 01241 855120
📄 01241 859737
e-mail: secretary@panmuregolfclub.co.uk
web: www.panmuregolfclub.co.uk
A nerve-testing, adventurous course which opens quietly and builds its challenge amongst the sandhills further out. The course is used for Open championship final qualifying rounds.
18 holes, 6317yds, Par 70, SSS 71, Course record 62.
Club membership 700.
Visitors Mon, Wed-Fri, Sun & BHs. Dress code. **Societies** Booking required. **Green Fees** £85 per day; £65 per round. **Prof** Neil Mackintosh **Course Designer** James Braid **Facilities** ⑪ ⽕🍴 ⬟ ⌷🛈⬡ 🏊 🖇🏌⚒⚐ **Conf** Corporate Hospitality Days **Location** S side of village off A930
Hotel BUD Premier Travel Inn Dundee East, 115-117 Lawers Dr, Panmurefield Village, BROUGHTY FERRY ☎ 0870 9906324 60 en suite

EDZELL

Edzell
High St DD9 7TF
☎ 01356 647283 (Secretary)
📄 01356 648094
e-mail: secretary@edzellgolfclub.net
web: www.edzellgolfclub.net
This delightful, gentle, flat course is situated in the foothills of the Highlands and provides good golf as well as conveying a feeling of peace and quiet to everyone who plays here. The village of Edzell is one of the most picturesque in Scotland.
18 holes, 6367yds, Par 71, SSS 71, Course record 62.
West Water: 9 holes, 2057yds, Par 32, SSS 31.
Club membership 855.
Visitors Mon-Sun & BHs. Booking required. Handicap certificate. Dress code. **Societies** Booking required. **Green Fees** £45 per day; £33 per round (£56/£40 Sat & Sun). West Water: £15 per 16 holes, £12 per 9 holes. **Prof** A J Webster **Course Designer** Bob Simpson **Facilities** ⑪ ⽕🍴 ⬟ ⌷🛈⬡ 🏊 🖇🏌⚒⚐ **Location** On B966, S end of Edzell
Hotel ★★★ 66% HL Glenesk Hotel, High St, EDZELL ☎ 01356 648319 24 en suite

MONIFIETH

Monifieth
Princes St DD5 4AW
☎ 01382 532767 (Medal) & 532967 (Ashludie)
📄 01382 535816
The chief of the two courses at Monifieth is the Medal Course. It has been one of the qualifying venues for the Open Championship on more than one occasion. A seaside links, but divided from the sand dunes by a railway which provides the principal hazard for the first few holes. The 10th hole is outstanding, the 17th is excellent and there is a delightful finishing hole. The other course here is the Ashludie, and both are played over by a number of clubs who share the links.

Medal Course: 18 holes, 6655yds, Par 71, SSS 72, Course record 63.
Ashludie Course: 18 holes, 5123yds, Par 68, SSS 66.
Club membership 1750.
Visitors Mon-Sun & BHs. Booking required. Handicap certificate. Dress code. **Societies** booking required. **Green Fees** not

continued

CHAMPIONSHIP COURSE
ANGUS — CARNOUSTIE

CARNOUSTIE GOLF LINKS

20 Links Pde DD7 7JE
☎ **01241 853789 bookings**
📠 **01241 852720**
e-mail: **golf@carnoustiegolflinks.co.uk**
web: **www.carnoustiegolflinks.co.uk**
Championship: 18 holes, 6941yds,
Par 72, SSS 75, Course record 64.
Burnside: 18 holes, 6028yds, Par 68, SSS 70.
Buddon Links: 18 holes, 5420yds, Par 66,
SSS 67. **Visitors** Mon-Sun & BHs. Booking
required. Dress code. **Societies** Booking
required. **Green Fees** Championship course
£115, Burnside £33, Buddon £28. Play all 3
courses £135. **Prof** Colin Sinclair **Course
Designer** James Braid **Facilities** ⑨ 🍴 🛍 🛒 🎣
🏌 📠 ⛳ ◇ ✎ 🏐 **Leisure** heated indoor pool,
sauna, solarium, gym. **Location** SW of town
centre off A930

This Championship Course has been voted
the top course in Britain by many golfing
greats and described as Scotland's ultimate
golfing challenge. The course developed
from origins in the 1560s; James Braid
added new bunkers, greens and tees in
the 1920s. The Open Championship first
came to the course in 1931 and Carnoustie
hosted the Scottish Open in 1995
and 1996, and was the venue for the 1999
Open Championship and will stage the
Championship in 2007. The Burnside
Course is enclosed on three sides by the
Championship Course and has been used
for Open Championship qualifying rounds.
The Buddon Course has been extensively
remodelled, making it ideal for mid to
high handicappers.

SCOTLAND

confirmed. **Prof** Ian McLeod **Facilities** ⓣ ⓘ◎ ⓛ ☑ ⓕⓛ ⚐ 🖨 🏌 ✐
Location NE side of town on A930
Hotel BUD Premier Travel Inn Dundee East, 115-117 Lawers Dr, Panmurefield Village, BROUGHTY FERRY ☎ 0870 9906324 60 en suite

MONTROSE

Montrose Golf Links
Traill Dr DD10 8SW
☎ 01674 672932
🖹 01674 671800
e-mail: secretary@montroselinks.co.uk
web: www.montroselinks.co.uk
The links at Montrose like many others in Scotland are on commonland and are shared by three clubs. The Medal Course at Montrose - the fifth oldest in the world - is typical of Scottish links, with narrow, undulating fairways and problems from the first hole to the last. The Broomfield course is flatter and easier.

Medal Course: 18 holes, 6544yds, Par 71, SSS 72, Course record 63.
Broomfield Course: 18 holes, 4830yds, Par 66, SSS 63.
Club membership 1300.
Visitors Mon-Sun & BHs. Booking required Sat & Sun. Handicap certificate. Dress code. Must contact in advance. **Societies** Booking required. **Green Fees** Medal: £57 per day; £45 per round (£65/£50 Sat & Sun). Broomfield: £18 per round (£20 weekends). **Prof** Jason J Boyd **Course Designer** W Park/Tom Morris **Facilities** ⓣ ⓘ◎ ⓛ ☑ ⓕ ⚐ 🖨 🏌 ✐ **Location** NE side of town off A92

ARGYLL & BUTE

MACHRIHANISH

Machrihanish
PA28 6PT
☎ 01586 810213
🖹 01586 810221
e-mail: secretary@machgolf.com
web: www.machgolf.com
Magnificent natural links of championship status. The 1st hole is the famous drive across the Atlantic. Sandy soil allows for play all year round. Large greens, easy walking, windy. Fishing.
18 holes, 6225yds, Par 70, SSS 71, Course record 63.
The Pans Course: 9 holes, 2376yds, Par 34, SSS 69.
Club membership 1400.
Visitors Mon-Sun & BHs. Booking Required Sat & Sun **Societies** Booking required. **Green Fees** Mon-Fri & Sun £60 per day, £40 per round. (Sat £75£50). The Pans course £12 per day. **Prof** Ken Campbell **Course Designer** Tom Morris **Facilities** ⓣ ⓘ◎ ⓛ ☑ ⓕⓛ ⚐ 🖨 🏌 🛒 ✐ **Location** 5m W of Campbeltown on B843

OBAN

Glencruitten
Glencruitten Rd PA34 4PU
☎ 01631 564604
e-mail: obangolf@btinternet.com
web: www.obangolf.com
There is plenty of space and considerable variety of hole on this downland course - popular with holidaymakers. In a beautiful, isolated situation, the course is hilly and testing, particularly the 1st and 12th (Par 4s) and 10th and 17th (Par 3s).
18 holes, 4452yds, Par 61, SSS 63, Course record 55.
Club membership 500.
Visitors Mon-Sun & BHs. Booking required Sat. Dress code. **Societies** Welcome. **Green Fees** Mon-Fri £25 per day. (£30 Sat & Sun). **Course Designer** James Braid **Facilities** ⓣ ⓘ◎ ⓛ ☑ ⓕⓛ 🏌 🖨 🛒 ✐ **Location** NE side of town centre off A816
Hotel ★★★ 80% HL Manor House Hotel, Gallanach Rd, OBAN ☎ 01631 562087 11 en suite

CITY OF EDINBURGH

EDINBURGH

Royal Burgess
181 Whitehouse Rd, Barnton EH4 6BU
☎ 0131 339 2075
🖹 0131 339 3712
e-mail: secretary@royalburgess.co.uk
web: www.royalburgess.co.uk
No mention of golf clubs would be complete without the Royal Burgess, which was instituted in 1735 and is the oldest golfing society in Scotland. Its course is a pleasant parkland, and one with a great deal of variety. A club which anyone interested in the history of the game should visit.
18 holes, 6111yds, Par 68, SSS 69.
Club membership 635.
Visitors Mon-Sun & BHs. Booking required. Handicap certificate. Dress code. **Societies** Booking requried. **Green Fees** £55 per day (£75 Sat & Sun). **Prof** Steven Brian **Course Designer** Tom Morris **Facilities** ⓣ ⓘ◎ ⓛ ☑ ⓕⓛ ⚐ 🖨 🏌 ✐ **Conf** Corporate Hospitality Days **Location** 5m W of city centre off A90

CHAMPIONSHIP COURSE

CITY OF EDINBURGH — EDINBURGH

MARRIOTT DALMAHOY HOTEL

Kirknewton EH27 8EB
☎ 0131 335 1845 📠 0131 335 1433
e-mail: mhrs.golf@marriotthotels.com
web: www.marriott.com/edigs
East Course: 18 holes, 7055yds, Par 73,
SSS 74, Course record 70.
West Course: 18 holes, 5168yds, Par 68,
SSS 66, Course record 60.
Club membership 822.
Visitors Mon-Sun & BHs. Booking required.
Handicap certificate. Dress code. **Societies**
Booking required. **Green Fees** East Course:
£65 per 18 holes (£80 Sat, Sun & BHs). West:
£40 (£45 Sat, Sun & BHs). Reduced winter
rates. **Prof** Scott Dixon **Course Designer**
James Braid **Facilities** ⊕ ⦿ ⛴ ☺ ⚑ 🗖 ⚲
🏠 ⛳ ◇ ⛾ ✦ 🏹 **Leisure** hard tennis courts,
heated indoor swimming pool, sauna,
solarium, gymnasium, fitness studio, golf
academy, health salon. **Location** 7m W of city
on A71

The Championship East Course has
hosted many major events including the
Solheim Cup and the Charles Church
Seniors PGA Championship of Scotland.
The course has long sweeping fairways
and generous greens protected by strategic
bunkers. Many of the long Par 4 holes
offer a serious challenge to any golfer.
The signature 18th hole has the green set
in front of Dalmahoy's historic hotel with
a testing approach over a wide ravine.
The shorter West Course offers a different
test with tighter fairways requiring more
accuracy from the tee. The finishing holes
incorporate the Golgar burn meandering
through the fairway to create a tough finish
to the course.

CHAMPIONSHIP COURSE

EAST LOTHIAN — GULLANE

MUIRFIELD

(HONOURABLE COMPANY OF EDINBURGH GOLFERS)

Muirfield EH31 2EG
☎ 01620 842123 📄 01620 842977
e-mail: hceg@muirfield.org.uk
web: www.muirfield.org.uk
Muirfield Course: 18 holes, 6673yds,
Par 70, SSS 73, Course record 63.
Club membership 700.
Visitors Tue & Thu. Booking required.
Handicap certificate. Dress code. **Societies**
Booking required. **Green Fees** £180
per 36 holes, £145 per 18 holes. **Course
Designer** Harry Colt **Facilities** ⑨ by prior
arrangement 🖥🖊🍴 ⚑ ✦ **Location** NE
of village, off A198 next to Greywalls Hotel

The course at Muirfield was designed by Old Tom Morris in 1891 and is generally considered to be one of the top ten courses in the world. The club itself has an excellent pedigree: it was founded in 1744, making it just 10 years older than the Royal and Ancient but not as old as Royal Blackheath. Muirfield is the only course to have hosted the Open (15 times, the most recent in 2002), the Amateur, the Mid Amateur, the Ryder Cup, the Walker Cup and the Curtis Cup. It is consistently ranked as one of the world's best golf courses.

CITY OF GLASGOW

GLASGOW

Haggs Castle
70 Dumbreck Rd, Dumbreck G41 4SN
☎ 0141 427 1157
🖷 0141 427 1157
e-mail: secretary@haggscastlegolfclub.com
web: www.haggscastlegolfclub.com
Wooded, parkland course where Scottish National Championships and the Glasgow and Scottish Open have been held.
18 holes, 6426yds, Par 72, SSS 71, Course record 63. Club membership 900.
Visitors Mon-Fri. Booking required. Handicap certificate. Dress code. **Societies** Booking required. **Green Fees** £40 per round; £50 per day. **Prof** Campbell Elliott **Course Designer** Dave Thomas (1998) **Facilities** ⑪ ⑩ ⑥ ⌑ ⅋ ⍨ ⚷ ⍩ ⚭ ⚷ **Conf** Corporate Hospitality Days **Location** M77 junct 1, 2.5m SW of city centre

DUMFRIES & GALLOWAY

CUMMERTREES

Powfoot
DG12 5QE
☎ 01461 204100
🖷 01461204111
e-mail: info@powfootgolfclub.com
web: www.powfootgolfclub.com
This British Championship course is on the Solway Firth, playing at this delightfully compact semi-links seaside course is a scenic treat. Lovely holes include the 2nd, the 8th and the 11th. The 9th includes a Second World War bomb crater.
18 holes, 6255yds, Par 69, SSS 69, Course record 63. Club membership 660.
Visitors Mon-Fri, Sun & BHs. Booking required. Handicap certificate.
Dress code. **Societies** Booking required. **Green Fees** £46 per day, £35 per round (£57/£41 Sat & Sun). **Course Designer** J Braid **Facilities** ⑪ ⑩ ⑥ ⌑ ⅋ ⍨ ⚭ ⚷ **Location** 0.5m off B724
Hotel ★★★ 73% HL Best Western Hetland Hall Hotel, CARRUTHERSTOWN ☎ 01387 840201   14 en suite 15 annexe en suite

CITY OF DUNDEE

DUNDEE3

Downfield
Turnberry Av DD2 3QP
☎ 01382 825595
🖷 01382 813111
e-mail: downfieldgc@aol.com
web: www.downfieldgolf.co.uk
A 2007 Open Qualifying venue. A course with championship credentials providing an enjoyable test for all golfers.
18 holes, 6803yds, Par 73, SSS 73, Course record 65. Club membership 750.
Visitors Mon-Fri, Sun & BHs. Booking required. Dress code. **Societies** Booking required. **Green Fees** £59 per day, £49 per round. **Prof** Kenny Hutton **Course Designer** James Braid **Facilities** ⑪ ⑩ ⑥ ⌑ ⅋ ⍨ ⚭ ⚷ ⚭ ⚷ **Leisure** snooker room. **Conf** Corporate Hospitality Days **Location** N of city centre, signed at junct A90

EAST LOTHIAN

DUNBAR

Dunbar
East Links EH42 1LL
☎ 01368 862317
🖷 01368 865202
e-mail: secretary@dunbargolfclub.sol.co.uk
web: www.dunbar-golfclub.co.uk
Another of Scotland's old links. It is said that it was some Dunbar members who first took the game of golf to the north of England. A natural links course on a narrow strip of land, following the contours of the sea shore. There is a wall bordering one side and the shore on the other side making this quite a challenging course for all levels of player. The wind, if blowing from the sea, is a problem. Qualifying course for the Open Championship.
18 holes, 6406yds, Par 71, SSS 71, Course record 62. Club membership 1000.
Visitors Mon-Wed, Fri-Sun & BHs. Booking required. Dress code. **Societies** Booking required. **Green Fees** £65 per day, £50 per round (£85/£60 Sat & Sun). Discounts after 3pm. **Prof** Jacky Montgomery **Course Designer** Tom Morris **Facilities** ⑪ ⑩ ⑥ ⌑ ⅋ ⍨ ⚭ ⚷ ⚭ ⚷ **Conf** Corporate Hospitality Days **Location** 0.5m E off A1087
Hotel ★★★★ 80% HL Macdonald Marine Hotel, Cromwell Rd, NORTH BERWICK ☎ 0870 400 8129   83 en suite

GULLANE

Gullane
West Links Rd EH31 2BB
☎ 01620 842255
🖹 01620 842327
e-mail: bookings@gullanegolfclub.com
web: www.gullanegolfclub.com
Gullane is a delightful village and one of Scotland's great golf centres. The game has been played on the 3 links courses for over 300 years and was formed in 1882. The first tee of the Championship No. 1 course (a Final Qualifier when The Open is played at Muirfield) is literally in the village and the three courses stretch out along the coast line. All have magnificent views over the Firth of the Fourth, standing on the highest point at the 7th Tee is reported as one of the "finest views in golf".
Course No 1: 18 holes, 6466yds, Par 71, SSS 72, Course record 65.
Course No 2: 18 holes, 6244yds, Par 71, SSS 71, Course record 64.
Course No 3: 18 holes, 5252yds, Par 68, SSS 66. Club membership 1200.
Visitors Mon-Sun & BHs. Booking required. Dress code. Handicap certificate required for Course 1 **Societies** Welcome. **Green Fees** Course 1: £85 per round (£100 Sat & Sun). Course 2: £40 per round (£45 Sat & Sun). Course 3: £25 per round (£30 Sat & Sun). **Prof** Alasdair Good **Course Designer** Various **Facilities** ⊕ ⁑◎ ⍒ ☑ ⛳ ⚑ ⚒ ☺ ⌖ ⚘ ✈ 🏌 ⚑ **Leisure** golf museum. **Conf** facs Corporate Hospitality Days
Location W end of village on A198
Hotel ★★★ HL Greywalls Hotel, Muirfield, GULLANE
☎ 01620 842144 17 en suite 6 annexe en suite

LONGNIDDRY

Longniddry
Links Rd EH32 0NL
☎ 01875 852141
🖹 01875 853371
e-mail: secretary@longniddrygolfclub.co.uk
web: www.longniddrygolfclub.co.uk
Undulating seaside links and partial woodland course with no Par 5s. One of the numerous courses which stretch east from Edinburgh to Dunbar. The inward half is more open than the wooded outward half, but can be difficult in prevailing west wind.
18 holes, 6260yds, Par 68, SSS 70, Course record 62. Club membership 1100.
Visitors Mon-Sun & BHs. Booking required. Handicap certificate. Dress code. **Societies** Booking required. **Green Fees** £65 per day, £42 per round (£60 Sat & Sun). **Prof** John Gray **Course Designer** H S Colt **Facilities** ⊕ ⁑◎ ⍒ ☑ ⛳ ⚒ ☺ ⌖ ✈ 🏌 ⚑
Conf Corporate Hospitality Days **Location** N side of village off A198
Hotel ★★★ HL Greywalls Hotel, Muirfield, GULLANE
☎ 01620 842144 17 en suite 6 annexe en suite

NORTH BERWICK

North Berwick
Beach Rd EH39 4BB
☎ 01620 892135
🖹 01620 893274
e-mail: secretary@northberwickgolfclub.com
web: www.northberwickgolfclub.com
Another of East Lothian's famous courses, the links at North Berwick is still popular. A classic championship links, it has many hazards including the beach, streams, bunkers, light rough and low walls. The great hole on the course is the 15th, the famous Redan.
West Links: 18 holes, 6420yds, Par 71, SSS 72, Course record 63. Club membership 730.
Visitors Mon-Sun & BHs. Booking required. Handicap certificate. Dress code. **Societies** booking required. **Green Fees** not confirmed. **Prof** D Huish **Facilities** ⊕ ⁑◎ ⍒ ☑ ⛳ ⚒ ☺ ⌖ ✈ 🏌 ⚘
Conf Corporate Hospitality Days **Location** W side of town on A198
Hotel ★★★★ 80% HL Macdonald Marine Hotel, Cromwell Rd, NORTH BERWICK ☎ 0870 400 8129 83 en suite

FIFE

CRAIL

Crail Golfing Society
Balcomie Clubhouse, Fifeness KY10 3XN
☎ 01333 450686 & 450960
🖹 01333 450416
e-mail: info@crailgolfingsociety.co.uk
web: www.crailgolfingsociety.co.uk
Perched on the edge of the North Sea, the Crail Golfing Society's courses at Balcomie are picturesque and sporting. Crail Golfing Society began its life in 1786 and the course is highly thought of by students of the game both for its testing holes and the standard of its greens. Craighead Links has panoramic seascape and country views. With wide sweeping fairways and USGA specification greens it is a testing but fair challenge.
Balcomie Links: 18 holes, 5922yds, Par 69, SSS 70, Course record 62.
Craighead Links: 18 holes, 6700yds, Par 72, SSS 74, Course record 69. Club membership 1600.
Visitors Mon-Sun & BHs. Booking required. Dress code **Societies** Booking required. **Green Fees** Balcomie £65 per day, (£78 Sat & Sun). Craighead Balcomie £55 per day, £40 per round (£68/£50 Sat & Sun). **Prof** Graeme Lennie **Course Designer** Tom Morris **Facilities** ⊕ ⁑◎ ⍒ ☑ ⛳ ⚒ ☺ ⌖ ⚘ ✈ 🏌 **Location** 2m NE off A917
Hotel ★★ 68% SHL Balcomie Links Hotel, Balcomie Rd, CRAIL ☎ 01333 450237 15 rms (13 en suite)
Hotel ★★★★ 81% GA The Spindrift, Pittenweem Rd, ANSTRUTHER ☎ 01333 310573 Fax 01333 310573 8 rms (7 en suite)

ELIE

Golf House Club
KY9 1AS
☎ 01333 330301
🖷 01333 330895
e-mail: secretary@golfhouseclub.org
web: www.golfhouseclub.org
One of Scotland's most delightful holiday courses
with panoramic views over the Firth of Forth. Some of
the holes out towards the rocky coastline are splendid.
This is the course which has produced many good
professionals, including James Braid.
18 holes, 6273yds, Par 70, SSS 70, Course record 62.
Club membership 600.
Visitors Mon-Sun & BHs. Booking required. Handicap certificate.
Dress code. **Societies** Booking required. **Green Fees** £80
per day, £60 per round (£90/£70 Sat & Sun). **Prof** Ian Muir
Facilities ⑪ ⑩ ⓛ ⬜ ⬛ ⚲ 🏌 **Leisure** hard tennis
courts. **Location** W side of village off A917

LEVEN

Leven Links
The Promenade KY8 4HS
☎ 01333 428859 & 421390
🖷 01333 428859
e-mail: secretary@leven-links.com
web: www.leven-links.com
Leven has the classic ingredients which make up a golf
links in Scotland; undulating fairways with hills and
hollows, out of bounds and a burn or stream. Turning
into the prevailing west wind at the 13th leaves the
golfer with a lot of work to do before one of the finest
finishing holes in golf. A top class championship links
course used for Open final qualifying stages, it has fine
views over Largo Bay.

18 holes, 6506yds, Par 71, SSS 72, Course record 63.
Club membership 1000.
Visitors Mon-Fri, Sun & BHs. Booking required Fri & Sun. Dress
code. **Societies** Welcome. **Green Fees** £60 per day, £45 per
round (weekends £70/£55). **Course Designer** Tom Morris
Facilities ⑪ ⑩ ⓛ ⬜ ⬛ ⚲ 🏌

LUNDIN LINKS

Lundin
Golf Rd KY8 6BA
☎ 01333 320202
🖷 01333 329743
e-mail: secretary@lundingolfclub.co.uk
web: www.lundingolfclub.co.uk
A complex links course with open burns, an internal out
of bounds(the old railway line), and strategic bunkering.
Lundin presents a challenge for the thinking golfer
where position from the tee rather than distance will
yield just rewards on the scorecard. Renowned for its
beautiful greens and some of the most demanding short
Par 4's in the game of golf.

18 holes, 6371yds, Par 71, SSS 71, Course record 63.
Club membership 895.
Visitors Mon-Sun & BHs. Booking required. Dress code.
Societies Booking required. **Green Fees** £65 per day, £47 per
round (£50 Sat & Sun). **Prof** David Webster **Course Designer**
James Braid **Facilities** ⑪ ⑩ ⓛ ⬜ ⬛ ⚲ 🏌 **Location** W side
of village off A915

ST ANDREWS

The Duke's Course
Craigtoun KY16 8NS
☎ 01334 474371
🖷 01334 479456
e-mail: reservations@oldcoursehotel.co.uk
web: www.oldcoursehotel.co.uk
Now owned and managed by the Old Course Hotel, with
a spectacular setting above St Andrews. Blending the
characteristics of a links course with an inland course,
Duke's offers rolling fairways, undulating greens and a
testing woodland section. Five separate tees at every hole
and buggy paths running throughout the course.
18 holes, 6749yds, Par 71, SSS 73, Course record 67.
Club membership 500.
Visitors Mon-Sun & BHs. Booking required. Dress code **Societies**
booking required. **Green Fees** not confirmed. **Prof** Ron Walker
Course Designer Tim Liddy **Facilities** ⑪ ⑩ ⓛ ⬜ ⬛ ⚲ ◇
🏌 🏌 **Leisure** heated indoor swimming pool, sauna, solarium,
gymnasium, computer swing analyses. **Conf** facs Corporate
Hospitality Days

continued

Location A91 to St Andrews, turn off for Strathkinness
Hotel ★★★★★ HL The Old Course Hotel, Golf Resort & Spa, ST ANDREWS ☎ 01334 474371 144 en suite

TAYPORT

Scotscraig
Golf Rd DD6 9DZ
☎ 01382 552515
🖨 01382 553130
e-mail: scotscraig@scotscraiggolfclub.com
web: www.scotscraiggolfclub.com
Combined with heather and rolling fairways, the course is part heathland, part links, with the greens being renowned for being fast and true.
18 holes, 6550yds, Par 71, SSS 72, Course record 62. Club membership 835.
Visitors Mon-Sun & BHs. Booking required. Dress code.
Societies Booking required. **Green Fees** £65 per day, £47 per round (£80/£60am/£52pm Sat & Sun). **Prof** Craig Mackie
Course Designer James Braid **Facilities** ⊕ ⑩ ⚑ ➘ ⛳ ⚚ ⚑ ⚑ 𝄄 ⚑ **Conf** Corporate Hospitality Days **Location** S side of village off B945
Hotel ★★ 68% HL Sandford Country House Hotel, Newton Hill, Wormit, DUNDEE ☎ 01382 541802 16 en suite

HIGHLAND

BOAT OF GARTEN

Boat of Garten
PH24 3BQ
☎ 01479 831282
🖨 01479 831523
e-mail: office@boatgolf.com
web: www.boatgolf.com
In the heart of the Cairngorm National Park, this prime example of James Braid's design genius is cut through moorland and birch forest, maximising the natural landscape. A beautiful and challenging course set amid stunning scenery.

DORNOCH

Royal Dornoch
Golf Rd IV25 3LW
☎ 01862 810219 ext.185
🖨 01862 810792
e-mail: bookings@royaldornoch.com
web: www.royaldornoch.com
The championship course was recently rated among the world's top courses and is a links of rare subtlety. It appears amicable but proves very challenging in play with stiff breezes and tight lies. The 18-hole Struie links course provides, in a gentler style, an enjoyable test of a golfer's accuracy for players of all abilities.

Championship: 18 holes, 6514yds, Par 70, SSS 73.
Struie Course: 18 holes, 6276yds, Par 72, SSS 70.
Club membership 1700.
Visitors Mon-Sun & BHs. Booking required for Championship Course. Handicap certificate. **Societies** Booking required.
Green Fees Championship course: £78 per round (£88 Sat & Sun).
Struie course: £45 per day, £35 per round. **Prof** A Skinner
Course Designer Tom Morris **Facilities** ⊕ ⑩ ⚑ ➘ ⛳ ⚚ ⚑ ⚑ ⚑ **Leisure** hard tennis courts. **Conf** facs Corporate Hospitality Days **Location** E side of town

NAIRN

Nairn
Seabank Rd IV12 4HB
☎ 01667 453208
🖨 01667 456328
e-mail: secretary@nairngolfclub.co.uk
web: www.nairngolfclub.co.uk
18 holes, 6430yds, Par 71, SSS 73, Course record 64.
Newton: 9 holes, 3542yds, Par 58, SSS 57.
Course Designer A Simpson/Old Tom Morris/James Braid
Location 16m E of Inverness on A96
Telephone for further details

MORAY

ELGIN

Elgin
Hardhillock, Birnie Rd, New Elgin IV30 8SX
☎ 01343 542338
🖨 01343 542341
e-mail: secretary@elgingolfclub.com
web: www.elgingolfclub.com
Possibly the finest inland course in the north of Scotland, with undulating greens and compact holes that demand the highest accuracy. There are 13 Par 4s and one Par 5 hole on its parkland layout, eight of the Par 4s being over 400yds long.

SCOTLAND

ST ANDREWS LINKS

Pilmour House KY16 9SF
☎ **01334 466666** 📠 **01334 479555**
e-mail: linkstrust@standrews.org.uk
web: www.standrews.org.uk
Old Course: 18 holes, 6609yds, Par 72, SSS 72, Course record 62.
New Course: 18 holes, 6604yds, Par 71, SSS 73. **Jubilee Course:** 18 holes, 6742yds, Par 72, SSS 73, Course record 63.
Eden Course: 18 holes, 6112yds, Par 70, SSS 70. **Strathtyrum Course:** 18 holes, 5094yds, Par 69, SSS 69.
Balgove Course: 9 holes, 1530yds, Par 30, SSS 30. **Visitors** Old Course: contact course for booking details. Handicap certificate required. Other courses: 1 month advance booking required New/Jubilee/Eden/Strath. **Societies** booking required. **Green Fees** Old £59-£120 according to season. New £28-£57. Jubilee £28-£57. Eden £17-£34. Strathtyrum £11-£23. Balgrove £7-£10. **Prof** Steve North
Facilities ⊕ 🍴 🛒 🖥 🍽 ⚐ ⛳ 🏌 🚌 ✂ 🏌
Location Off A91

Golf was first played here around 1400 and the Old Course is acknowledged worldwide as the home of golf. The Old Course has played host to the greatest golfers in the world and many of golf's most dramatic moments. The New Course (6604yds) was opened in 1895, having been laid out by Old Tom Morris. The Jubilee was opened in 1897 and is 6805yds long from the medal tees. A shorter version of the Jubilee Course is also available, known as the Bronze Course, measuring 5674yds. There is no handicap limit for the shorter course and it is best for lower and middle handicap golfers. The Starthtyrum has a shorter, less testing layout, best for high handicap golfers. The nine-hole Balgrove Course, upgraded and re-opened in 1993, is best for beginners and children. The facilities and courses at St Andrews make this the largest golf complex in Europe.

ELGIN GOLF CLUB

Hardhillock: 18 holes, 6416yds, Par 68, SSS 69, Course record 63. Club membership 1000.
Visitors Mon-Sun & BHs. Booking required. Handicap certificate. Dress code. **Societies** booking required. **Green Fees** not confirmed. **Prof** Kevin Stables **Course Designer** John Macpherson **Facilities** ⊕ 🍴 🛉 ⚑ 🖫 🏋 ☂ ✆ 🛒 ⚑ 🏌 **Conf** facs **Location** 1m S on A941
Hotel ★★★ 79% HL Mansion House Hotel, The Haugh, ELGIN ☎ 01343 548811 23 en suite

FORRES

Forres
Muiryshade IV36 2RD
☎ 01309 672250
📄 01309 672250
e-mail: sandy@forresgolf.demon.co.uk
web: www.forresgolf.demon.co.uk
An all-year parkland course laid on light, well-drained soil in wooded countryside. Walking is easy despite some hilly holes. A test for the best golfers.
18 holes, 6240yds, Par 70, SSS 70, Course record 60. Club membership 1000.
Visitors Mon-Sun & BHs. Dress code. **Societies** Booking required. **Green Fees** £30 per round/£40 per day. **Prof** Sandy Aird
Course Designer James Braid/Willie Park **Facilities** ⊕ 🍴 🛉 🖫 🏋 🏋 ☂ 🛒 🏌 **Conf** Corporate Hospitality Days **Location** SE side of town centre off B9010
Hotel ★★★ 73% HL Ramnee Hotel, Victoria Rd, FORRES ☎ 01309 672410 20 en suite

LOSSIEMOUTH

Moray
Stotfield Rd IV31 6QS
☎ 01343 812018
📄 01343 815102
e-mail: secretary@moraygolf.co.uk
web: www.moraygolf.co.uk
Two fine Scottish Championship links courses, known as Old and New (Moray), and situated on the Moray Firth where the weather is unusually mild.
Old Course: 18 holes, 6643yds, Par 71, SSS 73, Course record 65. New Course: 18 holes,

6004yds, Par 69, SSS 69, Course record 62. Club membership 1550.
Visitors Mon-Sun & BHs. Booking required. Dress code. **Societies** Booking required. **Green Fees** Phone. **Prof** Alistair Thomson **Course Designer** Tom Morris & Henry Cotton **Facilities** ⊕ 🍴 🛉 🖫 🏋 ☂ 🛒 ✆ ✆ **Conf** Corporate Hospitality Days **Location** N side of town
Hotel ★★★ 79% HL Mansion House Hotel, The Haugh, ELGIN ☎ 01343 548811 23 en suite

NORTH AYRSHIRE

IRVINE

Glasgow
Gailes KA11 5AE
☎ 0141 942 2011
📄 0141 942 0770
e-mail: secretary@glasgow-golf.com
web: www.glasgowgailes-golf.com
A lovely seaside links. The turf of the fairways and all the greens is truly glorious and provides tireless play. Established in 1882, this is a qualifying course for the Open Championship.
Glasgow Gailes: 18 holes, 6535yds, Par 71, SSS 72, Course record 63. Club membership 1200.
Visitors Mon-Sun & BHs. Booking required. Contact club for details. **Societies** booking required. **Green Fees** not confirmed. **Prof** J Steven **Course Designer** W Park Jnr **Facilities** ⊕ 🍴 by prior arrangement 🛉 🖫 🏋 🏋 ☂ 🛒 ✆ **Conf** Corporate Hospitality Days **Location** Off A78 at Newhouse junct, S of Irvine
Hotel ★★★ 75% HL Montgreenan Mansion House Hotel, Montgreenan Estate, KILWINNING ☎ 01294 850005 21 en suite

Western Gailes
Gailes by Irvine KA11 5AE
☎ 01294 311649
📄 01294 312312
e-mail: enquiries@westerngailes.com
web: www.westerngailes.com
A magnificent seaside links with glorious turf and wonderful greens. The view is open across the Firth of Clyde to the neighbouring islands. It is a well-balanced course crossed by three burns. There are two Par 5s, the 6th and 14th, and the 11th is a testing 445yd Par 4 dog-leg.
18 holes, 6639yds, Par 71, SSS 74, Course record 65.
Visitors Mon, Wed, Fri & BHs. Sun pm. Booking required. Dress code. **Societies** Booking required. **Green Fees** £110 per 18 holes, £160 per 36 holes (both including lunch). £120 Sun (no lunch). **Facilities** ⊕ 🍴 by prior arrangement 🛉 🖫 🏋 🏋 ☂ ✆ **Conf** Corporate Hospitality Days **Location** 2m S off A737
Hotel ★★★ 75% HL Montgreenan Mansion House Hotel, Montgreenan Estate, KILWINNING ☎ 01294 850005 21 en suite

PERTH & KINROSS

BLAIRGOWRIE

Blairgowrie
Golf Course Rd, Rosemount PH10 6LG
☎ 01250 872622
🖷 01250 875451
e-mail: office@theblairgowriegolfclub.co.uk
web: www.theblairgowriegolfclub.co.uk
Two 18-hole championship heathland/woodland
courses, also a nine-hole course.

Rosemount Course: 18 holes, 6590yds, Par 72,
SSS 72, Course record 64.
Lansdowne Course: 18 holes, 6834yds, Par 72,
SSS 73, Course record 66.
Wee Course: 9 holes, 2352yds, Par 32.
Club membership 1724.
Visitors Mon-Sun & BHs. Booking required. Handicap certificate.
Dress
code. **Societies** Booking required. **Green Fees** Phone. **Prof**
Charles Dernie **Course Designer** J Braid/P Allis/D Thomas/
Old Tom Morris **Facilities** ⓘ ⓘ ⓛ ☐ ⓗ ⤓ ☕ ☂ ☃ ☄ **Conf**
Corporate Hospitality Days **Location** Off A93 Rosemount
Hotel ★★★ 67% HL Angus Hotel, Wellmeadow, BLAIRGOWRIE
☎ 01250 872455 81 en suite

CRIEFF

Crieff
Ferntower, Perth Rd PH7 3LR
☎ 01764 652909
🖷 01764 655096
e-mail: bookings@crieffgolf.co.uk
web: www.crieffgolf.co.uk
Set in dramatic countryside, Crieff Golf Club was
established in 1891. The Ferntower championship course
has magnificent views over the Strathearn valley and
offers all golfers an enjoyable round. The short nine-hole
Dornoch course, which incorporates some of the James
Braid designed holes from the original 18 holes, provides
an interesting challenge for juniors, beginners and
others short of time.

Ferntower Course: 18 holes, 6502yds, Par 71, SSS 72,
Course record 63.
Dornock Course: 9 holes, 2372yds, Par 32, SSS 63.
Club membership 720.
Visitors Mon-Sun & BHs. Booking required. Handicap certificate.
Societies Booking required. **Green Fees** Ferntower: May &
Oct £30, Jun-Sep £33 per round (£36/£40 Sat & Sun). Dornock
£12 for 9 holes, £16 for 18 holes. **Prof** David Murchie **Course
Designer** James Braid **Facilities** ☐ ⓗ ☐ ☕ ⤓ ☃ ☄ ☂ **Conf**
Corporate Hospitality Days **Location** 0.5m NE on A85
Hotel ★★★ 80% HL Royal Hotel, Melville Square, COMRIE
☎ 01764 679200 11 en suite

PITLOCHRY

Pitlochry
Golf Course Rd PH16 5QY
☎ 01796 472792
🖷 01796 473947
e-mail: pro@pitlochrygolf.co.uk
web: www.pitlochrygolf.co.uk
A varied and interesting heathland course with fine
views and posing many problems. Its SSS permits few
errors in its achievement.
18 holes, 5670yds, Par 69, SSS 69, Course record 60.
Club membership 400.
Societies Booking required. **Green Fees** £37 per day, £27 per
round (£45/£35 weekends). **Prof** Mark Pirie **Course Designer**
Willy Fernie **Facilities** ⓘ ⓘ ⓛ ☐ ⓗ ⤓ ☕ ☃ ☄ **Location**
Off A924 onto Larchwood Rd
Hotel ★★ 76% HL Moulin Hotel, 11-13 Kirkmichael Rd, Moulin,
PITLOCHRY ☎ 01796 472196 15 en suite

GLENEAGLES HOTEL

PH3 1NF
☎ 01764 662231 📠 01764 662134
e-mail: resort.sales@gleneagles.com
web: www.gleneagles.com
King's Course: 18 holes, 6471yds, Par 70,
SSS 73, Course record 60.
Queen's Course: 18 holes, 5965yds, Par 68,
SSS 70, Course record 62.
PGA Centenary Course: 18 holes, 6787yds,
Par 73, SSS 74, Course record 63.
Visitors Booking required. **Societies** Booking
required. **Green Fees** May-Sept £115 up
to 3pm, £75 after 3pm, £40 after 5pm.
Reduced rates rest of the year. **Prof** Russell
Smith **Course Designer** James Braid/Jack
Nicklaus **Facilities** ⑪ 🍴 🛏 🖥 🍷🍴 🏌 📷 ⛳
◇ 🏌 🛺 🏌 🎣 **Leisure** hard and grass tennis
courts, outdoor and indoor heated pools,
fishing, sauna, gym, golf academy, horse
riding, shooting, falconry, off road driving.
Location 2m SW of A823

The PGA Centenary Course, created by
Jack Nicklaus, and launched in May 1993,
has an American-Scottish layout with many
water hazards, elevated tees and raised
contoured greens. It is the selected venue
for the Ryder Cup 2014. It has a five-tier
tee structure making it both the longest
and shortest playable course, as well as
the most accommodating to all standards
of golfer. The King's Course, with its
abundance of heather, gorse, raised greens
and plateau tees, is set within the valley of
Strathearn with the Grampian mountains
spectacularly in view to the north. The
shorter Queen's Course, with fairways lined
with Scots pines and water hazards, is set
in a softer landscape and is considered
an easier test of golf. You can improve
your game at the golf academy where the
philosophy is that golf should be fun and
fun in golf comes from playing better.
A corporate golf package is available.

CHAMPIONSHIP COURSE

WESTIN TURNBERRY RESORT

KA26 9LT
☎ 01655 331000 📄 01655 331069
e-mail: turnberry@westin.com
web: www.westin.com/turnberry
Ailsa Course: 18 holes, 6440yds, Par 69,
SSS 72, Course record 63.
Kintyre Course: 18 holes, 6376yds, Par 71,
SSS 72, Course record 63.
Arran Course: 9 holes, 1996, Par 31, SSS 31.
Visitors Mon-Sun & BHs. Booking required.
Dress code. **Societies** booking required.
Green Fees Phone. **Prof** Paul Burley
Course Designer Mackenzie Ross/Donald
Steel **Facilities** ⑪ ⑩ 🍴 🔧 🏊 📷 ⚐ ◇
🚗 ✎ ⚑ **Leisure** hard tennis courts, heated
indoor swimming pool, fishing, sauna,
solarium, gymnasium, Colin Montgomerie
Links Golf Academy. **Location** 15m SW of Ayr
on A77

For thousands of players of all nationalities, Turnberry is one of the finest of all golf destinations, where some of the most remarkable moments in Open history have taken place. The legendary Ailsa Course is complemented by the new highly acclaimed Kintyre Course, while the nine-hole Arran Course, created by Donald Steel and Colin Montgomerie, has similar challenges such as undulating greens, tight tee shots, pot bunkers and thick Scottish rough. With the famous hotel on the left and the magnificent Ailsa Craig away to the right, there are few vistas in world golf to match the 1st tee here. To help you prepare for your game the Colin Montgomerie Links Golf Academy, alongside the luxurious and extensive clubhouse, was opened in April 2000; it features 12 driving bays, four short-game bays, two dedicated teaching rooms and a group teaching room.

SCOTLAND

SCOTTISH BORDERS

KELSO

Roxburghe
Heiton TD5 8JZ
☎ 01573 450331
🖨 01573 450611
e-mail: hotel@roxburghe.net
web: www.roxburghe.net
An exceptional parkland layout designed by Dave Thomas and opened in 1997. Surrounded by natural woodland on the banks of the River Teviot. Owned by the Duke of Roxburghe, this course has numerous bunkers, wide rolling and sloping fairways and strategically placed water features. The signature hole is the 14th.

18 holes, 6925yds, Par 72, SSS 74, Course record 66. Club membership 300.
Visitors Mon-Sun & BHs. Booking required. Handicap certificate. Dress code. **Societies** booking required. **Green Fees** not confirmed. **Prof** Craig Montgomerie **Course Designer** Dave Thomas
Facilities ⑪ ⑩ ⚑ ⌾ 🖵 🏵 ⚘ ⏱ ◇ ⚫ ⚓ ⚐ ℱ **Leisure** fishing, Clay pigeon shooting, falconry, archery, mountain bikes. **Conf** facs Corporate Hospitality Days **Location** 2m W of Kelso on A698
Hotel ★★★ 83% HL The Roxburghe Hotel & Golf Course, Heiton, KELSO ☎ 01573 450331 16 en suite 6 annexe en suite

SOUTH AYRSHIRE

BARASSIE

Kilmarnock (Barassie)
29 Hillhouse Rd KA10 6SY
☎ 01292 313920
🖨 01292 318300
e-mail: secretary@kbgc.co.uk
web: www.kbgc.co.uk
The club has a 27-hole layout. Magnificent seaside links, relatively flat with much heather and small, undulating greens.
18 holes, 6817yds, Par 72, SSS 74, Course record 63.
9 hole course: 9 holes, 2888yds, Par 34.
Club membership 600.

Visitors Mon, Tue, Thu & Fri. Booking required. Dress code.
Societies Booking required. **Green Fees** £65 for up to 36 holes.
Prof Gregor Howie **Course Designer** Theodore Moone
Facilities ⑪ ⑩ ⚑ 🖵 🏵 ⚘ ⚫ ⚓ ⚐ ℱ **Location** E side of village on B746, 2m N of Troon
Hotel ★★★★ 75% HL Paramount Marine Hotel, Crosbie Rd, TROON ☎ 01292 314444 89 en suite

PRESTWICK

Prestwick
2 Links Rd KA9 1QG
☎ 01292 477404
🖨 01292 477255
e-mail: bookings@prestwickgc.co.uk
web: www.prestwickgc.co.uk
Seaside links with natural hazards, tight fairways and difficult fast undulating greens.
18 holes, 6544yds, Par 71, SSS 73, Course record 67. Club membership 575.
Visitors Mon-Fri, Sun & BHs. Booking required. Handicap certificate. Dress code. **Societies** Booking required. **Green Fees** £110 per round, £165 per day (Sun £140 per round). **Prof** D A Fleming **Course Designer** Tom Morris **Facilities** ⑪ ⚑ 🖵 🏵 ⚘ ⚫ ⚓ ⚐ **Conf** Corporate Hospitality Days **Location** In town centre off A79
Hotel ★★★ 75% HL Parkstone Hotel, Esplanade, PRESTWICK ☎ 01292 477286 30 en suite

SOUTH LANARKSHIRE

LANARK

Lanark
The Moor, Whitelees Rd ML11 7RX
☎ 01555 663219 & 661456
🖨 01555 663219
e-mail: lanarkgolfclub@supanet.com
web: www.lanarkgolfclub.co.uk
Lanark is renowned for its smooth fast greens, natural moorland fairways and beautiful scenery. The course is built on a substrate of glacial sands, providing a unique feeling of tackling a links course at 600ft above sea level. The Par of 70 can be a real test when the prevailing wind blows.
Old Course: 18 holes, 6306yds, Par 70, SSS 71, Course record 62.
Wee Course: 9 holes, 1489yds, Par 28.
Club membership 880.
Visitors Mon-Fri. Booking required. Dress code. **Societies** Booking required. **Green Fees** £50 per day, £40 per round. Wee Course £8 per day. **Prof** Alan White **Course Designer** Tom Morris **Facilities** ⑪ ⑩ ⚑ 🖵 🏵 ⚘ ⚫ ⚓ ⚐ **Conf** Corporate Hospitality Days **Location** E side of town centre off A73
Hotel ★★★ 75% CHH Cartland Bridge Hotel, Glasgow Rd, LANARK ☎ 01555 664426 20 rms (18 en suite)

CHAMPIONSHIP COURSE

ROYAL TROON

Craigend Rd KA10 6EP
☎ **01292 311555** 🖷 **01292 318204**
e-mail: bookings@royaltroon.com
web: www.royaltroon.com
Old Course: 18 holes, 6641yds, Par 71,
SSS 73, Course record 64.
Portland: 18 holes, 6289yds, Par 71, SSS 71,
Course record 65.
Craigend: 9 holes.
Club membership 800.
Visitors Mon-Tue & Thu. Booking required.
Handicap certificate. Dress code.
Societies Booking required. **Green Fees**
£220 per day including coffee/lunch, 1 round
over Old & 1 round over Portland **Prof** R B
Anderson **Course Designer** C Hunter/G
Strath/W Fernie **Facilities** ⑨ ⑩ 🍴 🍷 🏌 **Location** S of town on B749. 5m
from Prestwick airport

Troon was founded in 1878 with just
five holes on linksland. In its first decade
it grew from five holes to six, then 12,
and finally 18 holes. It became Royal
Troon in 1978 on its 100th anniversary.
Royal Troon's reputation is based on its
combination of rough and sandy hills,
bunkers, and a severity of finish that has
diminished the championship hopes of
many. The most successful players have
relied on an equal blend of finesse and
power. The British Open Championship
has been played at Troon eight times -
in 1923, 1950, 1962, 1973, 1982, 1989,
1997, and lastly in 2004 when it hosted
the 133rd tournament. It has the shortest
hole of courses hosting the Open. Ten new
bunkers and four new tees were added after
the 1997 competition. It is recommended
that you apply to the course in advance for
full visitor information.

STIRLING

BANNOCKBURN

Brucefields Family Golfing Centre
Pirnhall Rd FK7 8EH
☎ 01786 818184
🖹 01786 817770
e-mail: christine.frost@brucefields.co.uk
Gently rolling parkland with fine views. Most holes can
be played without too much difficulty with the exception
of the 2nd which is a long and tricky Par 4 and the 6th, a
Par 3 which requires exact club selection and a straight
shot.
Main Course: 9 holes, 2513yds, Par 68, SSS 68,
Course record 66. Club membership 300.
Visitors Mon-Sun & BHs. Dress code. **Societies** Booking
required. **Green Fees** £18 per 18 holes, £11 per 9 holes
(£20/£12 Sat & Sun). **Prof** Gregor Monks **Course Designer**
Souters Sportsturf **Facilities** ⑪ ⑩ ⓛ ⓛ ⓛ ⓛ ⓛ ⓛ ⓛ ⓛ
Leisure golf academy, Par 3 9 hole course. **Conf** facs Corporate
Hospitality Days **Location** M80/M9 junct 9, A91, 1st left signed

SCOTTISH ISLANDS

ISLAY, ISLE OF

PORT ELLEN

Machrie Hotel
Machrie PA42 7AN
☎ 01496 302310
🖹 01496 302404
e-mail: machrie@machrie.com
web: www.machrie.com
Championship links course opened in 1891, where golf's
first £100 Open Championship was played in 1901. Fine
turf and many blind holes. Par 4.
18 holes, 6226yds, Par 71, SSS 71, Course record 66.
Club membership 340.
Visitors Mon-Sun & BHs. Dress code **Societies** Booking
required. **Green Fees** £65 per day, £47 per round. **Course
Designer** W Campbell **Facilities** ⑪ ⑩ ⓛ ⓛ ⓛ ⓛ ⓛ ⓛ
ⓛ ⓛ ⓛ ⓛ **Leisure** fishing, snooker, table tennis. **Conf** facs
Corporate Hospitality Days **Location** 4m N off A846
Guest Accommodation ★★★★★ RR The Harbour Inn and
Restaurant, BOWMORE ☎ 01496 810330 7 en suite

ANGLESEY, ISLE OF

BEAUMARIS

Henllys
Henllys Hall LL58 8HU
☎ 01248 811717
🖹 01248 811511
e-mail: hg@hpb.co.uk
web: www.henllysgolfclub.co.uk
The Menai Straits and the Snowdonia mountains form
a magnificent backdrop to the course. Full use has been
made of the mature parkland trees and natural water
hazards to provide a really testing and enjoyable game
of golf.
18 holes, 6062yards, Par 71, SSS 69,
Course record 65. Club membership 300.
Visitors Mon-Sun & BHs. Booking required. **Societies** Booking
required. **Green Fees** £24 (£30 Sat & Sun). **Prof** Peter Maton &
David Gadsby **Course Designer** Roger Jones **Facilities** ⑪ ⑩ ⓛ
ⓛ ⓛ ⓛ ⓛ ⓛ ⓛ **Location** A545 through Beaumaris, 0.25m
Henllys Hall signed on left
Hotel ★★ 83% HL Ye Olde Bulls Head Inn, Castle St,
BEAUMARIS ☎ 01248 810329 12 en suite 1 annexe en suite

HOLYHEAD

Holyhead
Lon Garreg Fawr, Trearddur Bay LL65 2YL
☎ 01407 763279
🖹 01407 763279
web: www.holyheadgolfclub.co.uk
Treeless, undulating seaside course which provides a
varied and testing game, particularly in a south wind.
The fairways are bordered by gorse, heather and rugged
outcrops of rock. Accuracy from most tees is paramount
as there are 43 fairway and greenside bunkers and
lakes. Designed by James Braid.

18 holes, 6058yds, Par 70, SSS 70, Course record 64.
Club membership 1350.
Visitors Mon-Sun & BHs. Booking required. Handicap certificate.
Dress code. **Societies** Booking required **Green Fees** £35 per
day (£40 Sat & Sun). ⑧ **Prof** Stephen Elliot **Course Designer**
James Braid **Facilities** ⑪ ⑩ ⓛ ⓛ ⓛ ⓛ ⓛ ⓛ ⓛ ⓛ

Conf facs Corporate Hospitality Days **Location** A55 to rdbt at Holyhead, left onto B4545 to Trearddur Bay 1m
Hotel ★★★ 79% HL Trearddur Bay Hotel, TREARDDUR BAY
☎ 01407 860301 34 en suite 6 annexe en suite

BRIDGEND

BRIDGEND

Southerndown
Ogmore By Sea CF32 0QP
☎ 01656 880476
🖹 01656 880317
e-mail: southerndowngolf@btconnect.com
web: www.southerndowngolfclub.co.uk
Downland-links championship course with rolling fairways and fast greens. Golfers who successfully negotiate the four Par 3s still face a testing finish with three of the last four holes played into the prevailing wind. The Par 3 5th is played across a valley and the 18th, with its split-level fairway, is a demanding finishing hole. Superb views.
18 holes, 6449yds, Par 70, SSS 72, Course record 63. Club membership 710.
Visitors Mon-Sun & BHs. Booking required. Handicap certificate. Dress
code. **Societies** Booking required. **Green Fees** £50 per 18 holes £65 per day (£70 Sat & Sun). **Prof** D G McMonagle **Course Designer** W Park/W Fernie & others **Facilities** ⊕ ⏨ ⌷ ☡ ✆ ⌢ ↗
🏠 ♟ ✆ ✆ ✆ **Conf** Corporate Hospitality Days **Location** 3m SW of Bridgend on B4524
Hotel ★★★ 73% HL Best Western Heronston Hotel, Ewenny Rd, BRIDGEND ☎ 01656 668811 & 666084
🖹 01656 767391 69 en suite 6 annexe en suite

PORTHCAWL

Royal Porthcawl
Rest Bay CF36 3UW
☎ 01656 782251
🖹 01656 771687
e-mail: royalporthcawl@btconnect.com
web: www.royalporthcawl.com
One of the great links courses, Royal Porthcawl is unique in that the sea is in full view from every single hole. The course enjoys a substantial reputation with heather, broom, gorse and a challenging wind demanding a player's full skill and attention.
18 holes, 6440yds, Par 72, SSS 73. Club membership 800.
Visitors Tue, Thu & Fri. Booking required. Handicap certificate. Dress code. **Societies** booking required. **Green Fees** not confirmed. **Prof** Peter Evans **Course Designer** Ramsey Hunter **Facilities** ⊕ ⏨ ⌷ ☡ ✆ ⌢ ↗ 🏠 ♟ ✆ ✆ **Location** M4 junct 37, proceed to Rest Bay
Hotel ★★★ 68% HL Seabank Hotel, The Promenade, PORTHCAWL ☎ 01656 782261 67 en suite

CARDIFF

CARDIFF

St Mellons
St Mellons CF3 2XS
☎ 01633 680408
🖹 01633 681219
e-mail: stmellons@golf2003.fsnet.co.uk
web: www.stmellonsgolfclub.co.uk
Opened in 1936, St Mellons is a parkland course on the eastern edge of Cardiff. The course is laid out in the shape of a clover leaf and provides one of the best tests of golf in south Wales. The course comprises three Par 5s, five Par 3s and 10 Par 4s. The Par 3s will make or break your card but the two finishing Par 4 holes are absolutely superb.
18 holes, 6275yds, Par 70, SSS 70, Course record 63. Club membership 700.
Visitors Mon, Tue & Thu. Fri am only. Booking required. Handicap certificate. Dress code. **Societies** Booking required.
Green Fees £32 per round, £40 per day. **Prof** Barry Thomas
Course Designer Colt & Morrison **Facilities** ⊕ ⏨ ⌷ ☡ ✆ ✆
↗ 🏠 ♟ ✆ ✆ **Conf** Corporate Hospitality Days **Location** M4 junct 30, 2m E off A48
Hotel ★★★ 72% HL Best Western St Mellons Hotel & Country Club, Castleton, CARDIFF ☎ 01633 680355 21 en suite 20 annexe en suite

CARMARTHENSHIRE

BURRY PORT

Ashburnham
Cliffe Ter SA16 0HN
☎ 01554 832269 & 833846
e-mail: golf@ashburnhamgolfclub.co.uk
web: www.ashburnhamgolfclub.co.uk
This course has a lot of variety. In the main it is of the seaside type although the holes in front of the clubhouse are of an inland character. The front nine are played in a westerly direction into the prevailing wind, which can vary from a mild breeze to a near gale, the 1st and 9th being particularly tough. The second nine, usually wind assisted, opens with a long Par 5 and has a testing last few holes finishing with an elevated treacherous green at the 18th.

continued

ABERDOVEY

LL35 0RT
☎ **01654 767493** 📄 **01654 767027**
e-mail: info@aberdoveygolf.co.uk
web: www.aberdoveygolf.co.uk
18 holes, 6454yds, Par 71, SSS 72,
Course record 66.
Club membership 1000.
Visitors Mon-Sun & BHs. Booking required.
Handicap certificate. Dress code.
Societies Booking required. **Green Fees** £50
per day, £40 per round (£60/£45 Sat & Sun).
Prof John Davies **Course Designer** J Braid
Facilities ⑪ ⑩ 🍴 📇 ⛱ 🏠 ◇ ⚷ 🛒 ✎
Leisure snooker. **Conf** facs **Location** 0.5m W
on A493

Golf was first played at Aberdovey in 1886, with the club founded six years later. The links has since developed into one of the finest championship courses in Wales. The club has hosted many prestigious events over the years, and is popular with golfing societies and clubs who regularly return here. Golfers can enjoy spectacular views and easy walking alongside the dunes of this characteristic seaside links. Fine holes include the 3rd, 11th and a good short hole at the 12th. The late Bernard Darwin, a former president and captain at the club, was a golf correspondent for the Times. Many of his writings feature the course, which he referred to as 'the course that my soul loves best of all the courses in the world.' Darwin was a major contributor to its success, and he would easily recognise the course today.

CHAMPIONSHIP COURSE

MONMOUTHSHIRE — CHEPSTOW

MARRIOTT ST PIERRE HOTEL

St Pierre Park NP16 6YA
☎ **01291 625261** 📄 **01291 627977**
e-mail: **mhrs.cwlgs.golf@marriotthotels.co.uk**
web: **www.marriottstpierre.co.uk**
Old Course: 18 holes, 6733yds, Par 71, SSS 72, Course record 64.
Mathern Course: 18 holes, 5732yds, Par 68, SSS 67.
Club membership 800.
Visitors Mon-Sun & BHs. Booking required. Dress code. **Societies** Booking required.
Green Fees Old from £68, Mathern from £37. Winter: Old Course from £32, Mathern from £25. **Prof** Craig Dun **Course Designer** Henry Cotton **Facilities** ⑨ ⑩ 🏋 ⌨ 🏌 ⚲ 🏠 ⛴ ◇ 🚜
🏊 🏇 **Leisure** hard tennis courts, heated indoor pool, fishing, sauna, solarium, gymnasium, halfway house on Old Course, health & beauty suite, chipping green. **Conf** facs Corporate Hospitality Days **Location** M48 junct 2, A466 towards Chepstow, at 2nd rdbt take exit for Caerwent. Hotel after 2m

Set in 400 acres of beautiful parkland, Marriott St Pierre offers two 18-hole courses. The Old Course is one of the finest in the country and has played host to over 14 European Tour events. The Par 3 18th hole is famous for its tee shot over the lake to an elevated green. The Mathern has its own challenges and is highly enjoyable for golfers of all abilities. The hotel has teaching professionals as well as hire of clubs and equipment.

18 holes, 6916yds, Par 72, SSS 74, Course record 66. Club membership 650.
Visitors Mon-Sun & BHs. Booking required Sun, Sat & BHs. Handicap certificate. Dress code **Societies** Booking required. **Green Fees** £60 per day, £50 per round (£75/£65 Sat, Sun & BHs). **Prof** Martin Stimson **Course Designer** J H Taylor **Facilities** ⑪ by prior arrangement ⑩ by prior arrangement ⑤ ♥ ⑪ ㅅ 🏌 ☂ 🛆 ✔ **Conf** facs Corporate Hospitality Days **Location** W of town centre on A484
Hotel ★★ 72% HL Ashburnham Hotel, Ashburnham Rd, Pembrey, LLANELLI ☎ 01554 834343 & 834455 📄 01554 834483 13 en suite

CONWY

CONWY

Conwy (Caernarvonshire)
Beacons Way, Morfa LL32 8ER
☎ 01492 592423
📄 01492 593363
e-mail: secretary@conwygolfclub.co.uk
web: www.conwygolfclub.co.uk
Founded in 1890, Conwy has hosted national and international championships since 1898. Set among sand hills, possessing true links greens and a profusion of gorse on the latter holes, especially the 16th, 17th and 18th. This course provides the visitor with real golfing enjoyment in stunning scenery.
18 holes, 6100yds, Par 72, SSS 72. Club membership 1050.
Visitors Mon-Sun & BHs. Booking required. Handicap certificate. Dress code. **Societies** Booking required. **Green Fees** £43 per day, £38 per round (£48/£42 Sat, Sun & BHs). **Prof** Peter Lees **Facilities** ⑪ ⑩ ⑤ ♥ ⑪ ㅅ 🏌 ☂ ✔ 🛆 ✔ **Leisure** snooker tables. **Location** 1m W of town centre on A55

Hotel ★★★ 78% HL Castle Hotel Conwy, High St, CONWY ☎ 01492 582800 28 en suite

LLANDUDNO

Llandudno (Maesdu)
Hospital Rd LL30 1HU
☎ 01492 876450
📄 01492 876450
e-mail: secretary@maesdugolfclub.co.uk
web: www.maesdugolfclub.co.uk
Part links, part parkland, this championship course starts and finishes on one side of the main road, the remaining holes, more seaside in nature, being played on the other side. The holes are pleasantly undulating and present a pretty picture when the gorse is in bloom. Often windy, this varied and testing course is not for beginners.
18 holes, 6545yds, Par 72, SSS 72, Course record 62. Club membership 1120.
Visitors Mon-Sun & BHs. Dress code. **Societies** Booking required. **Green Fees** £35 per day, £25 per round (£40/£30 Sat & Sun). **Prof** Simon Boulden **Facilities** ⑪ ⑩ ⑤ ♥ ⑪ ㅅ 🏌 ☂ ✔ 🛆 ✔ **Leisure** snooker. **Location** S of town centre on A546
Hotel ★★★ 81% HL Imperial Hotel, The Promenade, LLANDUDNO ☎ 01492 877466 100 en suite

North Wales
72 Bryniau Rd, West Shore LL30 2DZ
☎ 01492 875325
📄 01492 873355
e-mail: golf@nwgc.freeserve.co.uk
web: www.northwalesgolfclub.co.uk
Challenging seaside links with superb views of Anglesey and Snowdonia. It possesses hillocky fairways, awkward stances and the occasional blind shot. Heather and gorse lurk beyond the fairways and several of the greens are defended by deep bunkers. The first outstanding hole is the 5th, a Par 5 that dog-legs into the wind along a rollercoasting, bottleneck fairway. Best Par 4s include the 8th, played through a narrow valley menaced by a railway line and the beach and the 11th, which runs uphill into the wind and where the beach again threatens. The finest Par 3 is the 16th, with a bunker to the left of a partially hidden, bowl-shape green.

WALES

18 holes, 6287yds, Par 71, SSS 71, Course record 66. Club membership 670.

Visitors Mon-Sun & BHs. Booking required. Dress code. **Societies** booking required. **Green Fees** not confirmed. **Prof** Richard Bradbury **Course Designer** Tancred Cummins **Facilities** ⑨ ⑩ 🄻 ⌨ 🍴 🏌 ⛳ 🚗 ✈ ✓ **Leisure** snooker.
Location W side of town on A546
Hotel ★★ HL St Tudno Hotel and Restaurant, The Promenade, LLANDUDNO ☎ 01492 874411 18 en suite

GWYNEDD

HARLECH

Royal St Davids
LL46 2UB
☎ 01766 780361
🖹 01766 781110
e-mail: secretary@royalstdavids.co.uk
web: www.royalstdavids.co.uk
Championship links with easy walking. Natural hazards demand strength and accuracy. Under the gaze of Harlech Castle, with a magnificent backdrop of the Snowdonia mountains.

18 holes, 6263yds, Par 69, SSS 71, Course record 61. Club membership 900.

Visitors Mon-Sun & BHs. Booking required. Handicap certificate. Dress code. **Societies** Booking required. **Green Fees** £55 per day, £45 per round, £28 after 3pm (£65/£55/£34 Sat & Sun). **Prof** John Barnett **Course Designer** Harold Finch-Hatton **Facilities** ⑨ ⑩ 🄻 ⌨ 🍴 🏌 🚗 ✓ 🏌 ✈ **Conf** facs Corporate Hospitality Days **Location** W side of town on A496
Hotel ★★ 68% SHL Ty Mawr Hotel, LLANBEDR ☎ 01341 241440 10 en suite

MORFA NEFYN

Nefyn & District
LL53 6DA
☎ 01758 720966
🖹 01758 720476
e-mail: nefyngolf@tesco.net
web: nefyn-golf-club.com
A 27-hole course played as two separate 18s, Nefyn is a cliff-top links where you never lose sight of the sea. A well-maintained course which will be a very tough

test for the serious golfer, but still user friendly for the casual visitor. Every hole has a different challenge and the old 13th fairway is some 30yds across from sea to sea. The
course has the bonus of a pub on the beach roughly halfway round
for those whose golf may need some bolstering.
Old Course: 18 holes, 6201yds, Par 71, SSS 71, Course record 67. New Course: 18 holes, 6317yds, Par 71, SSS 71, Course record 66. Club membership 800.

Societies booking required. **Prof** John Froom **Course Designer** James Braid **Facilities** ⑨ ⑩ 🄻 ⌨ 🍴 🏌 🚗 🏌 ✈ ✓ **Conf** facs **Location** 0.75m NW
Hotel ★★★ 78% CHH Porth Tocyn Hotel, Bwlch Tocyn, ABERSOCH ☎ 01758 713303 17 en suite

MONMOUTHSHIRE

ABERGAVENNY

Monmouthshire
Gypsy Ln, LLanfoist NP7 9HE
☎ 01873 852606
🖹 01873 850470
e-mail: monmouthshiregc@btconnect.com
web: www.themonmouthshiregolfclub.com
This parkland course is very picturesque, with the beautifully wooded River Usk running alongside. There are a number of Par 3 holes and a testing Par 4 at the 15th.
18 holes, 5806yds, Par 70, SSS 69, Course record 65. Club membership 600.

Visitors Mon-Sun. Booking required Mon & Thu-Sun. Handicap certificate. Dress code. **Societies** Booking required. **Green Fees** Phone. **Prof** B Edwards **Course Designer** James Braid **Facilities** ⑨ ⑩ by prior arrangement 🄻 ⌨ 🍴 🏌 🚗 🏌 ✓
Location 2m S off B4269
Hotel ★★ 79% HL Llanwenarth Hotel & Riverside Restaurant, Brecon Rd, ABERGAVENNY ☎ 01873 810550 17 en suite
Hotel ★★★★★ 86% GA Glangrwyney Court, CRICKHOWELL ☎ 01873 811288 Fax 01873 810317 5 rms (4 en suite)

MONMOUTH

Rolls of Monmouth
The Hendre NP25 5HG
☎ 01600 715353
🖨 01600 713115
e-mail: sandra@therollsgolfclub.co.uk
web: www.therollsgolfclub.co.uk
A hilly and challenging parkland course encompassing
several lakes and ponds and surrounded by woodland.
Set within a beautiful private estate complete with
listed mansion and panoramic views towards the Black
Mountains. The short 4th has a lake beyond the green
and both the 17th and 18th holes are magnificent holes
with which to end your round.
18 holes, 6733yds, Par 72, SSS 73, Course record 69.
Club membership 160.
Visitors Mon-Sun & BHs. Booking required. Dress code.
Societies Booking required. **Green Fees** £40 per day (£44 Sat
& Sun). **Facilities** ⑪ ⑩ ⓛ 🖵 ⑪ 🔏 🖻 ⊶ ◇ 🍴 ✔ **Location** 4m
W on B4233

NEWPORT

Newport
Great Oak, Rogerstone NP10 9FX
☎ 01633 892643
🖨 01633 896676
e-mail: newportgolfclub.gwent@euphony.net
web: newportgolfclub.org.uk
Undulating parkland on an inland plateau 300ft above
sea level, with views over the surrounding wooded
countryside. There are no blind holes, but plenty of
natural hazards and bunkers.
18 holes, 6460yds, Par 72, SSS 71, Course record 63.
Club membership 800.
Visitors Mon-Sun except BHs. Booking required. Dress code.
Societies Booking required. **Green Fees** £35 per day; £30 per
round (£40 weekends & bank holidays). ✆ **Prof** Paul Mayo
Course Designer W Fernie **Facilities** ⑪ ⑩ ⓛ 🖵 ⑪ 🔏 🖻 ✔
🍴 ✔ **Conf** Corporate Hospitality Days **Location** M4 junct 27,
1m NW on B4591
Hotel ★★★★★ 85% HL The Celtic Manor Resort, Coldra
Woods, NEWPORT ☎ 01633 413000 400 en suite

Tredegar Park
Parc-y-Brain Rd, Rogerstone NP10 9TG
☎ 01633 894433
🖨 01633 897152
e-mail: secretary@tredegarparkgolfclub.co.uk
web: www.tredegarparkgolfclub.co.uk
A course completed in 1999 with two balanced halves,
mostly in view from the clubhouse. A rolling, open
course with fine scenic views.
18 holes, 6545yds, Par 72, SSS 72.
Club membership 822.
Visitors Mon-Sun & BHs. Booking required. Handicap
certificate. Dress code. **Societies** Booking required. **Green Fees**

Phone. **Prof** Lee Pagett **Course Designer** R Sandow **Facilities**
⑪ ⑩ ⓛ 🖵 ⑪ 🔏 🖻 ⊶ 🍴 ✔ **Conf** facs **Location** M4 junct 27,
B4591 N, club signed
Hotel ★★★ 68% HL The Kings Hotel, High St, NEWPORT
☎ 01633 842020 61 en suite

PEMBROKESHIRE

TENBY

Tenby
The Burrows SA70 7NP
☎ 01834 844447 & 842978
🖨 01834 842978
e-mail: tenbygolfclub@uku.co.uk
web: www.tenbygolf.co.uk
The oldest club in Wales, this fine seaside links, with sea
views and natural hazards, provides good golf all the
year round.
18 holes, 6224yds, Par 69, SSS 71, Course record 65.
Club membership 700.
Visitors Mon-Sun & BHs. Booking required. Handicap certificate.
Dress code. **Societies** Booking required. **Green Fees** Phone ✆
Prof Mark Hawkey **Course Designer** James Braid **Facilities** ⑪
⑩ ⓛ 🖵 ⑪ 🔏 🖻 ⊶ ✔ 🍴 ✔ **Conf** Corporate Hospitality Days
Location Near railway station
Hotel ★★★ 77% HL Atlantic Hotel, The Esplanade, TENBY
☎ 01834 842881 42 en suite

SWANSEA

CLYDACH

Inco SA6 5QR
☎ 01792 842929
e-mail: secretaryinco.golf@amserve.com
Flat meadowland course bordered by meandering River
Tawe and the Swansea valley. Recently completed an
ambitious development programme.
18 holes, 6064yds, Par 70, SSS 69, Course record 68.
Club membership 450.
Visitors Mon-Sun & BHs. Dress code. **Societies** Booking required.
Green Fees £18 per round (£23 Sat & Sun). ✆ **Facilities** ⑪ ⑩
ⓛ 🖵 ⑪ 🔏 **Leisure** outdoor bowling green. **Conf** Corporate
Hospitality Days **Location** M4 junct 45, 1.5m NE on A4067
Hotel BUD Premier Travel Inn Swansea North, Upper Fforest Way,
Morriston, SWANSEA ☎ 08701 977246 40 en suite

SOUTHGATE

Pennard 2 Southgate Rd SA3 2BT
☎ 01792 233131 & 233451 🖨 01792 234797
e-mail: sec@pennardgolfclub.com
web: www.pennardgolfclub.com
Undulating, cliff-top seaside links with good coastal views.
At first sight it can be intimidating with steep hills that make
club selection important - there are a few blind shots to
contend with. The difficulties are not insurmountable unless

CELTIC MANOR RESORT

Coldra Woods NP18 1HQ
☎ **01633 413000** 🖨 **01633 410269**
e-mail: golf@celtic-manor.com
web: www.celtic-manor.com
Roman Road: 18 holes, 6030yds, Par 70, SSS 72, Course record 63.
Coldra Woods: 18 holes, 3539yds, Par 59, SSS 61. **Wentwood Hills:** 18 holes, 6211yds, Par 71, SSS 75, Course record 61.
Club membership 580.
Visitors Mon-Sun & BHs. Booking required. Dress code. **Societies** booking required.
Green Fees Apr-Oct: Wentworth Hills £60, Roman Road £60, Coldra Woods £25.
Prof Kevin Carpenter **Course Designer** Robert Trent Jones **Facilities** 🏌 🍽 ⛳ 🖥 🍴 ⛳ 🏠 ⛳ ◇ 🏌 🚃 🏌 ⛳ **Leisure** hard tennis courts, heated indoor pool, fishing, sauna, solarium, gym, Health spa, Golf Academy with 18 hole course, Shooting school. **Conf** facs Corporate Hospitality Days **Location** M4 junct 24, B4237 towards Newport, 300yds right

This relatively new resort has quickly become a world-renowned venue for golf, set in 1400 acres of beautiful, unspoiled parkland at the southern gateway to Wales. Boasting three championship courses, Celtic Manor offers a challenge for all levels of play, complemented by a golf school and one of the largest clubhouses in Europe, as well as extensive leisure facilities. In 2010, The Celtic Manor Resort will host the 38th Ryder Cup on the world's first ever course to be specifically designed for this prestigious tournament. The new course opened in spring 2007, featuring nine holes from the original Wentwood Hills course and nine spectacular new holes in the valley of the River Usk.

the wind begins to blow in calm weather. Greens are slick and firm all year.
18 holes, 6265yds, Par 71, SSS 72, Course record 69. Club membership 1020.
Visitors Mon & Wed-Sun. Contact club for details. Handicap certificate. Dress code. **Societies** booking required. **Green Fees** not confirmed. **Prof** M V Bennett **Course Designer** James Braid **Facilities** ⓘ ⏀ ⒧ ⌷
⏀ ⚄ 🛎 ❤ ⚑ **Location** 8m W of Swansea by A4067 and B4436
Hotel ★★★ CHH Fairyhill, REYNOLDSTON ☎ 01792 390139 8 en suite

SWANSEA

Clyne

120 Owls Lodge Ln, The Mayals, Blackpyl SA3 5DP
☎ 01792 401989 📄 01792 401078
e-mail: clynegolfclub@supanet.com
web: www.clynegolfclub.com
Challenging moorland course with excellent greens and scenic views of Swansea Bay and the Gower. Many natural hazards with a large number of bunkers and gorse and bracken in profusion,
18 holes, 6334yds, Par 70, SSS 72, Course record 64. Club membership 900.
Visitors Mon-Sun & BHs. Booking required. Handicap certificate. Dress code. **Societies** Booking required. **Green Fees** £30 per round (£40 Sat, Sun & BHs), Winter £20 including bar meal. ⊜
Prof Jonathan Clewett **Course Designer** H S Colt & Harries **Facilities** ⓘ ⏀ ⒧ ⌷ ⏀ ⚄ 🛎 ❤ ⚑ **Leisure** chipping green,driving nets,indoor practice net. **Location** 3.5m SW on B4436

VALE OF GLAMORGAN

HENSOL

Vale Hotel Golf & Spa Resort
Hensol Park CF72 8JY
☎ 01443 665899
📄 01443 222220
e-mail: smetson@vale-hotel.com
web: www.vale-hotel.com
Two championship courses set in 200 acres of glorious countryside, with views over Hensol Lake and castle. The Wales National with greens constructed to USGA standard will prove a stern test for even the very best players. The aptly named Lake course has water coming into play on 12 holes. The signature hole, the 12th, has an island green reached via a stone bridge. The club is also home to the Welsh PGA.
Lake: 18 holes, 6426yds, Par 72, SSS 71.
Wales National: 18 holes, 7414yds, Par 73, SSS 73, Course record 64. Club membership 1100.
Visitors Mon-Sun & BHs. Booking required. Handicap certificate. Dress code. **Societies** Booking required **Green Fees** Phone.
Prof Llewellyn, Coombs, Williams **Course Designer** Peter Johnson & Terry Jones **Facilities** ⓘ ⏀ ⒧ ⌷ ⏀ ⚄ 🛎 ❤ ⚑ ◇ ❤ 🛍

⚑ ❤ **Leisure** hard tennis courts, heated indoor swimming pool, squash, fishing, sauna, solarium, gymnasium, short game area, video analysis. **Conf** facs Corporate Hospitality Days **Location** M4 junct 34, signed
Hotel ★★★★ 79% HL Vale Hotel Golf & Spa Resort, Hensol Park, HENSOL ☎ 01443 667800 29 en suite 114 annexe en suite

WREXHAM

CHIRK

Chirk Golf Club LL14 5AD
☎ 01691 774407 📄 01691 773878
e-mail: chirkjackbarker@btinternet.com
web: www.jackbarker.com
Overlooked by the National Trust's Chirk Castle, a championship-standard 18-hole course with a 664yd Par 5 at the 9th - one of the longest in Europe. Also a nine-hole course, driving range and golf academy.
18 holes, 7045yds, Par 72, SSS 73, Course record 69. Club membership 300.
Visitors Mon-Sun & BHs. Booking required. Dress code. **Societies** Booking required. **Green Fees** £14 per round (£16 Fri, £18 Sat & Sun). **Prof** M Maddison **Facilities** ⓘ ⏀ ⒧ ⌷ ⏀ ⚄ 🛎 ❤ ❤
❤ **Leisure** 9 hole Par 3 course. **Conf** facs **Location** 1m NW of Chirk, near Chirk Castle

WREXHAM

Clays Bryn Estyn Rd, Llan-y-Pwll LL13 9UB
☎ 01978 661406 📄 01978 661406
e-mail: claysgolf@claysgolf.co.uk
web: www.claysgolf.co.uk
Gently undulating parkland course in countryside with views of the Welsh mountains. Noted for its difficult Par 3s.
18 holes, 6010yds, Par 69, SSS 69, Course record 62. Club membership 420.
Visitors Mon-Sun & BHs **Societies** Welcome. **Green Fees** £19 per round (£25 Sat & Sun). **Prof** David Larvin **Course Designer** R D Jones **Facilities** ⓘ ⏀ ⒧ ⌷ ⏀ ⚄ 🛎 ❤ ❤ 🛍 ❤ ❤ **Conf** facs Corporate Hospitality Days **Location** Off A534

NORTHERN IRELAND
CO ANTRIM

ANTRIM

Massereene
51 Lough Rd BT41 4DQ
☎ 028 9442 8096
📠 028 9448 7661
e-mail: info@massereene.com
web: www.massereene.com
The first nine holes are parkland, while the second, adjacent to the shore of Lough Neagh, have more of a links character with sandy ground.
18 holes, 6602yds, Par 72, SSS 72, Course record 63.
Club membership 1050.
Visitors Mon-Sun & BHs. Booking required. Dress code. **Societies** Booking required. **Green Fees** £22 per round (£30 Sun & Sat). **Prof** Jim Smyth **Course Designer** F Hawtree/H Swan
Facilities ⊕ ⏦ ⬛ ♨ ⬚ ⚘ ⚑ 🛒 🚗 ✎ **Conf** facs Corporate Hospitality Days **Location** 1m SW of town
Hotel ★★★★ 69% HL Galgorm Manor, BALLYMENA
☎ 028 2588 1001 24 en suite

BALLYCASTLE

Ballycastle
Cushendall Rd BT54 6QP
☎ 028 2076 2536
📠 028 2076 9909
e-mail: info@ballycastlegolfclub.com
web: www.ballycastlegolfclub.com
An unusual mixture of terrain beside the sea, lying at the foot of one of the nine glens of Antrim, with magnificent views from all parts. The first five holes are parkland with natural hazards; the middle holes are links type and the rest on adjacent upland. Accurate iron play is essential for good scoring while the undulating greens will test putting skills.
18 holes, 5927mtrs, Par 71, SSS 70, Course record 64.
Club membership 825.
Visitors Mon-Sun & BHs. Booking required Sat, Sun & BHs. Dress code. **Societies** Booking required. **Green Fees** £25 per round (£35 Sat, Sun & BHs). **Prof** Ian McLaughlin **Facilities** ⊕ ⏦ ⬛ ⬚ ⚘ ♨ 🚗 ✎ **Conf** facs Corporate Hospitality Days **Location** Between Portrush & Cushendall (A2)
Hotel ★★★ 74% HL Bayview Hotel, 2 Bayhead Rd, PORTBALLINTRAE ☎ 028 2073 4100 25 en suite

BALLYCLARE

Greenacres
153 Ballyrobert Rd BT39 9RT
☎ 028 9335 4111
📠 028 9335 4166
Designed and built into the rolling countryside, and with the addition of lakes at five of the holes, provides a challenge for both the seasoned golfer and the higher-handicapped player.
18 holes, 6031yds, Par 71, SSS 69.
Club membership 520.
Visitors Mon-Fri, Sun & BHs. Dress code **Societies** Booking required. **Green Fees** not confirmed. **Facilities** ⊕ ⏦ ⬛ ⬚ ♨ ⚘ ⚑ ✎ ✿ **Conf** facs Corporate Hospitality Days **Location** 12m from Belfast city centre
Hotel ★★★ 72% HL Headfort Arms Hotel, Headfort Place, KELLS ☎ 0818 222800 & 046 9240063 📠 046 9240587 45 en suite

BALLYGALLY

Cairndhu
192 Coast Rd BT40 2QG
☎ 028 2858 3954
📠 028 2858 3324
e-mail: cairndhugc@btconnect.com
Built on a hilly headland, this course is both testing and scenic, with wonderful coastal views. The Par 3 second hole can require anything from a 9 to a 3 iron depending on the wind, while the 3rd has a carry of 165 metres over a headland to the fairway. The 10th, 11th and 12th holes constitute Cairndhu's Amen Corner, feared and respected by any standard of golfer.
18 holes, 5611mtrs, Par 70, SSS 69, Course record 64.
Club membership 905.
Visitors Mon-Fri , Sun & BHs. Booking required Thu, Fri, Sun & BHs. Handicap certificate. Dress code. **Societies** Booking required **Green Fees** £20 per round (£25 Sun). **Prof** Stephen Hood **Course Designer** Mr Morrison **Facilities** ⊕ ⏦ ⬛ ⬚ ♨ ⚘ ✎ 🚗 ✿ **Conf** facs **Location** 4m N of Larne on coast road
Guesthouse ★★★★ GH Manor Guest House, 23 Older Fleet Rd, Harbour Highway, LARNE ☎ 028 2827 3305 8 en suite

BALLYMENA

Ballymena 128 Raceview Rd BT42 4HY
☎ 028 2586 1487
📠 028 2586 1487
18 holes, 5299mtrs, Par 68, SSS 67, Course record 62.
Location 2m E on A42
Telephone for further details
Hotel ★★★★ 69% HL Galgorm Manor, BALLYMENA
☎ 028 2588 1001 24 en suite

Galgorm Castle Golf & Country Club

Galgorm Rd BT42 1HL
☎ 028 2564 6161 ▤ 028 2565 1151
e-mail: golf@galgormcastle.co.uk
web: www.galgormcastle.com
An 18-hole USGA championship course set in 220 acres
of mature parkland in the grounds of one of Ireland's
most historic castles. The course is bordered by two rivers
which come into play and includes five lakes. A course of
outstanding beauty offering a challenge to both the novice
and low handicapped golfer.

18 holes, 6736yds, Par 72, SSS 72, Course record 67.
Club membership 600.
Visitors Mon-Sun & BHs. Booking required. Dress code. **Societies**
Booking required. **Green Fees** £32 per round (£40 Sat & Sun).
Prof Phil Collins **Course Designer** Simon Gidman **Facilities**
⑪ ⑩ ♨ ☕ ⌑ ⚑ ♨ ⬚ ⊶ ✔ ☎ ✔ 𝔽 **Leisure** fishing, PGA staffed
Academy. **Conf** facs Corporate Hospitality Days **Location** 1m S of
Ballymena on A42
Hotel ★★★★ 69% HL Galgorm Manor, BALLYMENA
☎ 028 2588 1001 24 en suite

BALLYMONEY

Gracehill

141 Ballinlea Rd, Stranocum BT53 8PX
☎ 028 2075 1209
▤ 028 2075 1074
e-mail: info@gracehillgolfclub.co.uk
web: www.gracehillgolfclub.co.uk
Challenging parkland course with some holes played over
water and many mature trees coming into play.
18 holes, 6553yds, Par 72, SSS 73, Course record 69.
Club membership 400.
Visitors Mon-Sun & BHs. Booking required. Dress code. **Societies**
Booking required. **Green Fees** £25 per round (£30 Sat & Sun).
Course Designer Frank Ainsworth **Facilities** ⑪ ⑩ ♨ ☕ ⌑
⬚ ✔ ✔ 𝔽 **Conf** Corporate Hospitality Days **Location** M2 N
from Belfast, onto A26 N to Ballymoney, signs for Coleraine. At
Ballymoney bypass onto B147/A2 to Sranocum/Ballintoy
Hotel ★★ 76% HL Brown Trout Golf & Country Inn, 209 Agivey Rd,
AGHADOWEY ☎ 028 7086 8209 15 en suite

CARRICKFERGUS

Carrickfergus

35 North Rd BT38 8LP
☎ 028 9336 3713
▤ 028 9336 3023
e-mail: carrickfergusgc@btconnect.com
Parkland course, fairly level but nevertheless demanding,
with a notorious water hazard at the 1st. Well-maintained,
with an interesting in-course riverway and fine views
across Belfast Lough.
18 holes, 5768yds, Par 68, SSS 68.
Club membership 850.
Visitors Mon-Fri, Sun & BHs. Booking required. Handicap
certificate. Dress code. **Societies** Booking required. **Green Fees**
£19 per day, £12 per round (£25/£15 Sat, Sun & BHs). **Prof** Gary
Mercer **Facilities** ⑪ ⑩ ♨ ☕ ⌑ ⚑ ⬚ ✔ **Conf** facs Corporate
Hospitality Days **Location** 9m NE of Belfast on A2
Hotel ★★ 68% HL Dobbins Inn Hotel, 6-8 High St, CARRICKFERGUS
☎ 028 9335 1905 15 en suite

Greenisland

156 Upper Rd, Greenisland BT38 8RW
☎ 028 9086 2236
A parkland course nestling at the foot of Knockagh Hill,
with scenic views over Belfast Lough.
9 holes, 6045yds, Par 71, SSS 69.
Club membership 660.
Visitors Mon-Sun & BHs. **Societies** Welcome. **Green Fees** £12
(£18 Sat & Sun). ⊛ **Facilities** ⑪ ⑩ ♨ ☕ ⌑ ⬚ **Location** N of
Belfast, close to Carrickfergus
Hotel ★★ 68% HL Dobbins Inn Hotel, 6-8 High St, CARRICKFERGUS
☎ 028 9335 1905 15 en suite

CUSHENDALL

Cushendall

21 Shore Rd BT44 0NG
☎ 028 2177 1318
e-mail: cushendallgc@btconnect.com
Scenic course with spectacular views over the Sea of
Moyle and Red Bay to the Mull of Kintyre. The River Dall
winds through the course, coming into play in seven of the
nine holes. This demands a premium on accuracy rather
than length. The signature hole is the Par 3 2nd, requiring
a tee shot across the river to a plateau green with a steep
slope in front and out of bounds behind.
9 holes, 4386mtrs, Par 66, SSS 63, Course record 59.
Club membership 824.
Visitors Mon-Wed, Fri & BHs. Booking required Thu. Dress
code. **Societies** Booking required. **Green Fees** £13 per day (£18
BHs). ⊛ **Course Designer** D Delargy **Facilities** ♨ ☕ ⌑ ⬚ ✔
Location In Cushendall beside beach on Antrim coast road

continued

CHAMPIONSHIP COURSE

CO ANTRIM — PORTRUSH

ROYAL PORTRUSH

Dunluce Rd BT56 8JQ
☎ **028 7082 2311** 🖷 **028 7082 3139**
e-mail: info@royalportrushgolfclub.com
web: www.royalportrushgolfclub.com
Dunluce: 18 holes, 6641yds, Par 72, SSS 73.
Valley: 18 holes, 6054yds, Par 70, SSS 72.
Club membership 1300.
Visitors Mon-Sun & BHs. Handicap
certificate. Dress code. **Societies** Booking
required. **Green Fees** Dunluce: £105 per
round, £120 weekends. Valley: £35 per
round, £40 weekends. **Prof** Gary McNeill
Course Designer Harry Colt **Facilities** ⑨
⑩ ⓛ ⛳ ⑭ ⚓ ☕ ⚑ ✐ ⚘ **Location** 0.8km
from Portrush on Bushmills road

This course, designed by Harry S Colt, is
considered to be among the best six in the
UK. Founded in 1888, it was the venue of
the first professional golf event in Ireland,
held in 1895, when Sandy Herd beat Harry
Vardon in the final. Royal Portrush is
spectacular and breathtaking, one of the
tightest driving courses known to golfers.
On a clear day there's a fine view of Islay
and the Paps of Jura from the 3rd tee, and
the Giant's Causeway from the 5th. While
the greens have to be 'read' from the start,
there are fairways up and down valleys,
and holes called Calamity Corner and
Purgatory (for good reason). The 2nd hole,
Giant's Grave, is 509yds, but the 17th is
even longer.

Guesthouse (AA Appointed) The Villa Farm House, 185 Torr Rd, CUSHENDUN ☎ 028 2176 1252 3 en suite

LARNE

Larne

54 Ferris Bay Rd, Islandmagee BT40 3RT
☎ 028 9338 2228
📄 028 9338 2088
e-mail: info@larnegolfclub.co.uk
web: www.larnegolfclub.co.uk
An exposed part links, part heathland course offering a good test, particularly on the last three holes along the sea shore.
9 holes, 6686yds, Par 70, SSS 70, Course record 64. Club membership 430.
Visitors Contact club for details. **Societies** welcome. **Green Fees** not confirmed. ☻ **Course Designer** G L Bailie **Facilities** ⊕ ⏲ 🍺 ⬜ 🌱 ⛳ **Location** 6m N of Whitehead on Browns Bay road

PORTBALLINTRAE

Bushfoot

50 Bushfoot Rd, Portballintrae BT57 8RR
☎ 028 2073 1317
📄 028 2073 1852
e-mail: bushfootgolfclub@btconnect.com
A seaside links course with superb views in an area of outstanding beauty. A challenging Par 3 7th is ringed by bunkers with out of bounds beyond, while the 3rd has a blind approach. Also a putting green and pitch and putt course.
9 holes, 6075yds, Par 70, SSS 68, Course record 68. Club membership 850.
Visitors Mon, Wed-Fri, Sun & BHs. Booking required. **Societies** Booking required. **Green Fees** £16 per round (£20 Sat, Sun & BHs). ☻ **Facilities** ⊕ ⏲ 🍺 ⬜ 🌱 ⛳ ⚑ ⛳ **Location** Off Ballaghmore road
Hotel ★★★ 74% HL Bayview Hotel, 2 Bayhead Rd, PORTBALLINTRAE ☎ 028 2073 4100 25 en suite

WHITEHEAD

Whitehead

McCrae's Brae BT38 9NZ
☎ 028 9337 0820 & 9337 0822
📄 028 9337 0825
e-mail: robin@whiteheadgc.fsnet.co.uk
web: www.whiteheadgolfclub.com
Undulating parkland course with magnificent sea views.
18 holes, 5952yds, Par 70, SSS 69, Course record 65. Club membership 962.
Visitors Mon-Fri, Sun & BHs. Booking required Thu & Sun. Dress code. **Societies** Booking required. **Green Fees** £18 per round (£22 Sun & BHs). ☻ **Prof** Colin Farr **Course Designer** A B Armstrong **Facilities** ⊕ ⏲ 🍺 ⬜ 🌱 ⛳ ⚑ 🛒 ⛳ **Conf** Corporate Hospitality Days **Location** 1m from town
Hotel ★★ 68% HL Dobbins Inn Hotel, 6-8 High St, CARRICKFERGUS ☎ 028 9335 1905 15 en suite

CO ARMAGH

ARMAGH

County Armagh

The Demesne, Newry Rd BT60 1EN
☎ 028 3752 5861 & 3752 8768
📄 028 3752 5861
e-mail: june@golfarmagh.co.uk
web: www.golfarmagh.co.uk
Mature parkland course with excellent views of Armagh city and its surroundings.
18 holes, 6212yds, Par 70, SSS 69, Course record 63. Club membership 1300.
Visitors Booking required Tue, Thu, Sat, Sun & BHs. Handicap certificate. Dress code. **Societies** Booking required. **Green Fees** not confirmed. **Prof** Alan Rankin **Facilities** ⊕ ⏲ 🍺 ⬜ 🌱 ⬜ 🛒 ⛳ 🛒 ⛳ ⚑ **Leisure** snooker. **Conf** Corporate Hospitality Days **Location** On Newry Rd
Hotel ★★ 68% HL The Cohannon Inn & Autolodge, 212 Ballynakilly Rd, DUNGANNON ☎ 028 8772 4488 42 en suite

LURGAN

Lurgan

The Demesne BT67 9BN
☎ 028 3832 2087
📄 028 3831 6166
e-mail: lurgangolfclub@btconnect.com
web: www.lurgangolfclub.co.uk
Testing parkland course bordering Lurgan Park Lake with a need for accurate shots. Drains well in wet weather and suits a long straight hitter.
18 holes, 6257yds, Par 70, SSS 70, Course record 66. Club membership 903.
Visitors Mon-Tue, Thu-Fri, Sun & BHs. Booking required. Dress code. **Societies** Booking required. **Green Fees** not confirmed. ☻ **Prof** Des Paul **Course Designer** A Pennink **Facilities** ⊕

🍴 🛏 ⛳🏌 ⛳ 🏊 🛋 ✧ **Conf** facs Corporate Hospitality Days
Location 0.5m from town centre near Lurgan Park

PORTADOWN

Portadown
192 Gilford Rd BT63 5LF
☎ 028 3835 5356
📄 028 3839 1394
e-mail: portadown.gc@btconnect.com
web: www.portadowngolfclub.co.uk
Well-wooded parkland on the banks of the River Bann,
which is one of the water hazards.
18 holes, 6130yds, Par 70, SSS 69, Course record 65.
Club membership 800.
Visitors Mon-Sun & BHs. Booking required. Dress code. **Societies**
Booking required. **Green Fees** not confirmed. ☺ **Prof** Paul
Stevenson **Facilities** ⑪ 🍴 🛏 ⛳🏌 🏊 🛋 ✧ **Leisure** squash.
Conf facs Corporate Hospitality Days **Location** SE via A59
Hotel ★★ 68% HL The Cohannon Inn & Autolodge, 212 Ballynakilly
Rd, DUNGANNON ☎ 028 8772 4488 42 en suite

TANDRAGEE

Tandragee
Markethill Rd BT62 2ER
☎ 028 3884 1272
📄 028 3884 0664
e-mail: office@tandragee.co.uk
web: www.tandragee.co.uk
Pleasant parkland course, the signature hole is the
demanding Par 3 16th known as 'The Quarry Hole'; the
real strength of Tandragee is in the short holes. Pleasant
views with the Mourne mountains in the distance.
18 holes, 5747mtrs, Par 71, SSS 70, Course record 65.
Club membership 1018.
Visitors Mon-Fri, Sun & BHs. Booking required. Dress code.
Societies Booking required. **Green Fees** £16 per round (£21 Sat
& Sun). ☺ **Prof** Dympna Keenan **Course Designer** John Stone
Facilities ⑪ 🍴 🛏 ⛳🏌 🏊 🛋 ✧ **Leisure** snooker. **Conf**
facs Corporate Hospitality Days **Location** On B3 from Tandragee
towards Markethill

CO BELFAST

BELFAST

Dunmurry
91 Dunmurry Ln, Dunmurry BT17 9JS
☎ 028 9061 0834
📄 028 9060 2540
e-mail: dunmurrygc@hotmail.com
web: www.dunmurrygolfclub.co.uk
Maturing very nicely, this tricky parkland course has several
memorable holes which call for skilful shots.
18 holes, 6156yds, Par 70, SSS 69, Course record 65.
Club membership 1100.

Visitors Mon-Fri, Sun & BHs. Booking required Fri, Sun & BHs.
Dress code. **Societies** Booking required **Green Fees** £27 per
round (£37 Sat, Sun & BHs). ☺ **Prof** John Dolan **Facilities** ⑪ 🍴
🛏 ⛳🏌 🏊 🛋 ✧
Hotel ★★★ 75% HL Malone Lodge Hotel, 60 Eglantine Av,
BELFAST ☎ 028 9038 8000 51 en suite

Malone
240 Upper Malone Rd, Dunmurry BT17 9LB
☎ 028 9061 2758 (Office) & 9061 4917 (Pro)
📄 028 9043 1394
e-mail: manager@malonegolfclub.co.uk
web: www.malonegolfclub.co.uk
Two parkland courses, extremely attractive with a large
lake, mature trees and flowering shrubs and bordered
by the River Lagan. Very well maintained and offering a
challenging round.

Main Course: 18 holes, 6706yds, Par 71, SSS 72,
Course record 65.
Edenderry: 9 holes, 6320yds, Par 72, SSS 70.
Club membership 1450.
Visitors Mon, Thu-Fri, Sun & BHs. Wed am only. Booking
required. Dress code. **Societies** Booking required. **Green Fees**
Main Course: £65 per day, Edenderry: £20 per day (£75/£25
Sat & Sun). **Prof** Michael McGee **Course Designer** C K Cotton
Facilities ⑪ 🍴 🛏 ⛳🏌 🏊 🛋 ✧ 🍴 **Leisure** fishing,
Outdoor bowling green. **Conf** Corporate Hospitality Days
Location 4.5m S opposite Lady Dixon Park
Hotel ★★★ 75% HL Malone Lodge Hotel, 60 Eglantine Av,
BELFAST ☎ 028 9038 8000 51 en suite

Mount Ober Golf & Country Club
24 Ballymaconaghy Rd BT8 6SB
☎ 028 9040 1811 & 9079 5666
📄 028 9070 5862
web: www.mountober.com
Inland parkland course which is a great test of golf for all
handicaps.
18 holes, 5022yds, Par 67, SSS 66, Course record 67.
Club membership 400.
Visitors Mon-Fri, Sun & BHs. Contact club for details. Dress
code. **Societies** Booking required. **Green Fees** £16.50 per
round (£18.50 Sun & BHs). **Prof** Wesley Ramsay **Facilities** ⑪ 🍴
🛏 ⛳🏌 🏊 🛋 ✧ 🐾 **Leisure** American billiards & snooker.

continued

ROYAL COUNTY DOWN

36 Golf Links Rd BT33 0AN
☎ **028 43723314** 🖨 **028 43726281**
e-mail: golf@royalcountydown.org
web: www.royalcountydown.org
Championship Course: 18 holes, 7181yds, Par 71, SSS 74, Course record 66.
Annesley: 18 holes, 4681yds, Par 66, SSS 63.
Club membership 450.
Visitors Mon, Tue, Thu, Fri, Sun & BHs. Booking required. Dress code. **Societies** Booking required. **Green Fees** Championship Course: £135 weekdays, £120 afternoon (£150 Sun). **Prof** Kevan Whitson **Course Designer** Tom Morris **Facilities** ⑨ by prior arrangement 🏌 🛢 🍴 🏌 🏌 🛒 ☂ ✎ **Location** N of town centre off A24

The Championship Course is consistently rated among the world's top ten courses. Laid out beneath the imperious Mourne Mountains, the course has a magnificent setting as it stretches out along the shores of Dundrum Bay. As well as being one of the most-beautiful courses, it is also one of the most challenging, with great swathes of heather and gorse lining fairways that tumble beneath vast sand hills, and wild tussock-faced bunkers defending small, subtly contoured greens. The Annesley Links offers a less formidable yet extremely characterful game, played against the same incomparable backdrop. Recently substantially revised under the direction of Donald Steel, the course begins quite benignly before charging headlong into the dunes. Several charming and one or two teasing holes have been carved out amid the gorse, heather and bracken.

Conf facs Corporate Hospitality Days **Location** Off Saintfield Rd
Hotel ★★★ 75% HL The Crescent Townhouse, 13 Lower
Crescent, BELFAST ☎ 028 9032 3349 17 en suite

Ormeau

50 Park Rd BT7 2FX
☎ 028 9064 0700
☷ 028 9064 6250
e-mail: ormeau.golfclub@virgin.net

Nine hole parkland course which provides a challenge for
low and high handicap golfers, good shots being rewarded
and those that stray offline receiving due punishment. The
long Par 4 5th hole has an intimidating out of bounds on
the right and a narrow sloping green, well protected by
trees and bunkers. Two long Par 3 holes each demand an
accurate drive and when playing the 3rd and 12th holes,
visitors are advised to look for the Fairy Tree which graces
the middle of the fairway. Club folklore states that if a golfer
hits this tree he should apologise to the fairies or his game
will suffer!

9 holes, 2688yds, Par 68, SSS 66.
Club membership 520.

Visitors Mon, Wed-Fri, Sun & BHs. Booking required Fri, Sun &
BHs. Dress code. **Societies** Booking required. **Green Fees** not
confirmed. ◉ **Prof** Mr Stephen Rourke **Facilities** ⑨ ◉ ⓚ ➿
☂ ⚐ ➾ ⚲ **Location** S of city centre between Ravenhill &
Ormeau roads

Hotel ★★★ 75% HL The Crescent Townhouse, 13 Lower
Crescent, BELFAST ☎ 028 9032 3349 17 en suite

CO DOWN

ARDGLASS

Ardglass

Castle Place BT30 7TP
☎ 028 4484 1219 ☷ 028 4484 1841
e-mail: info@ardglassgolfclub.com
web: www.ardglassgolfclub.com

A scenic clifftop seaside course with championship standard
greens. The first five holes, with the Irish Sea and cliffs
tight to the left, should be treated with respect as anything
resembling a hook will meet with disaster. The 2nd hole is
a daunting Par 3. The tee shot must carry a cliff and canyon
- meanwhile the superb views of the Mountains of Mourne
should not be missed.

18 holes, 6268yds, Par 70, SSS 69, Course record 65.
Club membership 900.

Visitors Mon-Sun & BHs. Booking required **Societies** Booking
required **Green Fees** £37 per round (£51 Sat & Sun). **Prof** Philip
Farrell **Course Designer** David Jones **Facilities** ⑨ ◉ ⓚ ➿ ☂⚐
⚲ ⚐ ➾ ⚲ **Conf** facs **Location** 7m from Downpatrick on
the B1

Hotel ★★ 69% HL Enniskeen House Hotel, 98 Bryansford Rd,
NEWCASTLE ☎ 028 4372 2392 12 en suite

HOLYWOOD

The Royal Belfast

Station Rd, Craigavad BT18 0BP
☎ 028 9042 8165
☷ 028 9042 1404
e-mail: royalbelfastgc@btclick.com
web: www.royalbelfast.com

18 holes, 6185yds, Par 70, SSS 69.

Course Designer H C Colt **Location** 2m E on A2
Telephone for further details
Hotel ★★★ 87% HL The Old Inn, 15 Main St,
CRAWFORDSBURN ☎ 028 9185 3255 29 en suite 1 annexe
en suite

CO FERMANAGH

ENNISKILLEN

Castle Hume

Castle Hume, Belleek Rd BT93 7ED
☎ 028 6632 7077
☷ 028 6632 7076
e-mail: info@castlehumegolf.com
web: www.castlehumegolf.com

Castle Hume is a particularly scenic and challenging course.
Set in undulating parkland with large rolling greens, rivers,
lakes and water hazards all in play on a championship
standard course.

18 holes, 5770mtrs, Par 72, SSS 70, Course record 69.
Club membership 350.

Visitors Mon-Sun & BHs. Booking required Wed, Sat & Sun.
Dress code. **Societies** booking required. **Green Fees** not
confirmed. **Prof** Shaun Donnelly **Course Designer** B Browne
Facilities ⑨ ◉ ⓚ ➿ ☂⚐ ⚲ ⚐ ➾ ⚲ ⚐ **Leisure** fishing.
Conf facs Corporate Hospitality Days **Location** 4m from
Enniskillen on A46 Belleek-Donegal road
Hotel ★★★★ 80% HL Killyhevlin Hotel, ENNISKILLEN
☎ 028 6632 3481 70 en suite

CO LONDONDERRY

CASTLEROCK

Castlerock

65 Circular Rd BT51 4TJ
☎ 028 7084 8314
☷ 028 7084 9440
e-mail: info@castlerockgc.co.uk
web: www.castlerockgc.co.uk

A most exhilarating course with three superb Par 4s, four
testing short holes and five Par 5s. After an uphill start,
the hazards are many, including the river and a railway,
and both judgement and accuracy are called for. The
signature hole is the 4th, Leg of Mutton. A challenge in
calm weather, any trouble from the elements will test
your golf to the limits.

continued

IRELAND

Mussenden Course: 18 holes, 6499yds, Par 73,
SSS 71, Course record 64.
Bann Course: 9 holes, 2938yds, Par 34, SSS 33,
Course record 60. Club membership 1250.
Visitors Mon-Sun & BHs. Booking required. Dress code.
Societies Booking required. **Green Fees** £60 per day (£75
Sat, Sun & BHs). **Prof** Ian Blair **Course Designer** Ben Sayers
Facilities ⑪ ⑩ 🛏 ☐ ⑪ 👥 🏌 🍴 ⛴ 🚗 🏌 **Location** 6m from
Coleraine on A2

CO TYRONE

COOKSTOWN

Killymoon
200 Killymoon Rd BT80 8TW
☎ 028 8676 3762 & 8676 2254
🖨 028 8676 3762
e-mail: killymoongolf@btconnect.com
web: www.killymoongolfclub.com
Parkland course on elevated, well-drained land. The
signature hole is the aptly named 10th hole - the Giant's
Grave. Accuracy is paramount here and a daunting tee
shot into a narrow-necked fairway will challenge even the
most seasoned golfer. The enclosing influence of the trees
continues the whole way to the green.
18 holes, 6202yds, Par 70, SSS 70, Course record 64.
Club membership 830.
Visitors Mon-Wed, Fri, Sun & BHs. Booking required Sun.
Dress code. **Societies** Booking required. **Green Fees** Tue-Fri
£22 per round (£15 Mon, £28 Sat-Sun). **Prof** Gary Chambers
Course Designer John Nash **Facilities** ⑪ ⑩ 🛏 ☐ ⑪ 👥 🏌 🍴
🚗 🏌 **Leisure** snooker. **Conf** facs Corporate Hospitality Days
Location S of Cookstown
Hotel ★★ 68% HL The Cohannon Inn & Autolodge, 212
Ballynakilly Rd, DUNGANNON ☎ 028 8772 4488 42 en suite

DUNGANNON

Dungannon
34 Springfield Ln BT70 1QX
☎ 028 8772 2098
🖨 028 8772 7338
e-mail: info@dungannongolfclub.com
web: www.dungannongolfclub.com
Parkland course with five Par 3s and tree-lined fairways.
18 holes, 6046yds, Par 72, SSS 69, Course record 62.
Club membership 1100.
Visitors Mon-Fri, Sun & BHs. Booking required Sun & BHs.
Handicap certificate. Dress code. **Societies** Welcome. **Green
Fees** £18 per round (£22 Sat & Sun). ⚕ **Prof** Vivian Teague
Course Designer Sam Bacon **Facilities** 🏌 🍴 🏌 🚗 🏌
Location 0.5m outside town on Donaghmore road
Hotel ★★ 68% HL The Cohannon Inn & Autolodge, 212
Ballynakilly Rd, DUNGANNON ☎ 028 8772 4488 42 en suite

REPUBLIC OF IRELAND

CO CARLOW

CARLOW

Carlow Deerpark
☎ 059 9131695
🖨 059 9140065
e-mail: carlowgolfclub@eircom.net
web: www.carlowgolfclub.com
Created in 1922 to a design by Cecil Barcroft, this testing
and enjoyable course is set in a wild deer park, with
beautiful dry terrain and a varied character. With sandy
subsoil, the course is playable all year round. There are
water hazards at the 2nd, 10th and 11th and only two
Par 5s, both offering genuine birdie opportunities.
18 holes, 6025mtrs, Par 70, SSS 71, Course record 63.
Oakpark: 9 holes, 5650mtrs, Par 70, SSS 69,
Course record 67. Club membership 1200.
Visitors Mon-Sun & BHs. Handicap certificate. Dress code.
Societies Booking required. **Green Fees** €50 per round (€60
Sat). Oakpark: €20 per 9/18 holes. **Prof** Andrew Gilbert **Course
Designer** Cecil Barcroft/Tom Simpson **Facilities** ⑪ ⑩ 🛏 ☐ ⑪
🏌 🍴 🏌 🚗 🏌 **Location** 3km N of Carlow on N9
Hotel ★★★ 75% HL Seven Oaks Hotel, Athy Rd, CARLOW
☎ 059 9131308 89 en suite

CO CAVAN

BALLYCONNELL

Slieve Russell Hotel Golf & Country Club
☎ 049 9525090
🖨 049 9526640
e-mail: slieve-russell@quinn-hotels.com
web: www.quinnhotels.com
An 18-hole course opened in 1992 and rapidly
establishing itself as one of the finest parkland courses
in the country. Forming part of a 300 acre estate,
including 50 acres of lakes, the course has been
sensitively wrapped around the surrounding landscape.
On the main course, the 2nd plays across water while
the 16th has water surrounding the green. The course
finishes with a 519yd, Par 5 18th.
18 holes, 6048mtrs, Par 72, SSS 72, Course record 65.
Club membership 400.
Visitors Mon-Sun & BHs. Booking required. Dress code.
Societies Booking required **Green Fees** €72 per round (€90
Sat). **Prof** Liam McCool/ Tristan Mullally **Course Designer**
Paddy Merrigan **Facilities** ⑪ ⑩ 🛏 ☐ ⑪ 🏌 🍴 🏌 ◇ 🚗 🏌 ⚘
Leisure hard tennis courts, heated indoor swimming pool,
sauna, solarium, gymnasium. **Conf** facs Corporate Hospitality
Days **Location** 4km E of Ballyconnel
Hotel ★★★★ 76% HL Slieve Russell Hotel Golf and Country
Club, BALLYCONNELL ☎ 049 9526444 219 en suite

CO CLARE

LAHINCH

Lahinch
☎ 065 708 1592
🖶 065 708 1592
e-mail: info@lahinchgolf.com
web: www.lahinchgolf.com
Old Course: 18 holes, 6123metres, Par 72, SSS 73.
Castle Course: 18 holes, 5115metres, Par 70, SSS 70.
Course Designer Alister MacKenzie **Location** 3km W of
Ennisstymon on N67
Telephone for further details

CO CORK

BLARNEY

Muskerry
Carrigrohane
☎ 021 4385297
🖶 021 4516860
e-mail: muskgc@eircom.net
web: www.muskerrygolfclub.ie
An adventurous game is guaranteed at this course, with
its wooded hillsides and the meandering Shournagh
River coming into play at a number of holes. The 15th is
a notable hole - not long, but very deep - and after that
all you need to do to get back to the clubhouse is stay
out of the water.
18 holes, 5520mtrs, Par 71, SSS 70.
Club membership 851.
Visitors Mon & Tue, Wed am only & Thu, Sat & Sun pm only.
Booking required. Handicap certificate. Dress code. **Societies**
Booking required. **Green Fees** €40 per round (€50 Sat & Sun).
Prof W M Lehane **Course Designer** Dr A McKenzie **Facilities**
⑪ ⅃ ⌸ ⽸ ⴢ 🛉 ⵁ 🏌 **Location** 4km W of Blarney
Hotel ★★★ 70% HL Blarney Castle Hotel, The Village Green,
BLARNEY ☎ 021 4385116 13 en suite

CORK

Cork Little Island
☎ 021 4353451
🖶 021 4353410
e-mail: corkgolfclub@eircom.net
web: www.corkgolfclub.ie
This championship-standard course is kept in superb
condition and is playable all year round. Memorable
and distinctive features include holes at the water's edge
and in a disused quarry. The 4th hole is considered to be
among the most attractive and testing holes in Irish golf.

18 holes, 5910mtrs, Par 72, SSS 72, Course record 67.
Club membership 750.
Visitors Mon-Wed, Fri-Sun & BHs. Booking required. Handicap
certificate. Dress code. **Societies** Booking required. **Green Fees**
€85 (€95 Sat & Sun). **Prof** Peter Hickey **Course Designer**
Alister Mackenzie **Facilities** ⑪ ⅃🍵 ⌸ ⽸ ⴢ 🛉 ⵁ 🏌 ⵗ
🍂 **Conf** Corporate Hospitality Days **Location** 8km E of Cork
on N25

MALLOW

Mallow Ballyellis
☎ 022 21145
🖶 022 42501
e-mail: mallowgolfclubmanager@eircom.net
web: www.mallowgolfclub.net
Mallow Golf Club was established in the late 19th
century. A well-wooded parkland course overlooking the
Blackwater Valley, Mallow is straightforward, but no less
of a challenge for it. The front nine is by far the longer,
but the back nine is demanding in its call for accuracy
and the Par 3 18th provides a tough finish.

continued

IRELAND

18 holes, 5769mtrs, Par 72, SSS 71, Course record 66. Club membership 1100.
Visitors Mon-Sun & BHs. Booking required Tue, Wed, Fri-Sun & BHs. Dress code. **Societies** Booking required **Green Fees** €45 per round (€50 Sat, Sun & BHs). **Prof** Sean Conway **Course Designer** D W Wishart **Facilities** ⏱ ⓘⓄ ☐ ⌧ ⓕ ☐ ⚐ ⚑ ⚒ ✦ **Leisure** hard tennis courts, squash. **Location** 1.6km E of Mallow
Hotel ★★★ CHH Longueville House Hotel, MALLOW
☎ 022 47156 & 47306 ◫ 022 47459 20 en suite

MONKSTOWN

Monkstown
Parkgariffe, Monkstown
☎ 021 4841376
e-mail: office@monkstowngolfclub.com
web: www.monkstowngolfclub.com
Undulating parkland with five tough finishing holes.

18 holes, 5441mtrs, Par 70, SSS 68, Course record 66. Club membership 960.
Visitors Mon & Thu-Sun. Booking required Fri-Sun. Handicap certificate. Dress code. **Societies** Welcome. **Green Fees** €43 per day (€50 Sat & Sun). **Prof** Batt Murphy **Course Designer** Peter O'Hare & Tom Carey **Facilities** ⏱ ⓘⓄ ☐ ⌧ ⓕ ☐ ⚐ ⚑ ⚒ ✦ ⚒ ✦ **Conf** Corporate Hospitality Days **Location** 0.8km SE of Monkstown
Hotel ★★★★ 73% HL Carrigaline Court Hotel, CARRIGALINE
☎ 021 4852100 91 en suite

YOUGHAL

Youghal
Knockaverry
☎ 024 92787 & 92861
◫ 024 92641
e-mail: youghalgolfclub@eircom.ie
web: www.youghalgolfclub.ie
For many years the host of various Golfing Union championships, Youghal offers a good test of golf and is well maintained for year-round play. The Parkland course has recently been extended with the addition of two new holes. There are panoramic views of Youghal Bay and the Blackwater estuary.
18 holes, 6175mtrs, Par 72, SSS 72, Course record 68. Club membership 1050.

Visitors Mon, Tue, Thu-Sun & BHs. Booking required. Handicap certificate. Dress code. **Societies** Booking required. **Green Fees** €30 per round (€40 Sat & Sun). **Prof** Liam Burns **Course Designer** Jeff Howes Golf Design **Facilities** ⏱ ⓘⓄ ☐ ⌧ ⓕ ☐ ⚐ ⚒ ✦ **Conf** Corporate Hospitality Days **Location** Off N25

CO DONEGAL
(DÚN NA NGALL)

BUNCRANA

North West
Lisfannon, Fahan, Buncrana
☎ 074 9361715
◫ 074 9363284
e-mail: secretary@northwestgolfclub.com
web: www.northwestgolfclub.com
A traditional links course on gently rolling sandy terrain with some long Par 4s. Good judgement is required on the approaches and the course offers a satisfying test coupled with undemanding walking.
18 holes, 5457mtrs, Par 70, SSS 70, Course record 64. Club membership 580.
Visitors Mon-Sun & BHs. Booking required. **Societies** Booking required. **Green Fees** €30 per round (€35 Sat & Sun). **Prof** Seamus McBriarty **Course Designer** Thompson Davy **Facilities** ⏱ ⓘⓄ ☐ ⌧ ⓕ ☐ ⚒ ☐ ✦ ✦ **Location** 1.6km S of Buncrana on R238

BUNDORAN

Bundoran
☎ 071 9841302
◫ 071 9842014
e-mail: bundorangolfclub@eircom.net
web: www.bundorangolfclub.com
This popular course, acknowledged as one of the best in the country, runs along the high cliffs above Bundoran beach and has a difficult Par of 70. Designed by Harry Vardon, it offers a challenging game of golf in beautiful surroundings and has been the venue for a number of Irish golf championships.
18 holes, 5688metres, Par 70, SSS 70, Course record 67. Club membership 770.
Visitors Mon-Sun & BHs. Booking required. Handicap certificate. Dress code. **Societies** welcome. **Green Fees** not confirmed. ◉ **Prof** David T Robinson **Course Designer** Harry Vardon **Facilities** ⚒ ☐ ⚐ ✦ **Conf** Corporate Hospitality Days **Location** Off Main St onto Sligo-Derry road
Hotel ★★★ 85% HL Sandhouse Hotel, ROSSNOWLAGH
☎ 071 9851777 55 en suite

CO DUBLIN

CASTLEKNOCK

Elm Green
☎ 01 8200797
📄 01 8226668
e-mail: elmgreen@golfdublin.com
web: www.golfdublin.com
Located a short distance from Dublin, beside Phoenix Park, with a fine layout, tricky greens and year round playability.
18 holes, 5300mtrs, Par 71, SSS 66, Course record 65. Club membership 650.
Visitors Mon-Sat & BHs. Booking required. **Societies** Booking required. **Green Fees** €20 per round (€36 Sat, Sun & BHs).
Prof Arnold O'Connor/Paul McGavan **Course Designer** Eddie Hackett **Facilities** ⑨ 🏌 ⌷ 🛒 ♥ 🏌 ⚑ 🏌 **Leisure** pitch and putt course. **Conf** facs Corporate Hospitality Days **Location** Off N3
Hotel ★★★ 74% HL Finnstown Country House Hotel, Newcastle Rd, Lucan, DUBLIN ☎ 01 6010700 25 en suite 28 annexe en suite

DONABATE

Island
Corballis
☎ 01 8436205 📄 01 8436860
e-mail: info@theislandgolfclub.com
web: www.theislandgolfclub.com

18 holes, 6206mtrs, Par 71, SSS 63.
Course Designer Martin Hawtree **Location** Off R126
Telephone for further details
Hotel ★★★ 72% HL Deer Park Hotel, Golf & Spa, HOWTH
☎ 01 8322624 80 en suite

DUBLIN

Royal Dublin North Bull Island Reserve, Dollymount
☎ 01 8336346
📄 01 8336504
e-mail: info@theroyaldublingolfclub.com
web: www.theroyaldublingolfclub.com
A popular course with visitors, for its design subtleties, the condition of the links and the friendly atmosphere. Founded in 1885, the club moved to its present site in 1889 and received its Royal designation in 1891. A notable former club professional was Christy O'Connor, who was appointed in 1959 and immediately made his name. Along with its many notable holes, Royal Dublin has a fine and testing finish. The 18th is a sharp dog-leg Par 4, with out of bounds along the right-hand side. The decision to try the long carry over the 'garden' is one many visitors have regretted.
18 holes, 6297mtrs, Par 72, SSS 74, Course record 63. Club membership 1250.
Visitors Mon, Tue, Thu and Fri. Booking required. Handicap certificate. Dress code. **Societies** Booking required. **Green Fees** €150 per round. **Prof** Leonard Owens **Course Designer** H S Colt **Facilities** ⑨ 🍴 🏌 ⌷ 🍴 ⚌ 🛒 🏌 ♥ 🏌 🏌 **Conf** facs Corporate Hospitality Days **Location** 5.5km NE of city centre
Hotel Ⓤ Longfield's Hotel, Fitzwilliam St Lower, DUBLIN 2 ☎ 01 6761367 26 en suite

St Margaret's Golf & Country Club
St Margaret's
☎ 01 8640400
📄 01 8640408
e-mail: reservations@stmargaretsgolf.com
web: www.stmargaretsgolf.com
A championship standard course which measures nearly 7,000 yards off the back tees, but flexible teeing offers a fairer challenge to the middle and high handicap golfer. The modern design makes wide use of water hazards and mounding. The Par 5 8th hole is set to become notorious - featuring lakes to the left and right of the tee and a third lake in front of the green. Ryder Cup player, Sam Torrance, has described the 18th as 'possibly the strongest and most exciting in the world'.
18 holes, 6325metres, Par 73, SSS 73, Course record 69. Club membership 260.
Visitors Mon-Sun & BHs. Booking required. Dress code. **Societies** booking required. **Green Fees** not confirmed. **Prof** John Kelly **Course Designer** Craddock/Ruddy **Facilities** ⑨ 🍴 🏌 ⌷ 🍴 ⚌ 🛒 🏌 ♥ 🏌 🏌 **Location** 9km N of city centre off R122

PORTMARNOCK

Strand Road, Portmarnock
☎ 01 8462968 📠 01 8462601
e-mail: emer@portmarnockgolfclub.ie
web: www.portmarnockgolfclub.ie
Old Course: 18 holes, 6567metres, Par 72, SSS 73.
New Course: 9 holes, 3082metres, Par 37.
Club membership 1100.
Visitors booking required. Handicap certificate. Dress code. **Societies** booking required.
Green Fees Phone. **Prof** Joey Purcell
Course Designer W Pickeman **Facilities** 🍽
🍽 by prior arrangement 🏌 🛒 🏌 🏖 📷 🏌
⛳ 🛺 ⛳ **Location** S of town off R106

Widely acknowledged as one of the great links courses, Portmarnock has hosted many great events from the 1949 British Amateur Championships 1949 and the 1960 Canada Cup, to 12 stagings of the revised Irish Open. Founded in 1894, the winding championship course offers a classic challenge: with water on three sides, no two successive holes play in the same direction. Unlike many courses that play nine out and nine home, Portmarnock demands a continual awareness of wind direction. Extraordinary holes include the 14th, which Henry Cotton regarded as the best hole in golf; the 15th, which Arnold Palmer regards as the best Par 3 in the world; and the 5th, regarded as the best on the course by the late Harry Bradshaw, who was for 40 years Portmarnock's professional and runner-up to AD Locke in the 1949 British Open, playing his ball from an empty bottle of stout.

MALAHIDE

Malahide Beechwood, The Grange
☎ 01 8461611
🖹 01 8461270
e-mail: manager@malahidegolfclub.ie
web: www.malahidegolfclub.ie

Main Course: 18 holes, 6066mtrs, Par 71.
Course Designer E Hackett **Location** 1.6km from R106 coast road at Portmarnock
Telephone for further details
Hotel ★★★★ HL Portmarnock Hotel & Golf Links, Strand Rd, PORTMARNOCK ☎ 01 8460611   98 en suite

CO GALWAY

BALLYCONNEELY

Connemara
☎ 095 23502 & 23602
🖹 095 23662
e-mail: links@iol.ie
web: www.connemaragolflinks.com
This championship links course has a spectacular setting by the Atlantic Ocean, with the Twelve Bens Mountains in the background. Established in 1973, it is a tough challenge, due in no small part to its exposed location, with the back nine the equal of any in the world. The last six holes are exceptionally long and offer a great challenge to golfers of all abilities. When the wind blows, club selection is crucial. Notable holes are the 13th (200yd Par 3), the long Par 5 14th, the 15th with a green nestling in the hills, the 16th guarded by water and the 17th and 18th, both Par 5s over 500yds long.

Championship: 18 holes, 6095mtrs, Par 72, SSS 73, Course record 64.
New: 9 holes, 2754mtrs, Par 35.
Club membership 970.
Visitors Mon-Sun & BHs. **Societies** Booking required. **Green Fees** €60 per round (€70 Fri-Sun). **Prof** Hugh O'Neill **Course Designer** Eddie Hackett **Facilities** ⑪ ⑩ 🍴 🖺 ♨ 🍴 ⅄ 🖨 ⚑ ✔ 🚑
✔ 🏇 **Conf** Corporate Hospitality Days **Location** W of village off R342
Hotel ★★★★ 77% HL Abbeyglen Castle Hotel, Sky Rd, CLIFDEN ☎ 095 21201   45 en suite

BEARNA

Bearna Golf and Country Club
Corboley
☎ 091 592677
🖹 091 592674
e-mail: info@bearnagolfclub.com
web: www.bearnagolfclub.com
Set amid the beautiful landscape of the west of Ireland and enjoying commanding views of Galway Bay, the course covers more than 100 hectares. This has resulted in generously proportioned fairways, many elevated tees and some splendid carries. Water comes into play at thirteen holes and the final four holes provide a memorable finish. Lakes on 6th, 7th and 10th holes.

18 holes, 5746metres, Par 72, SSS 72, Course record 68. Club membership 600.
Visitors Mon-Sun & BHs. Dress code. **Societies** welcome. **Green Fees** not confirmed. **Prof** Declan Cunningham **Course Designer** Robert J Brown **Facilities** ⑪ ⑩ 🍴 🖺 ♨ 🍴 ⅄ 🖨 ⚑ 🚑
✔ **Conf** facs **Location** 3.5km N of Bearna, off R336
Hotel ★★★★ 76% HL Galway Bay Hotel Conference & Leisure Centre, The Promenade, Salthill, GALWAY ☎ 091 520520   153 en suite

IRELAND

GALWAY

Galway
Blackrock, Salthill
☎ 091 522033
🖹 091 529783
e-mail: galwaygolf@eircom.net
web: galwaygolf.com
Designed by Dr A McKenzie, this course is inland by
nature, although some of the fairways run close to the
ocean. The terrain is of gently sloping hillocks with
plenty of trees and furze bushes to catch out the unwary.
Although not a long course it continues to delight visiting
golfers.
18 holes, 5995metres, Par 70, SSS 71,
Course record 67. Club membership 1238.
Visitors Mon, Wed-Sat & BHs. Booking required. Handicap
certificate. Dress code. **Societies** booking required. **Green Fees**
not confirmed. **Prof** Don Wallace **Course Designer** McKenzie
Facilities ⓣ 🍴 🖴 🖵 🖥 ♨ 🏊 🏌 ♣ 🛥 🛺 **Conf** Corporate
Hospitality Days **Location** 3km W in Salthill

ORANMORE

Galway Bay Golf Resort
Renville
☎ 091 790711
🖹 091 792510
e-mail: info@galwaybaygolfresort.com
web: www.galwaybaygolfresort.com
A championship golf course surrounded on three sides
by the Atlantic Ocean and featuring water hazards on a
number of holes. Each hole has its own characteristics
made more obvious by the everchanging seaside winds.
The design of the course highlights and preserves the
ancient historic features of the Renville Peninsula.
The spectacular setting and distractingly beautiful and
cleverly designed mix of holes presents a real golfing
challenge, demanding total concentration.
18 holes, 6533metres, Par 72, SSS 73,
Course record 68. Club membership 280.
Visitors contact club for details. **Societies** booking required.
Green Fees not confirmed. **Prof** Eugene O'Connor **Course
Designer** Christy O'Connor Jnr **Facilities** ⓣ 🍴 🖴 🖵 🖥 🏊 🛥
🛺 🚗 🚘 🏌 **Leisure** sauna **Conf** Corporate Hospitality Days
Location 5km SW of village

CO KERRY (CIARRAÍ)

GLENBEIGH

Dooks
☎ 066 9768205
🖹 066 9768476
e-mail: office@dooks.com
web: dooks.com
Long-established course on the shore between the Kerry
mountains and Dingle Bay. Sand dunes are a feature
(the name Dooks is a derivation of the Gaelic word for
sand bank) and the course offers a fine challenge in a
superb Ring of Kerry location. Redesigned by Martin
Hantree.
18 holes, 5944mtrs, Par 71, SSS 70, Course record 73.
Club membership 1000.
Visitors Mon-Sat & BHs. Booking required. Dress code.
Societies Booking required. **Green Fees** €80 per 18 holes.
Course Designer Martin Hawtree **Facilities** ⓣ 🍴 🖴 🖵 🖥 🏊
🛥 🛺 🏌 ♣ **Conf** Corporate Hospitality Days **Location** NE of
village off on N70
Hotel ★★★ 74% HL Gleneagle Hotel, Muckross Rd, KILLARNEY
☎ 064 36000 250 en suite

KENMARE

Ring of Kerry Golf & Country Club
Templenoe
☎ 064 42000
🖹 064 42533
e-mail: reservations@ringofkerrygolf.com
web: www.ringofkerrygolf.com
A world class golf facility with spectacular views across
Kenmare Bay. Opened in 1998, the club has gone from
strength to strength and is fast becoming a must-play
course for golfers visiting the area.

18 holes, 6236mtrs, Par 72, SSS 73, Course record 68.
Club membership 260.
Visitors Mon-Sun & BHs. Booking required Sat & Sun. Handicap
certificate. Dress code. **Societies** Booking required. **Green Fees**
€80 per round, €120 per 36 holes (€90/€130 Sat & Sun). **Prof**
Adrian Whitehead **Course Designer** Eddie Hackett **Facilities** ⓣ
🍴 🖴 🖵 🖥 🏊 🛥 🛺 🚗 🚘 🏌 **Conf** facs Corporate Hospitality
Days **Location** 6.5km W of Kenmare

continued

CHAMPIONSHIP COURSE

BALLYBUNION

Sandhill Rd
☎ 068 27146 📄 068 27387
e-mail: bbgolfgc@ioe.ie
web: www.ballybuniongolfclub.ie
Old Course: 18 holes, 6083mtrs, Par 71,
SSS 72, Course record 67.
Cashen: 18 holes, Par 72, SSS 71,
Course record 69.
Club membership 1500.
Visitors Mon-Sat. Booking required.
Handicap certificate. Dress code. **Societies**
Booking required. **Green Fees** Old Course:
€165 per round, Cashen Course: €110
per round, Both courses: €240. **Prof** Brian
O'Callaghan
Course Designer Simpson **Facilities** 🍴 🍽
🛒 🖥 🍴 ⛳ 🏠 ⛳ 🏌 **Leisure** sauna
Location 2km S of town

Having excellent links, Ballybunion is recognised for its fine development of the natural terrain. Mr Murphy built the Old Course in 1906. With large sand dunes and an Atlantic backdrop, Ballybunion offers the golfer an exciting round of golf in a scenic location. But be warned, the Old course is difficult to play in the wind. President Clinton played Ballybunion on his historic visit to Ireland in 1998. Although overshadowed by the Old Course, the Cashen Course designed by Robert Trent Jones is also world class, characterised by narrow fairways, small greens and large dunes.

IRELAND

Hotel ★★★★ CHH Sheen Falls Lodge, KENMARE ☎ 064 41600 66 en suite

Hotel ★★★★ 76% HL Meadowlands Hotel, Oakpark, TRALEE ☎ 066 7180444 57 en suite

KILLARNEY

Killarney Golf & Fishing Club
Mahony's Point
☎ 064 31034
🖹 064 33065
e-mail: reservations@killarney-golf.com
web: www.killarney-golf.com
The three courses are lakeside with tree-lined fairways; many bunkers and small lakes provide no mean challenge. Mahony's Point Course has a particularly testing Par 5, 4, 3 finish and the courses call for great skill from the tee. Killarney has been the venue for many important events and is a favourite of many famous golfers.
Mahony's Point: 18 holes, 5826mtrs, Par 72, SSS 72, Course record 64.
Killeen: 18 holes, 6047mtrs, Par 72, SSS 72, Course record 68.
Lackabane: 18 holes, 6011mtrs, Par 72, SSS 72, Course record 64. Club membership 1600.
Visitors Mon-Sun & BHs. Booking required. Handicap certificate. Dress code. **Societies** Booking required. **Green Fees** per 18 holes, Mahony's Point: €100, Killeen: €120, Lackabane: €80. **Prof** Tony Coveney
Course Designer H Longhurst/Sir Guy Campbell **Facilities** ⑪ ⑩ ⅃
⌨ ⅋ ⚑ 🏌 ⚐ Leisure sauna, gymnasium.
Conf Corporate Hospitality Days **Location** 3.5km W on N72
Hotel ★★★★★ HL Aghadoe Heights Hotel & Spa, KILLARNEY ☎ 064 31766 74 en suite

TRALEE

Tralee
West Barrow
☎ 066 7136379
🖹 066 7136008
e-mail: info@traleegolfclub.com
web: www.traleegolfclub.com
The first Arnold Palmer designed course in Europe, this magnificent 18-hole links is set in spectacular scenery on the Barrow peninsula, surrounded on three sides by the sea. Perhaps the most memorable hole is the Par 4 17th which plays from a high tee, across a deep gorge to a green perched high against a backdrop of mountains. The back nine is very difficult and challenging. Not suitable for beginners.
18 holes, 5970mtrs, Par 71, SSS 71, Course record 66. Club membership 1306.
Visitors Mon-Sat. Booking required. Handicap certificate. Dress code. **Green Fees** €170 per round. **Prof** David Power **Course Designer** Arnold Palmer **Facilities** ⑪ ⑩ ⅃ ⌨ ⅋ ⚑ 🏌 ⚐
Location 13km NW of Tralee off R558

WATERVILLE (AN COIREÁN)

Waterville House & Golf Links
☎ 066 9474102
🖹 066 9474482
e-mail: wvgolf@iol.ie
web: www.watervillegolflink.ie
On the western tip of the Ring of Kerry, this course is highly regarded by many top golfers. The feature holes are the Par 5 11th, which runs along a rugged valley between towering dunes, and the Par 3 17th, which features an exceptionally elevated tee. Needless to say, the surroundings are beautiful.
18 holes, 6202mtrs, Par 72, SSS 72, Course record 65.
Visitors Mon-Sun & BHs. Booking required. Handicap certificate. Dress code. **Societies** Booking required **Green Fees** €165 per round (€115 before 8am & after 4pm Mon-Thur). **Prof** Liam Higgins **Course Designer** Eddie Hackett/Tom Fazio **Facilities** ⑪
⑩ ⅃ ⌨ ⅋ ⚑ 🏌 ◇ ⚐ Leisure fishing, sauna, short game area. **Location** 0.5km from Waterville on N70
Hotel ★★★ 69% HL Derrynane Hotel, CAHERDANIEL ☎ 066 9475136 70 en suite

CO KILKENNY

KILKENNY

Kilkenny
Glendine
☎ 056 7765400
🖹 056 7723593
e-mail: enquiries@kilkennygolfclub.com
web: www.kilkennygolfclub.com
One of Ireland's most pleasant inland courses, noted for its tricky finishing holes and its Par 3s. Features of the course are its long 11th and 13th holes and the challenge increases year by year as thousands of trees planted over the last 30 years or so are maturing. As host of the Kilkenny Scratch Cup annually, the course is permanently maintained in championship condition.
18 holes, 5925mtrs, Par 71, SSS 70, Course record 68. Club membership 1368.
Visitors Mon-Sat & BHs. Booking required Fri, Sat & BHs. Dress code. **Societies** Booking required. **Green Fees** €35 per 18 holes (€40 Sat & BHs). **Prof** Jimmy Bolger **Facilities** ⑪
⑩ ⅃ ⌨ ⅋ ⚑ ⚐ 🏌 Leisure snooker & pool. **Conf** Corporate Hospitality Days **Location** 1.6km N of town on N77

CHAMPIONSHIP COURSE

CO KILDARE — STRAFFAN

THE K CLUB

☎ 01 6017300 📄 01 6017399
e-mail: golf@kclub.ie
web: www.kclub.ie
Palmer Course: 18 holes, 6526mtrs, Par 74, SSS 72, Course record 65.
Smurfit Course: 18 holes, 6636mtrs, Par 72, SSS 72.
Club membership 540.
Visitors booking required. **Societies** booking required. **Green Fees** Palmer £350, Smurfit £130. Reduced winter rates. **Prof** John McHenry/Peter O'Hagan
Course Designer Arnold Palmer **Facilities** ⑪
🍽 🛏 💻 🍴 ⚓ 🏠⛳ 🛒 🏌 🛺 🎣 🏹
Leisure heated indoor swimming pool, fishing, sauna, solarium, gymnasium.
Conf facs Corporate Hospitality Days
Location W of village off R403

The K Club was the Ryder Cup's venue in 2006, the first time that Ireland has hosted the event. The course reflects the personality of its architect, Arnold Palmer, covering 220 acres of Kildare woodland, with 14 man-made lakes and the River Liffey providing the water hazards. From the instant you arrive at the 1st tee, you are enveloped by a unique atmosphere: the courses are both cavalier and charismatic. The Palmer Course is one of Europe's most spectacular courses, charming, enticing, and invariably bringing out the very best in your game. The best way to describe the Smurfit Course is that of an inland links. It has many dramatic landscapes with dunes moulding throughout, while some 14 acres of water have been worked in to the design, especially through the holes 13-18. The course is entirely different from the Palmer Course located just across the River Liffey.

CHAMPIONSHIP COURSE
CO KILKENNY — THOMASTOWN

MOUNT JULIET HOTEL

☎ 056 7773064 📠 056 7773078
e-mail: golfinfo@mountjuliet.ie
web: www.mountjuliet.com
18 holes, 6639metres, Par 72, SSS 75,
Course record 62.
Club membership 500.
Visitors Mon-Sun & BHs. Booking required
Sat-Sun. Dress code. **Societies** booking
required. **Green Fees** from £75 in winter to
£160 weekend summer. **Prof** Sean Cotter
Course Designer Jack Nicklaus **Facilities** ⊕
🍽 🛍 💻 🍴 🏹 🏠 ⛳ ◇ ✦ ⛏ ✦ 🏌
Leisure hard tennis courts, heated indoor
swimming pool, fishing, sauna, solarium,
gymnasium, Archery/clay shooting/
equestrian. **Conf** facs Corporate Hospitality
Days **Location** 4km S of town off N9

Venue for the American Express
Championship in 2002 and 2004, Mount
Juliet's superb 18-hole course was designed
by Jack Nicklaus. It has also hosted many
prestigious events including the Irish
Open on three occasions. The course has a
cleverly concealed drainage and irrigation
system, perfect even when inclement
weather would otherwise halt play. It takes
advantage of the estate's mature landscape
to provide a world-class 72-Par challenge
for professionals and high-handicap
golfers alike. A unique three-hole golfing
academy has been added to allow novice
and experienced players ample opportunity
to improve their game, while a new 18-hole
putting course provides an extra dimension
of golfing pleasure and is the venue for the
National Putting Championship.

Hotel ★★★ 69% HL The Kilkenny Inn Hotel, 15/15 Vicar St, KILKENNY ☎ 056 7772828 30 en suite

CO LOUTH

BALTRAY

County Louth
☎ 041 9881530
📄 041 9881531
e-mail: reservations@countylouthgolfclub.com
web: www.countylouthgolfclub.com
Generally held to have the best greens in Ireland, this links course was designed by Tom Simpson to have well-guarded and attractive greens without being overly dependant on bunkers. It provides a good test for the modern champion, notably as the annual venue for the East of Ireland Amateur Open.
18 holes, 6141mtrs, Par 72, SSS 72, Course record 64. Club membership 1342.
Visitors Mon & Thu-Sat. Booking required. Handicap certificate. Dress code. **Societies** Booking required **Green Fees** €115 per round (€135 Sat). **Prof** Paddy McGuirk **Course Designer** Tom Simpson **Facilities** ⑪ ⑩ 🍴 🖥 🛢 ⛳ ▲ 🕏 🏌 ❖ 🏌 🏌 **Leisure** hard tennis courts. **Location** 8km NE of Drogheda

CO MAYO (MAIGH EO)

WESTPORT

Westport
Carrowholly
☎ 098 28262 & 27070
📄 098 27217
e-mail: info@westportgolfclub.com
web: www.westportgolfclub.com
This is a beautiful course with wonderful views of Clew Bay, with its 365 islands, and the holy mountain called Croagh Patrick, famous for the annual pilgrimage to its summit. Golfers indulge in a different kind of penance on this challenging course with many memorable holes. Perhaps the most exciting is the Par 5 15th, 580yds long and featuring a long carry from the tee over an inlet of Clew Bay.

18 holes, 6148mtrs, Par 73, SSS 71, Course record 61. Club membership 600.
Visitors Mon-Sun & BHs. Booking required Fri-Sun & BHs. Dress code. **Societies** Booking required. **Green Fees** €38/€45 per round (€42/€55 Sat & Sun). **Prof** Alex Mealia **Course Designer** Fred Hawtree **Facilities** ⑪ ⑩ 🍴 🖥 🛢 ⛳ ▲ 🕏 🏌 🏌 **Conf** Corporate Hospitality Days **Location** 4km from town off N59
Hotel ★★★ 82% HL Hotel Westport Leisure, Spa & Conference, Newport Rd, WESTPORT ☎ 098 25122 129 en suite

CO MEATH

KELLS

Headfort
☎ 046 9240146
📄 046 9249282
e-mail: info@headfortgolfclub.ie
web: www.headfortgolfclub.ie
Headfort Old Course is a delightful parkland course which is regarded as one of the best of its kind in Ireland. There are ample opportunities for birdies, but even if these are not achieved, provides a challenging test. The New Course is a modern course which criss-crosses the Blackwater river, making use of two islands.

Old Course: 18 holes, 5973mtrs, Par 72, SSS 71. New Course: 18 holes, 6164metres, Par 72, SSS 74. Club membership 1700.
Visitors Mon-Sun & BHs. Booking required. Dress code. **Societies** Booking required. **Green Fees** Old Course: €50 per round (€55 Fri-Sun). New Course; €65 per round (€70 Fri-Sun). **Prof** Brendan McGovern **Course Designer** Christy O'Connor jnr **Facilities** ⑪ ⑩ 🍴 🖥 🛢 ⛳ ▲ 🕏 🏌 🚗 🏌 **Location** 0.8km E of village on N3

CO SLIGO

INISHCRONE

Enniscrone
☎ 096 36297
🖷 096 36657
e-mail: enniscronegolf@eircom.net
web: www.enniscronegolf.com
27 holes, 6125metres, Par 73, SSS 72,
Course record 70.
Course Designer E Hackett/Donald Steel **Location** 0.8km S
of village
Telephone for further details
Hotel ★★★ 74% HL Teach Iorrais Hotel, Geesala, BALLINA
☎ 097 86888 31 en suite

SLIGO

County Sligo
Rosses Point
☎ 071 9177134 & 9177186
🖷 071 9177460
e-mail: teresa@countysligogolfclub.ie
web: countysligogolfclub.ie
Now considered to be one of the top links courses
in Ireland, County Sligo is host to a number
of competitions, including the West of Ireland
championships and internationals. Set in an elevated
position on cliffs above three large beaches, the
prevailing winds provide an additional challenge. Tom
Watson described it as 'a magnificent links, particularly
the stretch of holes from the 14th to the 17th'.
18 holes, 6136mtrs, Par 71, SSS 72, Course record 67.
Bomore: 9 holes, 2785mtrs, Par 35, SSS 69.
Club membership 1250.
Visitors Mon-Sun & BHs. Booking required. Handicap
certificate. Dress code. **Societies** Booking required. **Green
Fees** Championship Course: €75 per 18 holes (€90 Fri-Sun &
BHs), Bowmore: €25 9 holes €40 18 holes. **Prof** Jim Robinson
Course Designer Harry Colt **Facilities** ⑨ ⑩ ⧠ ⬚ ⵲ ⬚ ⴕ
⬚ ⬚ ⬚ **Conf** facs Corporate Hospitality Days **Location** N of
town off N15

CO TIPPERARY

CLONMEL

Clonmel
Lyreanearla, Mountain Rd
☎ 052 24050
🖷 052 83349
e-mail: cgc@indigo.ie
web: clonmelgolfclub.com
Set in the scenic, wooded slopes of the Comeragh
Mountains, this is a testing course with lots of open
space and plenty of interesting features. It provides an
enjoyable round in exceptionally tranquil surroundings.

18 holes, 5804metres, Par 72, SSS 71.
Club membership 850.
Visitors Mon-Sun & BHs. Booking required Wed, Sat & Sun.
Handicap certificate. Dress code. **Societies** booking required.
Green Fees not confirmed. **Prof** Robert Hayes **Course
Designer** Eddie Hackett **Facilities** ⑨ by prior arrangement ⬚
⬚ ⬚ ⬚ ⬚ ⴕ ⬚ ⬚ **Location** 5km from Clonmel off N24
Hotel ★★★ 76% HL Hotel Minella, CLONMEL ☎ 052 22388
70 en suite

CO WATERFORD

WATERFORD

Waterford Castle
The Island, Ballinakill
☎ 051 871633
🖷 051 871634
e-mail: golf@waterfordcastle.com
web: www.waterfordcastle.com/golf
A unique 130-hectare island course in the River Suir
and accessed by private ferry. The course has four
water features on the 2nd, 3rd, 4th and 16th holes
with a Swilken Bridge on the 3rd hole. Two of the
more challenging holes are the Par 4s at the 9th
and 12th, the 9th being a 379-metre uphill, dog-leg
right. The 417-metre 12th is a fine test of accuracy and
distance. The views from the course are superb.
18 holes, 6231mtrs, Par 72, SSS 71, Course record 65.
Club membership 770.
Visitors Mon-Sat & BHs. Booking required. Dress code.
Societies Booking required. **Green Fees** Winter €48-€52;
Summer €52-€62. **Course Designer** Des Smyth **Facilities**
⑨ ⑩ ⬚ ⬚ ⬚ ⬚ ⴕ ⬚ ⬚ ⬚ ⬚ **Leisure** hard tennis courts.
Conf facs Corporate Hospitality Days **Location** 3km E of town
via private ferry
Hotel ★★★★ HL Waterford Castle Hotel, The Island,
WATERFORD ☎ 051 878203 19 en suite

CO WESTMEATH

MULLINGAR

Mullingar
☎ 044 48366
🖷 044 41499
18 holes, 5858metres, Par 72, SSS 71,
Course record 63.
Course Designer James Braid **Location** 5km S of town on N52
Telephone for further details

Hotel ★★★★ 73% HL Mullingar Park Hotel, Dublin Rd, MULLINGAR ☎ 044 44446 & 37500 📠 044 35937 95 en suite

CO WEXFORD

GOREY

Courtown
Kiltennel
☎ 055 25166
📠 055 25553
e-mail: courtown@iol.ie
web: www.courtowngolfclub.com
18 holes, 5898mtrs, Par 71, SSS 71, Course record 65.
Course Designer Harris & Associates **Location** 5km SE of town off R742
Telephone for further details
Hotel ★★★★ 73% HL Ashdown Park Hotel, The Coach Rd, GOREY TOWN ☎ 053 9480500 79 en suite

ROSSLARE

Rosslare
Rosslare Strand
☎ 053 9132203 📠 053 9132263
e-mail: office@rosslaregolf.com
web: www.rosslaregolf.com
This traditional links course is within minutes of the ferry terminal at Rosslare. Many of the greens are sunken and are always in beautiful condition, but the semi-blind approaches are among features of this course which provide a healthy challenge. Celebrated 100 years of golf in 2005.

Old Course: 18 holes, 6042mtrs, Par 72, SSS 72, Course record 66.
Burrow: 12 holes, 3617metres, Par 46.
Club membership 1000.
Visitors Mon-Sun & BHs. Booking required. Dress code. **Societies** Booking required. **Green Fees** Phone. **Prof** Johnny Young **Course Designer** Hawtree/Taylor **Facilities** ⑪ ⑩ ℡ ☞ ℡ ⚒ ☎ ☂ ✔ ☎ ✔ **Leisure** sauna. **Conf** Corporate Hospitality Days **Location** N of Rosslare village
Hotel ★★★★ HL Kelly's Resort Hotel & Spa, ROSSLARE ☎ 053 32114 118 annexe en suite

CO WICKLOW

BRITTAS BAY

The European Club
☎ 0404 47415 📠 0404 47449
e-mail: info@europeanclub.com
web: www.theeuropeanclub.com
A links course that runs through a large dunes system. Since it was opened in 1992 it is rapidly gaining recognition as one of Irelands best courses. Notable holes include the 7th, 13th and 14th.
20 holes, 6737metres, Par 71, SSS 73, Course record 67. Club membership 100.
Visitors Mon-Sun & BHs. Booking required. Dress code. **Societies** welcome. **Green Fees** not confirmed. **Course Designer** Pat Ruddy **Facilities** ⑪ ⑩ ℡ ☞ ⚒ ☎ ☂ ✔ ☎ ✔ **Conf** Corporate Hospitality Days **Location** 1.6km from Brittas Bay

DUNLAVIN

Rathsallagh
☎ 045 403316 📠 045 403295
e-mail: info@rathsallagh.com
web: www.rathsallagh.com
Designed by Peter McEvoy and Christy O'Connor Jnr, this is a spectacular course which will test the pro's without intimidating the club golfer. Set in 525 acres of lush parkland with thousands of mature trees, natural water hazards and gently rolling landscape. The greens are of high quality, in design, construction and condition.
18 holes, 6324mtrs, Par 72, SSS 74, Course record 68.
Club membership 410.
Visitors Mon-Sun & BHs. Booking required. Dress code. **Societies** Booking required. **Green Fees** €60 per round (€80 Fri-Sat & BHs). **Prof** Brendan McDaid **Course Designer** McEvoy/O'Connor **Facilities** ⑪ ⑩ ℡ ☞ ⚒ ☎ ☂ ◇ ✔ ☎ ✔ ℱ **Leisure** hard tennis courts, sauna, private jacuzzi/steam room, croquet lawn, walled garden. **Conf** facs Corporate Hospitality Days **Location** SW of village off N9

CHAMPIONSHIP COURSE

CO WICKLOW — KILCOOLE

DRUIDS GLEN GOLF CLUB

Newtownmountkennedy
☎ 01 2873600 📠 01 2873699
e-mail: info@druidsglen.ie
web: www.druidsglen.ie
18 holes, 5987metres, Par 71, SSS 73,
Course record 62.
Club membership 219.
Visitors advance booking essential.
Societies advance booking essential
Green Fees Phone. **Prof** George Henry
Course Designer Tom Craddock/Pat Ruddy
Facilities ⑪ ⑪ 🔔 ⬛ 🍴 ⬛ 🛒 ♦ ⚐ 🚗
♦ ⚐ **Leisure** heated indoor swimming pool,
sauna, gymnasium. **Location** S of village on
R761

Druids Glen from the 1st tee to the 18th green
creates an exceptional golfing experience, with
its distinguished surroundings and spectacular
views. It is the culmination of years of
preparation, creating a unique inland course
that challenges and satisfies in equal parts.
Special features include an island green on
the 17th hole and a Celtic Cross on the 12th.
Druids Glen hosted the Murphy's Irish Open
in 1996, 1997, 1998 and for an unprecedented
fourth time in 1999. In 2000 Druids Glen
won the title of European Golf Course of the
Year and in 2002 it hosted the Seve trophy.
The world's top professionals and club golfers
alike, continue to enjoy the challenge here.
A variety of teeing positions are available
and there is a practice area, including three
full-length academy holes. Individual and
corporate members enjoy generous reserved
tee times; visitors are very welcome.